DEATH IN ADAM, LIFE IN CHRIST

Even when displaying sophisticated exegesis, conversations—and debates—over imputation are rarely informed by the history of interpretation. Fesko introduces us to seminal figures in this development and no engagement with original sin or justification should overlook his careful spade work.

MICHAEL HORTON
J. Gresham Machen Professor of Systematic Theology and Apologetics,
Westminster Seminary California, Escondido, California

Often books on imputation fall into three categories: confessional exposition, historical survey, or exegesis. In classic Reformed fashion, and with grace and style, John Fesko brings all three elements together in what is sure to become the standard Reformed work on Imputation for generations to come. From Augustine to Anslem, Lombard to Luther, and Calvin through Post-Reformation Reformed theologians, Fesko provides readers with the vital history and development of the doctrine from largely primary sources. He brings that rich history up to the present while interacting with the key voices in the modern discussions and debate—including some that are overlooked or unknown to many authors and readers. At the center of his history and theology lies a solid foundation of careful exegesis, Old and New Testaments, that goes beyond the handful of texts typically associated with imputation. All this is brought together in a thorough-going, accessible, covenant-theological statement of the doctrine of imputation.

BRIAN VICKERS
Professor of New Testament Interpretation and Biblical Theology,
The Southern Baptist Theological Seminary, Louisville, Kentucky

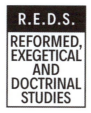

R.E.D.S.

REFORMED,
EXEGETICAL
AND
DOCTRINAL
STUDIES

DEATH IN ADAM, LIFE IN CHRIST

THE DOCTRINE OF IMPUTATION

J.V. FESKO

SERIES EDITORS J.V. FESKO & MATTHEW BARRETT

MENTOR
Encouraging Christians to Think

Unless otherwise indicated, Scripture quotations are from *The Holy Bible, English Standard Version*, copyright © 2001 by Crossway Bibles, a publishing ministry of Good News Publishers. Used by permission. All rights reserved. esv Text Edition: 2011.

Scripture quotations marked nlt are taken from *the Holy Bible, New Living Translation*, copyright © 1996. Used by permission of Tyndale House Publishers, Inc., Wheaton, Illinois 60189. All rights reserved.

Scripture quotations marked nrsv are taken from *the New Revised Standard Version* Bible, copyright 1989, Division of Christian Education of the National Council of the Churches of Christ in the United States of America. Used by permission. All rights reserved.

Scripture quotations marked kjv are taken from the *King James Version*.

Copyright © J. V. Fesko 2016

paperback ISBN 978-1-78191-908-8
epub ISBN 978-1-78191-975-0
mobi ISBN 978-1-78191-976-7

10 9 8 7 6 5 4 3 2 1

Published in 2016
in the
Mentor Imprint
by
Christian Focus Publications Ltd,
Geanies House, Fearn, Ross-shire,
IV20 1TW, Great Britain.

www.christianfocus.com

Cover design
by
Pete Barnsley

Printed
by
Bell & Bain, Glasgow

CONTENTS

ABBREVIATIONS

*	Author's translation
§, §§	article or paragraph, articles or paragraphs
AB	Anchor Bible
ANF	Ante-Nicene Fathers
BDAG	Bauer Arndt Gingrich and Danker, *Greek-English Lexicon*, 3rd ed.
BBR	*Bulletin for Biblical Research*
BCOTWP	Baker Commentary on the Old Testament Wisdom and Psalms
BNTC	Black's New Testament Commentary
ca.	*circa* ('about')
cf.	*confer* ('compare')
CH	*Church History*
CTJ	*Calvin Theological Journal*
CNTC	Calvin's New Testament Commentaries
CR	*Corpus Reformatorum*
esp.	especially
e.g.	*exempli gratia* ('for example')
ExpT	*Expository Times*
ff.	following
HTR	*Harvard Theological Review*
ICC	International Critical Commentary
JAOS	*Journal of the American Oriental Society*
JETS	*Journal of the Evangelical Theological Society*
JPS	Jewish Publication Society
JTS	*Journal of Theological Studies*

KJV	King James Version
LW	*Luther's Works*, ed. Jaroslav Pelikan, et al., 79 vols. (St. Louis: Concordia Publishing, 1955–)
LQ	*Lutheran Quarterly*
LXX	Septuagint
lect.	lecture
MAJT	*Mid-America Journal of Theology*
MT	Masoretic Text
NIB	New Interpreter's Bible
NICNT	New International Commentary on the New Testament
NICOT	New International Commentary on the Old Testament
NIGTC	New International Greek Testament Commentary
NIVAC	New International Version Application Commentary
NLT	New Living Translation
NPNF[1]	Nicene Post-Nicene Fathers, first series
NRSV	New Revised Standard Version
SCJ	*Sixteenth Century Journal*
SJOT	*Scandinavian Journal of the Old Testament*
s.v.	*sub verbo* ('under the word')
SVTQ	*St. Vladimir's Theological Quarterly*
TJ	*Trinity Journal*
TOTC	Tyndale Old Testament Commentary
TynB	*Tyndale Bulletin*
USQR	*Union Seminary Quarterly Review*
VT	*Vetus Testamentum*
WBC	Word Biblical Commentary
WTJ	*Westminster Theological Journal*

To my father-in-law,
Robert Mitchell Jones

Acknowledgements

Working on this book has been a joy for a number of reasons, and one of them has been the camaraderie of colleagues who have been willing to take the time to assist me along the way. I am grateful to David VanDrunen, a friend and model scholar, who is always willing to read material that I write and offer careful critique and feedback. Thanks goes to Matthew Barrett, my R.E.D.S. series co-editor, who also gave me excellent feedback and some helpful suggestions. Thank you Brian Hecker for assembling my bibliography and reading through the manuscript. Your assistance enabled me to get this book submitted on time. I am thankful for everyone at Christian Focus, especially Willie MacKenzie, for his support for the R.E.D.S. series and his continued encouragement and willingness to publish my work. Thank you, Zach Keele, for helping me iron out the wrinkles in one section of the book! Most of all, I want to thank my family—my wife, Anneke, my sons, Val and Rob, and my crazy daughter, Carmen Penelope. You always provide me with love, laughs, and the occasional lunacy. You also give me the support and encouragement I need to write.

I dedicate this book to my father-in-law, Robert Mitchell Jones, affectionately known around our home as 'Poppy.' You have warmly welcomed me into your family, continually show us your love, and you spend time with your grandchildren to give them memories they will never forget, like sailing on the Chesapeake or exploring the wonders of the Magic Kingdom. We look forward, dv, to making many more memories together. But most of all, I am thankful for your faithful service to Christ's church as a ruling elder for more than thirty years. Thank you for your sacrificial service to Christ's bride.

Most of all, I want to thank you, my faithful covenant Lord, for sending your only Son and freely giving me His righteousness through the work of your Spirit so that I may enter boldly into your presence to receive your blessing. I am hopeless without the glorious exchange: 'I will greatly rejoice in the LORD; my soul shall exult in my God, for he has clothed me with the garments of salvation; he has covered me with the robe of righteousness' (Isa. 61:10). SDG.

Series Preface

Reformed, Exegetical and Doctrinal Studies (R.E.D.S.) presents new studies informed by rigorous exegetical attention to the biblical text, engagement with the history of doctrine, with a goal of refined dogmatic formulation.

R.E.D.S. covers a spectrum of doctrinal topics, addresses contemporary challenges in theological studies, and is driven by the Word of God, seeking to draw theological conclusions based upon the authority and teaching of Scripture itself.

Each volume also explores pastoral implications so that they contribute to the church's theological and practical understanding of God's word. One of the virtues that sets R.E.D.S. apart is its ability to apply dogmatics to the Christian life. In doing so, these volumes are characterized by the rare combination of theological weightiness and warm, pastoral application, much in the tradition of John Calvin's *Institutes of the Christian Religion*.

These volumes do not merely repeat material accessible in other books but retrieve and remind the church of forgotten truths to enrich contemporary discussion.

MATTHEW BARRETT

J. V. FESKO

PREFACE

The doctrine of justification has been a balm for my soul ever since I discovered the glorious truth that by God's grace alone He declares sinners righteous on the basis of the obedience and suffering of Christ alone, and that sinners receive these wonderful blessings by faith alone. I have not only relished these truths in my heart, found solace in them in times when I have felt the burden of my sin, but also rested upon them when I have doubted my standing with God. I have to the best of my ability regularly pointed my family to the glories of justification, telling my children that they too can find forgiveness for their sins in Christ and receive His imputed righteousness. As a pastor, I taught this doctrine to my congregation, which became the occasion to write two books on the subject, *Justification: Understanding the Classic Reformed Doctrine* and *What Is Justification by Faith Alone?* As a seminary professor, I have continued to explore this doctrine in a number of essays published in journals as well as a book on the history of the doctrine, *Beyond Calvin: Union with Christ and Justification in Early Modern Reformed Theology (1517–1700)*. My personal goal is to continue to explore, historically, exegetically, and theologically this doctrine. I have written on broader theological topics, such as the covenant of redemption, but always with a view of seeing what more I can learn about the doctrine of justification as it lies nestled throughout the various corners of Scripture. But at the same time, I have mapped out a plan of various projects that I want to write as I continue to explore the doctrine of justification. This book represents one fulfilled part of that plan.

As I have studied the doctrine of justification, I have noted that there are very few monographs on the doctrine of imputation, a key load-bearing pillar within the doctrine of justification. Conversely, there are even fewer monographs on the doctrine of imputed guilt. Granted, numerous Reformed theologians treat these subjects as a part of larger systems of doctrine or in the many monographs on the doctrine of justification, but there are few, if any, books that treat both imputed guilt and righteousness. When it came to the history of the doctrine of imputation, there are hardly any monographs that treat the doctrine. When I saw this lacuna in Reformed theological literature, I wanted to fill in the hole. I wanted to write a book that would cover the history of the doctrine, present exegesis, and finally offer dogmatic formulation of the doctrine of imputation. In this respect, my hope is that this book fills the aims of the R.E.D.S. series, which is to present Reformed, exegetical and doctrinal studies that offer new contributions to the ongoing theological discussion in the broader church.

Unless otherwise indicated, all translations of foreign language texts are my own. I use the English Standard Version for Scripture quotations, unless otherwise noted by an asterisk (*) or give the different version in parentheses. All Scripture quotations with an asterisk are my own translations. And, all quoted confessions and catechisms, unless otherwise noted, come from Jaroslav Pelikan and Valerie Hotchkiss, eds., *Creeds and Confessions of Faith in the Christian Tradition*, 3 vols. (New Haven: Yale University Press, 2003).

Some might notice the absence of any reference to representatives of the so-called Federal Vision. I purposefully do not engage this theological movement for several reasons. First, numerous Reformed denominations have addressed this movement and have issued official reports. Second, others have thoughtfully engaged their claims. Noteworthy are two books by Guy Waters, *The Federal Vision and Covenant Theology: A Comparative Analysis* and *Justification and the New Perspectives On Paul: A Review and Response*. Third, much of the work of Federal Vision appears on the Internet, especially the blogosphere, which is difficult to track—it presents a moving target and is therefore difficult to pin down. Therefore, instead of trying to prune braches that sway in the wind, I have laid an axe to the root of the tree by engaging the history of the doctrine and addressing exegetically and theologically the fundamental errors that lie at the basis of the Federal Vision's rejection of imputation.

In the end, I hope and pray that this book serves to deepen the church's collective understanding of the doctrine of imputation— our corporate guilt in Adam and the sublime grace of God that comes to us by the imputed righteousness of Christ received by faith alone—the sole foundation for our right standing with God now or at the final judgment.

INTRODUCTION

'I am the master of my fate, I am the captain of my soul,' William Ernest Henley's (1849–1903) closing words to his famous poem, *Invictus*, aptly describe the spirit of the age.[1] In the Western post-Enlightenment world the individual is the hero and does not have to submit to anyone or anything. In other cultures and times, individuals were bound to communities and saw their identity wrapped up in these social bonds. But we now live in a world where we have turned our cameras, which once looked to the world around us, to ourselves. The 'selfie' has entered our cultural lexicon and is one more sign that the individual is accountable to no one and shapes his own life and destiny. In such an environment a book on the doctrine of imputation might seem out of place. Why discuss a doctrine that does not resonate with the prevailing cultural winds?

---

1. William Ernest Henley, *Echoes of Life and Death: Forty-Seven Lyrics by William Ernest Henley* (Portland, ME: Thomas B. Mosher, 1908), 7.

The simplest answer is, the doctrine of imputation is a biblical teaching and deserves serious study and reflection. Moreover it reminds us that, despite our claims of unfettered freedom, we are all bound to the actions of two people, Adam and Christ. The doctrine of imputation explains many key elements of these bonds. What, however, does the verb *to impute* mean? A basic definition is, to assign something to another. In accounting, someone can impute or assign a credit or debit to an account. In social interaction, someone can impute or assign false motives to someone's actions. In theological terms, *to impute* has historically been a term employed to explain how God assigns guilt, for example. In Leviticus 17:4, we read of the Lord *imputing* bloodguilt to the man who does not bring the required sacrifice to the tabernacle. In older translations of the Bible, we read of God assigning or crediting a person with the status of righteous, that is, they have fulfilled the requirements of the law: 'And therefore it was imputed to him for righteousness' (Rom. 4:22; KJV).

In historic Reformed theology theologians have reflected upon these and other texts and concluded that God employs a threefold imputation in the course of the redemption of the elect. First, God imputes Adam's first sin to all human beings. Second, in the redemption of the elect, He imputes the sins of the elect to Christ. And third, He imputes Christ's righteousness, or His obedience, to the elect. While they are not the only texts that discuss this threefold imputation, two Pauline passages have featured in the classic Reformed view. The first is Romans 5:12-21, though verse 19* sufficiently captures the essence of the passage: 'For as by the one man's disobedience the many were constituted sinners, so by the one man's obedience the many will be constituted righteous.' The second text is 2 Corinthians 5:17-21, though verse 21 contains the key statement: 'For our sake he made him to be sin who knew no sin, so that in him we might become the righteousness of God.' For historic Reformed theology, the doctrine of imputation typically incorporates these and other biblical texts in its treatment of the consequences of Adam's first sin and the effects of Christ's obedience.

The Westminster Confession (1647), for example, states: 'They,' Adam and Eve, 'being the root of all mankind, the guilt of this sin was imputed; and the same death in sin, and corrupted nature, conveyed to all their posterity descending from them by ordinary generation' (VI.iii). And conversely, in its explanation of the doctrine of justification, the Confession states, 'Those whom God effectually calleth, he also freely justifieth: not by infusing righteousness into them, but by pardoning their sins, and by accounting and accepting their persons as righteous; not for anything wrought in them, or done by them ... but by imputing the obedience and satisfaction of Christ unto them, they receiving and resting on him and his righteousness, by faith' (XI.i). But as common as these historic statements are, the broader church has not always agreed with such conclusions, and even some within the Reformed community have disagreed with elements of the classic doctrine of imputation.

CURRENT STATE OF THE DOCTRINE

Briefly stated, the history of the reception of the doctrine of imputation is complex and involves many twists and turns. As such, any treatment of the doctrine requires due attention to its origins, development, and reception. But in the big picture, the churches of the Protestant Reformation, both Lutheran and Reformed, have embraced the doctrine of imputation.[2] The Roman Catholic Church famously rejected it in its official response to the Reformation in the Council of Trent (1547).[3] Since the Reformation theologians of the Reformed tradition have defended classic threefold imputation, though there have undoubtedly been those who disagreed with portions of it, such as with the debates over the active obedience of Christ in the sixteenth and seventeenth centuries. Moreover,

---

2. See, e.g., Belgic Confession, §XXII-XXIII; Heidelberg Catechism, qq. 60-64; Westminster Confession of Faith, XI; Larger Catechism, qq. 70-73; Shorter Catechism, q. 33; Augsburg Confession, IV; Apology of the Augsburg Confession, IV; Formula of Concord, Epitome, III; Solid Declaration, III.

3. Council of Trent, Session VI, 13 Jan 1547, 'Decree on Justification.'

Reformed theologians in the sixteenth century debated the precise nature of Adam's imputed guilt, whether it came through means or apart from them, namely, mediate versus immediate imputation.

Debates over the precise nature of imputation raged in the nineteenth-century American Presbyterian scene, but the doctrine remained intact through the efforts of Old Princeton theologians like Charles Hodge (1797–1878) and B. B. Warfield (1851–1921).[4] In the contemporary period the doctrine of imputation has been criticized and defended. On this front, representatives of the so-called New Perspective on Paul have been some of the most vocal critics of the doctrine.[5] Theologians devoted to the traditional view of imputation have manned the ramparts of the Reformed system of doctrine and defended the imputation against criticisms and rejections.[6] In all of these debates, however, there are two noticeable trends.

First, critics and defenders typically fight on a very small Pauline battlefield—the so-called undisputed Pauline corpus.[7] Can

---

4. Charles Hodge, 'The Christian Spectator on The Doctrine of Imputation,' *The Biblical Repertory and Princeton Review* 3 (1831): 407-43; idem, 'Inquiries Respecting the Doctrine of Imputation,' *Biblical Repertory and Princeton Review* 2 (1830): 425-72; idem, 'The Doctrine of Imputation,' in *Theological Essays: Reprinted from the Princeton Review* (New York: Wiley and Putnam, 1846), 195-217; B. B. Warfield, 'Imputation,' in *Studies in Theology* (Edinburgh: Banner of Truth, 1988), 301-12.

5. See, e.g., N. T. Wright, *Justification: God's Plan and Paul's Vision* (Downers Grove: InterVarsity Press, 2009), 135-36, 157-58, 232-33; Michael F. Bird, 'Incorporated Righteousness: A Response to Recent Evangelical Discussion Concerning the Imputation of Christ's Righteousness in Justification,' *JETS* 476/2 (2004): 253-75.

6. See, e.g., Cornelis Venema, 'Calvin's Doctrine of the Imputation of Christ's Righteousness: Another Example of "Calvin vs. the Calvinists"?' *MAJT* 20 (2009): 15-47; D. A. Carson, 'The Vindication of Imputation: On Fields of Discourse and Semantic Fields,' in *Justification: What's At Stake in the Current Debates*, ed. Mark Husbands and Daniel J. Treier (Downers Grove: InterVarsity, 2004), 46-78; John Piper, *Counted Righteous in Christ: Should We Abandon the Imputation of Christ's Righteousness?* (Wheaton: Crossway, 2002).

7. Cf. e.g., N. T. Wright, *What St. Paul Really Said: Was Paul of Tarsus the Real Founder of Christianity?* (Grand Rapids: Eerdmans, 1997); Cornelis P.

such a narrow exegetical section decide a doctrine that purports to represent the teaching of the whole of Scripture? From one vantage point the answer to this question is, yes. We can draw correct global doctrinal conclusions from any one portion of Scripture and rest assured it will be consistent with the rest of Scripture given the Bible's verbal plenary inspiration. But if we only examine a small portion of Scripture and then attempt global conclusions, we run the risk of misinterpreting one part in the absence of the consideration of the whole. We also may present starved doctrinal conclusions that lack nourishment from the rest of the canon of Scripture. Such doctrinal accounts run the risk of being theologically anorexic. The doctrine of imputation, or any doctrine for that matter, must rest on the collective testimony of Scripture, not simply a few isolated Pauline texts.

Second, despite the doctrine's well-attested pedigree as a load-bearing pillar for the doctrine of justification, I have not found a treatment of imputation that deals with the history, exegesis, and both sides of the issue, namely, imputed guilt and righteousness. John Murray (1898–1975) wrote journal articles that were eventually published as a small book on the imputation of Adam's sin.[8] Conversely, Brian Vickers published his doctoral dissertation on Paul's theology of imputation, a book that focuses upon the question of imputed righteousness.[9] Various treatments of the doctrine either appear in broader treatments of the doctrines of justification or original sin but rarely can one find a monograph that deals with both imputed guilt and righteousness. One of the few treatments of threefold imputation appears in Caspar Wistar Hodge Jr.'s (1870–1937) brief article in the *International Standard Bible Encyclopedia*.[10] As useful and valuable as these resources are,

---

Venema, *The Gospel of Free Acceptance in Christ: An Assessment of the Reformation and New Perspective on Paul* (Edinburgh: Banner of Truth, 2006), 148.

8. John Murray, *The Imputation of Adam's Sin* (Philipsburg: P & R, 1977).

9. Brian Vickers, *Jesus' Blood and Righteousness: Paul's Theology of Imputation* (Wheaton: Crossway, 2006).

10. Caspar Wistar Hodge, Jr., 'Imputation,' *International Standard Bible Encyclo-*

the time has come for the doctrine of imputation that treats history, exegesis, and dogmatic formulation.

ARGUMENT

This essay, therefore, defends the thesis that the doctrine of the immediate threefold imputation (Adam's guilt to all human beings, the sins of the elect to Christ, and Christ's active and passive obedience to the elect) is a biblical doctrine. My goal is to present the doctrine as it rests in the cradle of classic Reformed covenant theology, not as an abstract mechanism where imputation is simply the means by which God accounts people guilty and righteous. Covenant theology is the necessary context for imputation because it clothes the doctrine in the robe of the blood, sweat, and tears of redemptive history. The Bible's teaching on the covenants act as a deterrent against presenting imputation as an abstract divine act of reconciling the ledgers of sin and righteousness rather than as an act of demerited favor and love—an inestimable gift forged on the anvil of the life, death, resurrection of Jesus Christ. While not a main focus of the book, as others have ably treated and explain classic threefold covenant theology (the covenants of redemption, works, and grace), we must locate the doctrine of imputation within the context of the respective works of the two Adams.[11] In the past some have treated imputation apart from consideration of the doctrine of the covenants.[12] In fact, this seems to be the present trend in contemporary discussions of imputation. As much as some

---

pedia, vol. 3, ed. James Orr (Grand Rapids: Eerdmans, 1974), 1462-66.

11. For recent examples, see Michael Horton, *God of Promise: Introducing Covenant Theology* (Grand Rapids: Baker, 2006); Zach Keele and Michael G. Brown, *Sacred Bond: Covenant Theology Explored* (Grandville, MI: Reformed Fellowship, 2012).

12. Murray (*Imputation of Adam's Sin*) does not mention the doctrine of the covenants, as he rejects the historic doctrine of the covenant of works. He instead prefers to label Adam's state in the garden as the 'Adamic Administration.' Murray holds the odd position of a non-covenantal but nevertheless federal imputation—cf. John Murray, 'The Adamic Administration,' in *Collected Writings of John Murray*, vol. 2, *Systematic Theology* (Edinburgh: Banner of Truth, 1977), 47-59.

might tout the importance of the covenants for Paul's theology, it never features in discussions on imputation.[13]

Granted, we can and should focus upon particular aspects of imputation, but at some point we should follow Paul's lead and place the two representative heads of mankind in parallel to explore the way in which God constitutes the many as sinners and righteous by virtue of the respective acts of the two Adams. Hence, we must explore imputation as a mechanism by which God accounts people guilty or righteous but do so within the historical matrix of the covenants of works and grace. Another important element of my defense of imputation is factoring the role of the Holy Spirit. As the history of the doctrine reveals, theologians account for the Spirit's work in terms of giving sinners faith in Christ, the instrument by which they lay hold of Christ's righteousness. But seldom do they factor the Spirit's work in other areas of the doctrine. I believe the Spirit has a greater role in imputation than theologians have historically acknowledged.

OUTLINE OF THE BOOK

This essay has three parts: history, exegesis, and dogmatic construction.

PART I: HISTORY

Any effort to offer a positive statement of the doctrine must be familiar with the various debates on both sides of the imputation coin, whether imputed guilt or righteousness. The early church wrestled with issues of inherited guilt, and in this period the views of Augustine (354–430) loom large. Theologians of the Middle Ages such as Anselm (ca. 1033–1109) and Thomas Aquinas (1225–74) employed Augustine's insights but also added their own unique accents. But the sixteenth-century reformers, including Martin Luther (1483–1546), challenged patristic and medieval views

---

13. N. T. Wright claims, 'Covenant theology is one of the main clues, usually neglected, for understanding Paul' (*The Climax of the Covenant: Christ and the Law in Pauline Theology* [Minneapolis: Fortress Press, 1993], xi).

on inherited guilt and especially righteousness as he moved the discussion in a legal-forensic direction. Luther no longer advocated a realistic view of righteousness but a legal one, which meant he believed that God imputed righteousness to sinners by faith alone. Similarly, John Calvin (1509–64) spoke of the imputation of righteousness and the non-imputation of sin, but he still held to medieval views of inherited guilt. His views are similar to those of Anselm and Aquinas, though he adds his own unique accents.

During the Reformation some of the most important but nevertheless largely unexplored terrain comes from the proceedings of the Council of Trent and its 1546 declarations on the doctrine of justification. Numerous Protestant historians and theologians have engaged the formal declarations of Trent, but few have explored the actual debates over imputed versus infused righteousness. Part I explores these debates to demonstrate that the Roman Catholic Church was very much aware of the Protestant position on imputed righteousness and roundly rejected it. In a three-hour speech before the council Jesuit theologian Diego Layñez (1512–1565) provided a dozen reasons why the Roman Catholic Church should reject and condemn the doctrine of imputed righteousness. Part I also surveys the Protestant responses to Trent, including the definitive rejoinder written by Lutheran theologian Martin Chemnitz (1522–1586). But just because Protestants were united in their rejection of Trent, does not mean they agreed on the precise nature of imputation.

Part I surveys, therefore, two key Protestant debates over imputation with the controversies over the views of Andreas Osiander (1498–1552) and Johannes Piscator (1546–1625). In the former Lutheran and Reformed theologians rejected the idea that believers, by virtue of their union with Christ, share in His essential righteousness. Both Lutheran and Reformed theologians believed that Christ's essential righteousness, what He possessed by virtue of His divine nature, was necessary but not the righteousness that believers received through justification. Both Lutherans and the Reformed maintained that God imputed the obedience, and therefore alien righteousness of Christ, which believers receive by faith alone. But within the Reformed churches significant debate erupted over the precise nature of Christ's imputed righteousness. Did God merely impute Christ's passive obedience, His life-long suffering that culminated in His crucifixion? Or did He also impute His active obedience, His life-long obedience to the law? Moreover, during the late-Reformation and Early Orthodox periods, theologians began to coordinate more closely the concepts of law and covenant. This added unique dimensions to the Reformed doctrine of imputation.

In Early Orthodoxy (1565–1630/40), Robert Rollock (ca. 1555–99) is a relatively unknown but important figure in the development of the doctrine of imputation. Rollock offers one of the first fully federal accounts of both imputed guilt and righteousness by means of the twofold architecture of the covenants of works and grace. As the doctrine develops in High Orthodoxy (1630/40–1700), there were debates regarding the precise nature of imputed righteousness at the Westminster Assembly, most notably over the question of Christ's imputed active obedience. Later Reformed theologians, such as Francis Turretin (1623–87), entered the fray and co-wrote the Formula Consensus Helvetica (1675) to reject officially the views of Piscator. During High Orthodoxy another debate broke out regarding the precise nature of Adam's imputed guilt—was it mediately or immediately imputed—did it come through means (procreation) or apart from means? Josua Placaeus (1596–1655) lobbied for his view of mediate imputation, but it was quickly rejected in Turretin's Formula Consensus.

Given the majority consensus in the seventeenth century for covenantally imputed guilt and righteousness, one might think that debates over these issues would dissipate. Nevertheless, controversy in the modern period intensified especially in the nineteenth-century Presbyterian Church. In many respects virtually every view advocated in the previous seventeen hundred years of the church re-surfaced: Pelagian imitation, immediate imputation, realistic imputation, and some, such as Robert L. Dabney (1820–98), claimed informed agnosticism on the matter. In the present day, there is a sense in which things have gone from bad to worse. Nineteenth-century theologians stood with the catholic faith and rejected Pelagian views of original sin, but in the twentieth century up to the present day, Pelagianism has come back with a vengeance. Fueled by source-critical views of Scripture and the latest scientific developments, theologians within both Roman Catholic and Reformed circles have denied the historicity of Adam and thus reconfigured the doctrines of original sin and Christ's satisfaction, which has led some self-professed Reformed theologians to scuttle entirely the doctrine of imputation.

All of these different twists and turns are necessary pieces of information that one must factor in the formulation of the doctrine of threefold imputation. In what sense do people receive Adam's guilt and by what, if any, means? Most agree that God imputes the sins of the elect to Christ, but not all agree on the precise nature of what God imputes to the elect, the active and / or passive obedience? Part I sets the stage for these questions by exploring the various debates over the doctrine of imputation.

PART II: EXEGESIS

All too often critics and proponents of imputation alike center the debate on a small cluster of Pauline texts. As important as Romans 5:12-19 and 2 Corinthians 5:17-21 are, they do not constitute its sole exegetical pillars. Part II therefore surveys a number of key Old Testament texts to establish exegetically the doctrine of imputation, including Joshua 7 and the sin of Achan, 2 Samuel 24 and David's sinful census, as well as Daniel 7. These texts show how God repeatedly binds the one (individuals) and the many together and holds the many accountable for the actions of the one, a key component of the doctrine of imputation. Beyond these texts, Part II surveys Leviticus 16 and the Day of Atonement, one of the crucial building blocks for imputation, a text that forms the foundation of Isaiah 53:11-12. Isaiah's famous song about the Suffering Servant is a vital Old Testament text that few critics or contemporary proponents factor. Part II surveys one last Old Testament text, Zechariah 3:1-5, a passage that seldom features in contemporary discussion but nevertheless provides fundamental data for imputation. Part II then segues to three New Testament texts: Romans 4, 5:12-21, and 2 Corinthians 5:17-21. This portion of Part II also engages recent rejections of the doctrine from various representatives of the New Testament guild who either embrace or are sympathetic to the so-called New Perspective on Paul. Part II establishes the legitimacy of threefold imputation: that God imputes Adam's sin to all humanity, that He imputes the sins of the elect to Christ, and Christ's active and passive obedience to the elect.

PART III: DOGMATIC CONSTRUCTION

Part III takes the gathered Old and New Testament exegetical data and situates the doctrinal truths within the scope of pre- and redemptive history. Part III explains that there are two necessary presuppositions for a proper biblical understanding of imputation: (1) affirming the historicity of Adam, and (2) factoring the covenantal nature of humanity's interactions with God. Given these two assumptions, Part III explores the respective works of Adam and Christ, the two epochal heads of humanity, which in classic Reformed theology receives the labels of the covenants of works and grace. While placing Adam in a covenantal relationship with God has come under criticism even within the Reformed community, it is a doctrinal conclusion affirmed by historic Jewish interpretation of the Old Testament. Moreover, the Israelite familiar with the rest of the Old Testament would have naturally recognized Adam's covenantal context. The covenantal context best explains the representative nature of the works of the two Adams. Rather than realistic or mediate categories, God's verbal, and hence forensic, dealings with humanity best explain the nature by which God holds all humanity accountable for Adam's first sin and the means by which He accredits Christ's active and passive righteousness to the elect. Part III does not merely assert these conclusions but rather bases them upon detailed exegesis of key passages, such as God's commands to Adam. Part III also factors the geography or location of Adam's covenantal dealings with God. Adam's covenant occurs in the context of the prototypical edenic temple, the realm of God's life-giving Spirit. When he sins, God banishes Adam from the temple and his exilic state is a significant factor in the doctrine of imputation that few take into account. Imputation, the forensic assignment of guilt, is a consequence of Adam's violation of the covenant for all of those federally bound to him, and Adam's offspring die because of this assignment of guilt, the consequence of which is dwelling in exile, under the state of death, east of Eden away from the life-giving power of the Spirit.

CONCLUSION

In the end, even though oft criticized and outright rejected, the doctrine of imputation is an essential component of the doctrine of justification, and more broadly the gospel. How do we account for the universality of death? Why do all human beings, regardless of age, place, culture, or language, succumb to this most unnatural state? Conversely, how do we account for the fact that Christ redeems fallen sinners? Even though some claim that the Bible only acknowledges our sin-fallen state but does not explain the connection between Adam and humanity, the Bible is clear. And even though some claim that imputation is an outdated and erroneous understanding of how God accounts sinners righteousness in His sight, the Bible is clear. What the apostle Paul succinctly presents in Romans 5:12-21 is a distillation of the uniform witness of Scripture—God covenantally binds the one and the many—no man is an island unto himself. No one can claim, 'I am the master of my fate, the captain of my soul,' and stand entirely alone before the divine bar of judgment. God has covenantally appointed two representatives, Adam and Christ, who determine the destinies of those whom they represent: 'For as by the one man's disobedience the many were constituted sinners, so by the one man's obedience the many will be constituted righteous' (Rom. 5:19*). Beneath Paul's simple statement lies the doctrine of imputation, namely, that we receive death in Adam but gain life in Christ.

PART I:

HISTORY OF THE DOCTRINE

1

The Early Church and the Middle Ages

Introduction

The story of the development of the doctrine of imputation naturally begins with the early church. One should not expect fully developed doctrinal expressions during this period as the church was just beginning to explicate and defend the various doctrines of the completed biblical canon. Theologians were aware of the presence of sin and humanity's sinfulness and the need for righteousness in salvation, but they only began to discuss and debate these ideas with great vigor in the effort to refute theological error, most notably with the rise of Pelagianism. This chapter, therefore, begins with a survey of the early church largely through the views of Augustine of Hippo (354–430), arguably the greatest theologian during the first millennium of church history. While other theologians certainly contributed to the development of imputation, Augustine stands heads and shoulders above the rest. It was his formulations that echoed into the middle ages. After expositing the views of Augustine, I treat three key figures during the middle ages, namely, Anselm (ca. 1033–1109), Peter Lombard (ca. 1100–60), and Thomas Aquinas (1225–74), towering theologians who made significant contributions to the ongoing discussion. This chapter shows that a legal-forensic concept of imputation was largely absent from the church during the early church and Middle Ages. Rather than employ legal categories, theologians spoke in ontological ones: sin and righteousness were physically transmitted, the former through procreation and the latter through the waters of baptism. The chapter concludes with key questions that arise in the course of surveying the early church and Middle Ages.

AUGUSTINE

In the post-Apostolic era theologians did not give great attention to the doctrine of imputation. They acknowledged the sinfulness of humanity and the need of righteousness for salvation. But they did not discuss these ideas under the rubric of imputation or trans-mission, whether in the case of the imputation of original sin or Christ's righteousness. One of the access points to the early church's understanding of original sin, for example, comes from various statements about why the church baptized infants. Clement of Alexandria (ca. 150–215) believed that children were 'pure in flesh, holy in soul by the abstinence from evil deeds,' which is how God 'generated us from our mother.'[1] Irenaeus (ca. 130–ca. 202) held that children were innocent and had no sense of evil.[2] Other Eastern theologians such as John Chrysostom (ca. 347–407) and Maximus the Confessor (580–662) held similar views. In other

---

1. Clement of Alexandria, *Stromata*, IV.25, in ANF II:439.

2. Irenaeus, *Against Heresies*, IV.xxviii.3, in ANF I:502.

words, Adam's sin did not bring guilt but mortality, and death, and suffering.[3] Chrysostom, for example, writes: 'We baptize even infants, although they are sinless, that they may be given the further gifts of sanctification, justice, filial adoption, and inheritance, that they may be brothers and members of Christ, and become dwelling places for the Spirit.'[4] In the West, theologians such as Tertullian (ca. 160–ca. 220) likewise thought that children were innocent and therefore should not be brought forward for baptism. In his mind, baptism committed the recipient to all of the obligations of discipleship, and hence all of the perils of apostasy.[5] A key idea for some of these theologians, such as Irenaeus and Clement, are the scriptural admonitions that sinners had to become like little children (Matt. 19:14; 1 Cor. 14:20). Other early church fathers held similar views.[6]

As theologians continued to reflect upon the idea of sin and how to account for human depravity, they began to posit the hereditary transmission of sin and guilt from one generation to the next. The hereditary transmission of sin was inherently connected to the dominant view of the origin of the human soul. Some, such as Tertullian, believed that the father generated the soul in the act

---

3. Chrysostom, 'Homily X,' in NPNF¹ XI:401-08, esp. 403-04; Fr. Panayiotis Papageorgiou, 'Chrysostom and Augustine on the Sin of Adam and Its Consequences,' *SVTQ* 39/4 (1995): 361-78, esp. 368-69; Maximus the Confessor, 'Ad Thalassium: On the Legacy of Adam's Transgression,' in *On the Cosmic Mystery of Jesus Christ* (New York: St. Vladimir's Seminary Press, 2003), 131-43; Daniel Haynes, 'The Transgression of Adam and Christ the New Adam: St. Augustine and St. Maximus the Confessor on the Doctrine of Original Sin,' *SVTQ* 55/3 (2011): 293-317, esp. 313-14; cf. Bradley L. Nassif, 'Toward a "Catholic" Understanding of St. Augustine's View of Original Sin,' *USQR* 39/4 (1984): 287-99, esp. 294-96.

4. Chrysostom, 'Third Instruction,' 3.6, in *Baptismal Instructions*, vol. 31, *Ancient Christian Writers*, eds. Johannes Quasten and Walter J. Burghardt (Mahwah: Paulist Press, 1963), 57.

5. Tertullian, *On Baptism*, 18, in ANF III:678.

6. See Pier Franco Beatrice, *The Transmission of Sin: Augustine and the Pre-Augustinian Sources*, trans. Adam Kamesar (Oxford: Oxford University Press, 2013), 77-94.

of procreation.[7] This view is known as *traducianism*. Others, such as Augustine and Jerome (ca. 347–420), believed that God created new souls every time a person was conceived, at which point God infuses the soul into the body, which has been called *creationism*.[8] And a third view, held by Origen (ca. 182–ca. 254), contends that God created a storehouse of souls from which He gathered and joined them to bodies conceived in the act of procreation. In other words, souls existed prior to the creation.[9] The dominant view regarding the origin of the soul was traducianism, a doctrine that was later rejected by the church. Nevertheless, within this context, souls bore the contagion of original sin as they were generated in procreation.[10] From within this thought-world Augustine developed his views on the transmission of original sin.

Augustine hammered out his views on original sin on the anvil of the Pelagian controversy.[11] One of the catalysts in the development of Augustine's view was the Pelagian claim that infants were born without any hereditary sin. Pelagius (fl. ca. 390–418) claimed that people did not inherit a sin nature but rather sinned because they followed Adam's negative example. In his explanation of Paul's famous text, 'Just as sin came into the world through one man, and death through sin, and so death spread to all men because all sinned' (Rom. 5:12), Pelagius argued that all people die because they follow Adam's bad example: 'As long as they sin the same

---

7. Tertullian, *A Treatise on the Soul*, § 27, in ANF III:207.

8. Augustine, *A Treatise on the Origin of the Human Soul, Addressed to Jerome (Letter 166)*, VIII.25, in NPNF¹ I:523-32.

9. Fifth Ecumenical (Constantinople) Council (553), *The Anathemas Against Origen*, §§1-15, in NPNF² XIV:318-20.

10. Beatrice, *Transmission of Sin*, 76-77. Cf. Peter Lombard, *The Sentences*, 4 vols., trans. Giulio Silano (Toronto: Pontifical Institutes of Medieval Studies, 2007–10), II.xviii.7; Thomas Aquinas, *Summa Theologica* (Allen: Christian Classics, 1948), Ia q. 118 arts. 1-3

11. For a theory on one of the chief sources of Augustine's doctrine, see Ernesto Bonaiuti, 'The Genesis of St. Augustine's Idea of Original Sin,' *HTR* 10/2 (1917): 159-75.

way, they likewise die.'[12] In this respect Pelagius was clear in his rejection of Adam's representative status: 'Thus, declaring it to be unjust that a soul which is born today, not from the lump of Adam, bears so ancient a sin belonging to another, they say that on no account should it be granted that God, who forgives a person his own sins, imputes to him another's.'[13] In Pelagius's view, each person stands personally and individually responsible for his own sin—he incurs no guilt, contagion, or hereditary defilement from Adam.

In Augustine's eyes, Pelagius threw down the gauntlet and rejected the necessity of God's grace. Early in Augustine's career, he advocated the idea of the sinfulness of the human race: 'Now all men are a mass of sin, since, as the apostle says, "In Adam all die" (1 Cor. 15:22), and to Adam the entire human race traces the origin of its sin against God. Sinful humanity must pay a debt of punishment to the supreme divine justice.'[14] Echoing Paul's lump of clay language from Romans 9:21, Augustine believed that humanity was formed from one mass, which 'inherited sin and the penalty of mortality.'[15] Augustine united all of humanity corporately in Adam, which bound all people to Adam's first sin and made them liable to punishment for it.

When Augustine later explained how Adam's sin was transmitted to his progeny, he appealed to Romans 5:12, but as many know, he mistranslated Paul's famous text. Augustine followed the Vulgate's rendering of the verse, which reads: 'Just as sin came into the world through one man, and death through sin, and so death spread to all men; in whom [Adam] all sinned [*in quo omnes peccaverunt*].' Numerous commentators have criticized

---

12. Pelagius, *Pelagius's Commentary on St Paul's Epistle to the Romans*, trans. Theodore de Bruyn (Oxford: Clarendon Press, 1998), 92.

13. Pelagius, *Commentary on Romans*, 94.

14. Augustine, *To Simplician*, II.16, in *Augustine: Earlier Writings*, vol. 6, Library of Christian Classics (Philadelphia: Westminster, 1953), 398; cf. II.17, 19, in *Augustine: Earlier Writings*, 398, 402.

15. Augustine, *To Simplician*, II.20, in *Augustine: Earlier Writings*, 403.

and noted Augustine's faulty translation.[16] Some have speculated that Augustine was ignorant of the Greek text, and since he only had the Latin before him, he consequently drew this erroneous conclusion. Others have pointed out that Augustine had access to the Greek text of Romans, was aware of the different readings, and nevertheless stuck to his interpretation.[17] Namely, all humanity sinned in Adam and was therefore guilty. Augustine was willing to hold to his view even in the face of what were difficult consequences. Unlike his predecessors, who taught that infants were born free of sin but were mortal because of Adam's sin, Augustine believed that infants 'are held in bondage by original sin alone, and because of this alone go into damnation.'[18] In other words, because infants bore the guilt of original sin they would be damned to hell if they died unbaptized. Baptism, according to Augustine, removed the stain and guilt of original sin, and without this remedy infants were subject to damnation even if they had committed no personal sins.[19]

Two church councils officially resolved the Augustine – Pelagius debate, the councils of Carthage (418) and Orange (529). The Council of Carthage was the first official ecclesiastical response to Pelagius. The council devotes eight canons to the question of original sin and bears the fingerprints of Augustine. The council anathematizes anyone who contends that Adam was created mortal. That is, he would have died whether or not he sinned.[20] The

---

16. Adolf von Harnack, *The History of Dogma*, vol. 5, trans. James Millar, ed. T. K. Cheyne and A. B. Bruce (London: Williams & Norgate, 1898), 215; John M. Rist, 'Augustine on Free Will and Predestination,' *JTS* 20/2 (1969): 430-31.

17. Gerald Bonner, 'Les Origens Africaines de la doctrine Augustinienne sur la chute et le péché originel,' in *God's Decree and Destiny: Studies on the Thought of Augustine of Hippo* (London: Variorum Reprints, 1987), 109.

18. Augustine, *Predestination of the Saints*, XIII.(24), in *Four Anti-Pelagian Writings*, Fathers of the Church, vol. 86, ed. Thomas P. Halton, et al. trans. John A. Mourant and William J. Collinge (Washington: Catholic University of America Press, 1992), 246.

19. Augustine, *On Forgiveness of Sins, and Baptism*, I.21, in NPNF[1] V:22-23.

20. Council of Carthage (418), canon 1, in Heinrich Denzinger, *Compendium of*

second canon anathematizes anyone who denies that infants must be baptized to remove original sin. To support this conclusion the council adopts Augustine's reading of Romans 5:12. The council states: 'For because of this tenet of faith even little children, who in themselves have not yet been able to commit any sins, are in consequence baptized truly for the remission of sins, so that in them that which has incurred by their birth may be cleansed by their rebirth.'[21]

The Council of Orange (529) reached similar conclusions but at certain points goes into greater detail regarding the transmission of original sin. In the second canon the council reaffirms Augustine's understanding of original sin: 'If anyone maintains that the fall harmed Adam alone and not his descendants or declares that only bodily death which is the punishment of sin, but no sin itself, which is the death of the soul, was passed on to the whole human race by one man, he ascribes injustice to God and contradicts the words of the apostle [i.e. Rom. 5:12].'[22] The council addresses a key Pelagian tenet, namely that the faculty of the will was unharmed by Adam's sin, and hence spoken of as free. The council counters this claim and argues that the will 'is wounded in all those who are born from the transgression of the first man.'[23] The council essentially affirmed Augustine's view and maintained that Adam's first sin, that is, its moral and judicial consequences, was transmitted to all of his progeny by virtue of their birth. In a word, like begets like, and hence a sinful man begets sinful offspring. Moreover, this sin affects the human race and subjects it to death and places the will under the noetic effects of sin.

Augustine's view was summarized and adopted at Carthage and Orange, and it was this doctrine that was eventually officially

Creeds, Definitions, and Declarations on Matters of Faith and Morals, 43rd ed., ed. Peter Hünermann, et al. (San Francisco: Ignatius Press, 2012), §222 (p. 82).

21. Council of Carthage (418), canon 2, in *Compendium*, §223 (pp. 82-83); cf. Beatrice, *Transmission of Sin*, 250-51.

22. Second Synod of Orange (529), canon 2, in *Compendium*, §372 (p. 135).

23. Second Synod of Orange (529), canon 8, in *Compendium*, §378 (p. 136).

received at the Council of Trent (1545–63). In one of its earliest sessions, the council issued a decree on original sin:

> If anyone does not acknowledge that the first man, Adam, when he acted against God's command in paradise, immediately lost that holiness and justice in which he had been created and, because of the sin of such a transgression, incurred the anger and displeasure of God and consequently death, with which God had previously threatened him, and with death a captivity under the power of him who, because of that sinful disobedience, was changed in body and soul for the worse: let him be anathema.[24]

In the subsequent paragraphs Trent condemns the idea that Adam's sin affected him alone, and once again like the earlier councils, they cite Romans 5:12. Trent condemns the Pelagian idea that sin is passed by imitation rather than propagation. They also affirm that infants must be baptized in order to remove the guilt and stain of original sin because they too contract it by virtue of their birth. They must be reborn through the waters of baptism.[25] By this point in the development of the doctrine the church argued that the necessity of infant baptism for the cleansing from original sin was part of the rule of faith transmitted from the apostles.[26]

A few observations are in order regarding the significance of Augustine's understanding of the transmission of original sin. First, Augustine's view has been designated as the *realistic* view of imputation.[27] Augustine's view, however, should instead be called the realistic view of the transmission of original sin, as his understanding does not involve a forensic-juridical imposition of guilt. We inherit Adam's guilt, not by a legal relationship, that is, a representative or federal one, but by our ontological connection

---

24. Dogmatic Decrees of the Council of Trent, 'Decree on Original Sin (17 June 1546),' sess. 5, § 1.

25. Council of Trent, 'Decree on Original Sin,' sess. 5, §§ 3-4.

26. Council of Trent, 'Decree on Original Sin,' sess. 5, § 4.

27. So, e.g., John Murray, *The Imputation of Adam's Sin* (Phillipsburg: P & R, 1959), 24.

to him.[28] We genetically inherit his sin and thus guilt and punishment. The act of procreation transmits guilt. The exegetical crux for Augustine's realistic view is not only Romans 5:12 but also Hebrews 7:4-10. This passage speaks of the occasion when Abraham paid tithes to Melchizedek (Heb. 7:4). The author contends that Levi paid tithes through Abraham: 'One might even say that Levi himself, who receives tithes, paid tithes through Abraham, for he was still in the loins of his ancestor when Melchizedek met him' (Heb. 7:9-10). Augustine invokes this passage to explain the link between Adam and his offspring.[29] Augustine writes: 'Not in vain, however, does Scripture say that even an infant is not free from sin if he has spent one day of life on earth. The Psalmist says, "In iniquity I was conceived, and in sin my mother nourished me in her womb." St. Paul says that all die in Adam, "in whom all have sinned".'[30] There is a sense in which the human race is seminally present in Adam, but Augustine also places weight upon the transmission of sin through the propagation of the race. By virtue of the natural and ontological union that humanity shares with Adam, all inherit original sin.[31]

Second, during the Augustine – Pelagius debate attention centered upon the question of original sin, although issues related to justification also surfaced. The relationship between grace, good works, merit, justification, and righteousness did arise, but were focused upon ontological rather than forensic categories. Augustine's realistic understanding of sin impacted his understanding of the nature of justification. If natural descent transmits original sin, then grace, and particularly righteousness, has a similar manner of transmission. In baptism God infuses grace into the sinner to

28. Gerald Hiestand, 'Augustine and the Justification Debates: Appropriating Augustine's Doctrine of Culpability,' *TJ* 28NS (2007): 120.

29. Augustine, *The Literal Meaning of Genesis*, vol. 41, *Ancient Christian Writers*, trans. John Hammond Taylor (New York: Paulist Press, 1982), VI.9 (p. 187).

30. Augustine, *Literal Meaning of Genesis*, VI.9 (p. 188); cf. Beatrice, *Transmission of Sin*, 100-101.

31. Murray, *Imputation*, 26-27.

counteract the effects of original sin. The water physically carries God's grace, that which extinguishes original sin and brings about a person's spiritual rebirth.[32] Upon their baptism, even infants are infused with the grace of the Holy Spirit and cleansed from original sin.[33] Given his realistic presuppositions, the ideological framework for the concept of imputed righteousness does not exist.[34] Sin and righteousness are primarily, though not exclusively, ontological categories. Their legal dimension comes about as an effect of their presence or absence in a person.

Hence, for Augustine, a person must actually be righteous in order to be declared just before the divine bar. Augustine illustrates this very point when he writes: 'Grace is therefore of him who calls, and the consequent good works of him who receive grace. Good works do not produce grace but are produced by grace. Fire is not hot in order that it may burn, but because it burns. A wheel does not run nicely in order that it may be round, but because it is round.'[35] A person must first receive God's grace before he can produce good works, which thereby demonstrate his righteous status. Augustine, therefore, does not distinguish between justification and sanctification as later early modern Protestant theologians do. Theologians of the patristic era follow this general pattern. Hence, one does not find widespread discussion in the patristic era of imputed righteousness as the doctrine later appears during the Protestant Reformation. The concept is present in inchoate form, but lacks the precision of later sixteenth-century formulations.[36] Rather, debate and discussion focuses upon the transmission of sin.

---

32. Augustine, *On Forgiveness of Sins, and Baptism*, I.20, in NPNF[1] V:22.

33. Augustine, *On Forgiveness of Sins, and Baptism*, I.10, in NPNF[1] V:18-19.

34. Hiesand, 'Augustine and Justification Debates,' 123, 129-30.

35. Augustine, *To Simplician*, I.ii.3, in *Augustine: Earlier Writings*, 388.

36. See Thomas C. Oden, *The Justification Reader* (Grand Rapids: Eerdmans, 2002), 60-106. In some respects Oden's gathered evidence shows that patristic theologians echoed and repeated statements from the biblical text that speak of imputation, but they infrequently say much more than this.

Third, and last, original sin corrupts the faculties of the soul (intellect and will) and brings mortality and ultimately death. Augustine believed that human beings retained their *liberum arbitrium* ('free choice'), but that they had lost *libertas* ('freedom') to choose to do spiritual good. Sin binds and corrupts the will.[37] In contrast to Pelagian views, Augustine affirmed the noetic and physical effects of original sin. Original sin brings death and corruption in its wake, and poisons all men, women, and children. Despite Augustine's prominence and esteem, later church councils did not completely endorse his views regarding the degree to which human nature had been vitiated by sin. This is not to say that the image of God was completly obliterated. Later church councils spoke of human nature being wounded, not vitiated. The Council of Orange states that Adam's whole person was 'changed for the worse' and the Council of Trent echoes these words.[38] Working from later medieval developments, which will be treated below, Trent affirms that Adam was not totally corrupted but that he lost his holiness and justice.[39]

MIDDLE AGES

Augustine's realistic doctrine of justification was dominant and was reaffirmed by numerous theologians for centuries to come. In other words, sin and righteousness were still primarily discussed in ontological rather than legal terms. Nevertheless, several key developments concerning the doctrine of original sin should be factored, most notably the contributions of Anselm, Lombard, and Aquinas. One late medieval theologian, Gabriel Biel (ca. 1420–95) explains that these three titans of the middle ages present the three major views on the nature of original sin. Anselm believed original

---

37. Augustine, *On Grace and Free Will*, in NPNF¹ V:436-65; cf. J. N. D. Kelly, *Early Christian Doctrines*, rev. ed. (San Francisco: Harper San Francisco, 1978), 357-66.

38. Cf. Augustine, *City of God*, XIII.3, 14, XXII.24; Second Synod of Orange (529), canon 1, in *Compendium*, §371 (p. 134); Dogmatic Decrees of Trent, 'Decree on Original Sin,' §1.

39. Dogmatic Decrees of Trent, 'Decree on Original Sin,' §2.

sin is the absence of original justice, Lombard that it is the presence of concupiscence, and Aquinas that it is the absence of original justice and positive presence of sin.[40]

ANSELM

For Anselm, original sin was not an added infection but rather a loss of original righteousness. Anselm viewed original sin in terms of a privation of nature rather than the positive presence of sin and guilt.[41] Adam's sin was a transgression of divine law and was an affront to God's honor.[42] What aggravated the nature of Adam's sin was Anselm's belief that Adam was created and given the divine gift of *iustitia* (righteousness), that which enabled him to distinguish between right and wrong.[43] When Adam sinned, he lost this gift of original righteousness for himself and his progeny. Anselm explains:

> If Adam and Eve had retained their original justice, their descendants would, like them, have been originally just. But they committed personal sin, and so whereas originally they had the strength and integrity to remain just without trouble, their whole being was now weakened and corrupted. Their bodies after their sin became like those of brute beasts, subject to corruption and carnal appetites, and their souls, ruled by this bodily corruption and these appetites, and deprived of the gifts they had lost, were themselves infected with carnal appetites. And because the whole human nature was contained in Adam and Eve, and nothing of it existed outside of them, the whole of human nature was weakened and corrupted.[44]

---

40. Heiko A. Oberman, *The Harvest of Medieval Theology* (1963; Grand Rapids: Baker, 1983), 121-23.

41. Wiley, *Original Sin*, 80.

42. Anselm, *Why God Became Man*, I.11, in *Anselm of Canterbury: The Major Works*, ed. Brian Davies: Oxford University Press, 1998), 282-83. Subsequent citations from Anselm will provide page numbers from the Davies edition in parentheses. Cf. Henri Rondet, *Original Sin: The Patristic and Theological Background* (Shannon, Ireland: Ecclesia Press, 1969), 148.

43. Anselm, *Why God Became Man*, II.i (*Works*, 315).

44. Anselm, *On the Virgin Conception and Original Sin*, §II (*Works*, 360).

While Anselm still retains the Augustinian realistic element, human fallenness is attributed to the absence of original righteousness, not the positive presence of sin. Moreover, Anselm's theory of the transmission of sin does not rest upon Augustine's idea of the seminal presence of humanity in Adam, but upon Platonist ideals: namely, Adam possesses the paradigmatic human nature, and thus the archetypal human nature falls with Adam's sin and all of his progeny with him.[45] In fact, Anselm contends that human seed, which Augustine saw as corrupted by sin, is no more defiled than spittle or blood. Sin does not reside in the body, per se, but in the human will.[46]

Anselm's definition of sin, the failure to render honor to God, naturally impacts his understanding of the function of righteousness in justification. He famously argues that Christ makes satisfaction on behalf of sinners through His obedience. Following the broad strokes of Romans 5:12-21, Anselm argues that just as death entered the human race through disobedience, that God brings salvation and restoration through a man's obedience.[47] Christ makes satisfaction, which brings the forgiveness of sins, but this does not automatically remedy the need for righteousness. Justice (or righteousness) does not rotate upon the axis of moral equity and obedience to the law but rather the state of the will: 'Justice is not rectitude of knowledge or action, but of will.'[48] Correlatively, Anselm maintains that truth is metaphysical rectitude, which he defines as 'rectitude perceptible by the mind alone.'[49] In his sin, Adam failed to live according to truth, moral rectitude, the standard that God establishes in the creation of the cosmos, and hence lost the divine gift of original

---

45. Anselm, *On the Virgin Conception and Original Sin*, §I (*Works*, 359); Rondet, *Original Sin*, 149.

46. Anselm, *On the Virgin Conception and Original Sin*, §VII (*Works*, 366-67).

47. Anselm, *Why God Became Man*, I.iii (*Works*, 268).

48. Anselm, *On Truth*, §XII (*Works*, 167).

49. Anselm, *On Truth*, §XII (*Works*, 166); cf. Alister E. McGrath, *Iustitia Dei: A History of the Christian Doctrine of Justification*, 3rd ed. (Cambridge: Cambridge University Press, 2005), 76-77.

righteousness. Christ makes satisfaction for Adam's sin, which then enables people to seek righteousness and justification.[50]

LOMBARD

Peter Lombard was familiar with the history of the Augustine–Pelagius debate and positively quotes Augustine's rejection of the Pelagian view. With Augustine Lombard believed that original sin was not simply a question of imitation but also 'by the vice of propagation and origin.'[51] Lombard then surveys the field of different opinions—according to unnamed theologians, some hold that original sin is the liability to punishment. In other words, Adam's offspring must suffer punishment for his act of disobedience.[52] Gregory of Nazianzus (ca. 329–90) defines original sin as a fault, which aligns with Augustine's views, which according to Lombard 'all people contract through concupiscence.' Lombard therefore concludes: 'Original sin is a fault, and that it is contracted by all who are born from their parents through concupiscence.'[53] He further explains that concupiscence is 'incentive to sin.'[54] In his judgment, Lombard believes concupiscence is the true nature of original sin: 'Through Adam, original sin, that is concupiscence, entered into all. From these statements, it is given to be understood what original sin is, namely the vice of concupiscence, which entered into all who were born from Adam through concupiscence and made them all sharers in its stain.'[55] Lombard believed that when Adam disobeyed, original sin proceeded from Adam's actual sin and he passed this on to all his offspring. According to Lombard, Adam passes original sin to his offspring through procreation because all humanity was formally, not materially or causally, in him. The

---

50. McGrath, *Iustitia Dei*, 78-81.

51. Peter Lombard, *The Sentences*, 4 vols., trans. Giulio Silano (Toronto: PIMS, 2007-10), II.xxx.4.

52. Lombard, *Sentences*, II.xxx.6.

53. Lombard, *Sentences*, II.xxx.7.

54. Lombard, *Sentences*, II.xxx.8.

55. Lombard, *Sentences*, II.xxx.10.

law of propagation, like begets like, governs the transmission of original sin.[56] Adam passed original sin to his offspring through the flesh, not through the soul.[57]

AQUINAS

Thomas Aquinas's contribution to the doctrine of the transmission of sin has been characterized as a synthesis of the Augustinian and Anselmian views.[58] Along Anselmian lines, Aquinas maintains that God created man and gave him the gift of original righteousness (*iustitia*), which held the disharmony of his soul at bay and staved off death.[59] For Aquinas original sin is the privation of justice (or righteousness); this is Anselm's view and Aquinas even cites his predecessor.[60] Thomas explains: 'The privation of original justice, whereby the will was made subject to God, is the formal element in original sin.'[61] Original justice was the glue that held the powers of the soul intact and ensured that (1) reason would remain in subjection to God, (2) the moral will would remain in subjection to reason, and (3) that the body would remain in subjection to the soul, which consists of the faculties of reason and will.[62] Aquinas writes: 'Now the cause of this corrupt disposition that is called original sin, is one only, viz. the privation of original justice, removing the subjection of man's mind to God.'[63] The disorder and chaos within

---

56. Lombard, *Sentences*, II.xxx.14.

57. Lombard, *Sentences*, II.xxxi.3.

58. Wiley, *Original Sin*, 83.

59. Thomas Aquinas, *Summa Theologica*, 5 vols. (Allen: Christian Classics, 1948), Ia q. 95 art. 1; Wiley, *Original Sin*, 85.

60. Aquinas, *Summa Theologica*, Ia IIae q. 83 art. 3; cf. Anselm, *On the Virgin Conception and Original Sin*, §III (*Works*, 361-62).

61. Aquinas, *Summa Theologica*, Ia IIae q. 82 art. 3.

62. Thomas Aquinas, *Commentary on the Letter of St. Paul to the Romans*, vol. 37, Latin/English Edition of the Works of St. Thomas Aquinas (Lander, Wyoming: Aquinas Institute for the Study of Sacred Doctrine, 2012), lect. 3, §416, pp. 141; Wiley, *Original Sin*, 85.

63. Aquinas, *Summa Theologica*, Ia IIae q. 82 art. 2

the human soul's faculties (reason and will) are due to the infection of original sin and the absence of original justice.[64]

Unlike Anselm, Aquinas believes that original sin is not merely the privation of original justice but also the infection and presence of sin. According to Thomas: 'Original sin spreads in two ways; from the flesh to the soul, and from the essence of the soul to the powers. The former follows the order of generation, the latter follows the order of perfection.'[65] That Thomas allows for the transmission of sin from flesh to soul means that, contrary to Anselm and in line with Augustine's and Lombard's earlier formulations, Adam transmits original sin to his progeny through the act of procreation. Aquinas cites Romans 5:12 in support of this claim and explicitly follows Augustine's exegesis of this text.[66] But Thomas also incorporates elements of Anselm's Platonic concept of human nature, as he believes that all individual persons are 'members of human nature,' which means, 'Sharing in the same species many men are one man.' Aquinas, then, maintains a twofold manner of the transmission of sin. Like two trains running on parallel tracks, Thomas maintains: 'Just as human nature is obtained through generation, so, too, by generation is passed on the defect it acquired from the sin of the first parent.'[67]

Original sin as the absence of original justice impacts Thomas's doctrine of justification. If original righteousness is an infused habit lost in the fall, then justification is about its recovery. Justification is a process that begins with the infusion of sanctifying grace in baptism, the movement of the will toward God through faith, the correlative movement of the will against sin, and the forgiveness of sin. Justification is both the remission of sin and the infusion of grace.[68] By this infusion of grace believers then seek to yield their

---

64. Aquinas, *Summa Theologica*, Ia IIae q. 82 art. 2.

65. Aquinas, *Summa Theologica*, Ia IIae q. 83 art. 2.

66. Aquinas, *Summa Theologica*, Ia IIae q. 82 art. 4, Ia IIae q. 81 art. 1; idem, *Romans*, lect. 3, §§406-20, pp. 137-42.

67. Aquinas, *Romans*, lect. 3, §410, p. 139.

68. Aquinas, *Summa Theologica*, Ia IIae q. 113 art. 2; idem, *Romans*, lect. 1, §§331-40, pp. 113-15; McGrath, *Iustitia Dei*, 64.

lives in obedience to God, or faith works through love (Gal. 5:6), in order to secure an indefectible standing before the divine bar.[69] For Thomas, original sin and justification, and hence righteousness, chiefly rest upon ontological rather than legal-forensic categories. For medieval theologians such as Anselm and Aquinas, we cannot describe their views in terms of imputed guilt and righteousness but rather the appropriate term is *transmitted*. Ontological rather than legal ligaments bind the human race. In fact, Thomas characterizes justification as deification, participation in the divine nature.[70] In this respect, union with Christ and justification go hand in hand in Aquinas's understanding.

CONCLUSION

In the early church and middle ages legal-forensic categories take a back seat to ontology. Exceptions always seem to hamper general rules, but there is little discussion of imputation in the early church or Middle Ages. Some have characterized early church views as realistic imputation, but *transmission* is a more accurate term. Theologians recognized the universal sinfulness of humanity, though there were dissenting voices regarding the innocence of infants. The Pelagian controversy, however, caused theologians such as Augustine to reexamine, drill down, and offer a full-fledged treatment of original sin. He argued for the physical transmission of sin through procreation, a conviction that endured for centuries to come; this view was codified in several different church councils, including Carthage, Orange, and Trent in the sixteenth century. But medieval theologians such as Anselm offered modifications to Augustinian views and contended that original sin was a privation of righteousness rather than the presence of sin. Moreover, rather than physical transmission, Anselm offered the idea of ordained

---

69. Thomas Aquinas, *Commentary on St. Paul's Letters to the Galatians and Ephesians*, vol. 39, Latin/English Edition of the Works of St. Thomas Aquinas (Lander, Wyoming: Aquinas Institute for the Study of Sacred Doctrine, 2012), lect. 2, §286, p. 128.

70. Aquinas, *Summa Theologica*, Ia IIae q. 112 art. 1.

transmission by virtue of Adam bearing the paradigmatic human nature. Aquinas incorporated both Augustinian and Anselmian elements in his own understanding of original sin and righteousness.

These developmental trends pose a number of questions that deserve consideration:

1. Is there a connection between Adam and his offspring? If so, what type of connection? Moral? Legal? Physical? Exemplary?

2. Is sin merely ontological and thereby something physically transmitted from one generation to the next?

3. If each successive generation inherits transmitted sin, then do they also physically receive righteousness through infusion?

4. Is original sin merely the absence of righteousness or the active presence of sin?

5. Do Platonic ideas best explain the biblical data? That is, does Adam bear the paradigmatic human nature, which when corrupted, affects all other human natures?

I address these questions in Parts II and III. Nevertheless, there is one more pressing question, namely, to what degree patristic views persist in the Reformation. On the one hand, the doctrine of imputed righteousness was part of the Reformation's renewed understanding of the doctrine of justification. But on the other hand, realistic and Anselmian views regarding the transmission of original sin still persisted.

2

THE REFORMATION

INTRODUCTION

An ontological view of sin and righteousness had a firm grip upon the church's collective understanding of original sin and justification, but during the Middle Ages the development of nominalism opened new vistas. Realism, the teaching that universals have an existence separate from specific concrete entities, colored the Augustinian doctrines of sin and justification. Hence, Augustine and others constructed these doctrines along realistic, or ontological, lines. But with the work of theologians like William of Ockham (ca. 1288 – ca. 1348), nominalism arose. Nominalism, the idea that universals do not have real existence but are merely names applied to qualities found in certain objects, created the intellectual space to consider sin and justification as something other than ontological.[1] This new philosophical development combined with renaissance humanism and the impulse to exegete the Scriptures from the original biblical languages prompted the reorientation of sin and righteousness around legal-forensic categories.

This chapter, therefore, explores Lutheran and Reformed views on imputation and the Roman Catholic response at the Council of Trent. Tridentine theologians believed one of the key issues of contention between Rome and the Protestant rebellion was the doctrine of imputation. Examining the Tridentine response is consequently important to understanding the full significance and scope of Protestant views. The chapter also explores the rise of covenant theology. Theologians combined categories of law and covenant, which impacted their doctrine of imputation. Many historians contend that the rise of federal theology, especially the doctrine of an Adamic covenant, originated with Reformed theologians. While this narrative is partially true, an Adamic covenant and covenantally imputed original guilt first appeared among Roman Catholic theologians. In fact, Roman Catholic theologians posited a twofold covenantal scheme long before Reformed theologians expressed similar views. A number of different factors, therefore, contribute to the articulation of a twofold imputation: the imputation of the sinner's guilt to Christ and Christ's righteousness to the believer. But early Roman Catholic formulations on covenantally imputed guilt provide at least one likely source for the development of a third form of imputation: the imputation of Adam's sin. This chapter, hence, covers Luther and Lutheranism, the Reformed tradition, the Tridentine response, and the Protestant rejoinder to Trent's rejection of imputation. The chapter also explores two related issues, namely, Andreas Osiander's (1498–1552) rejection of imputation and the coordination of law and covenant. The chapter

---

1. Millard J. Erickson, *Concise Dictionary of Christian Theology* (Grand Rapids: Baker, 1994), s. v. *realism, nominalism*, 116, 140.

then concludes with a summary of the developments during the Reformation and offers several key questions for further reflection and study.

LUTHER AND LUTHERANISM

While a number of forerunners contributed to the outbreak of the Protestant Reformation, Martin Luther (1483–1546) is often credited with moving things in a legal-forensic direction. Luther began his theological career embracing traditional dogmas of the church concerning original sin and justification but eventually questioned key tenets of the traditional doctrine of justification. Concerning original sin, Luther stayed within the boundaries of traditional views. He originally adhered to a creationist view regarding the origins of the human soul but then later moved to a traducianist position.[2] Borrowing biblical imagery, Luther contended that an evil tree produced evil fruit, and a righteous root produced good fruit (cf. Luke 6:43).[3] In Luther's view, people inherited the contagion of original sin by virtue of their birth.[4] In this respect, Luther was closely aligned with an Augustinian doctrine of original sin but differed from later medieval developments.[5] Luther was more insistent upon verbal concepts than ontological categories. But for Luther, God only deals with man through the word of promise, hence Adam's chief failure is ultimately unbelief, not a privation of justice.[6] This represents a break with medieval views of original sin. Luther wrote in 1522: 'As, therefore, faith alone makes a person

---

2. L'Ubomir Batka, 'Luther's Teaching on Sin and Evil,' in *The Oxford Handbook of Martin Luther's Theology*, eds. Robert Kolb, Irene Dingel, and L'Ubomir Batka (Oxford: Oxford University Press, 2014), 244.

3. Martin Luther, 'To George Spalatin, 19 Oct 1516,' LW 48:25. In this letter Luther rejects the idea presented by Aristotle, namely, that people become righteous by performing righteous deeds (cf. Aristotle, *Nicomachean Ethics*, 2nd ed., trans. Terence Irwin [Indianapolis: Hacket Publishing Co., 1999], II.1-7).

4. Martin Luther, 'Confession Concerning Christ's Supper,' LW 37:362.

5. Batka, 'Luther's Teaching on Sin and Evil,' 243.

6. Luther, 'The Babylonian Captivity of the Church,' LW 36:42; Batka, 'Luther's Teaching on Sin and Evil,' 244.

righteous and brings the Spirit and pleasure in good outward works, so, unbelief alone commits sin and brings forth the fleshly pleasure in bad outward works, as happened to Adam and Eve in paradise, Genesis 3.'[7] With statements like this, Luther introduced another concept by which to discuss matters of sin and righteousness, namely, verbal rather than ontological categories.[8]

The word-focused nature of Luther's theology comes to light especially in his doctrine of justification. In the medieval view, a person is justified by receiving an initial infusion of grace at baptism, which then equips him to pursue greater conformity to Christ. Only at the final judgment can a person be pronounced righteous, once he completes the process. In contrast to medieval views, Luther distinguished between the categories of law and gospel. Stated simply, the law demands and the gospel promises.[9] Luther's law – gospel distinction led him to conclude that there are two kinds of righteousness, active and passive.[10] Passive righteousness is alien; according to Luther it is 'the righteousness of another, instilled from without. This is the righteousness of Christ by which he justifies through faith.'[11] Active righteousness, on the other hand, belongs to the believer, which is expressed through love and good works.[12] In a 1519 sermon, Luther places passive righteousness in antithetical parallel to original sin: 'Therefore

---

7. Martin Luther, 'Preface to the Acts of the Apostles,' LW 35:369.

8. Robert Kolb, 'Luther on the Two Kinds of Righteousness: Reflections on His Two-Dimensional Definition of Humanity at the Heart of His Theology,' LQ 13 (1999): 449-66.

9. Mark Mattes, 'Luther on Justification as Forensic and Effective,' in The Oxford Handbook of Martin Luther's Theology, eds. Robert Kolb, Irene Dingel, and L'Ubomir Batka (Oxford: Oxford University Press, 2014), 268-69.

10. Robert Kolb, 'Luther on Two Kinds of Righteousness,' in Harvesting Martin Luther's Reflections on Theology, Ethics, and the Church, ed. Timothy J. Wengert (Grand Rapids: Eerdmans, 2004), 38-55; Charles P. Arand, 'Two Kinds of Righteousness as a Framework for Law and Gospel in the Apology,' LQ 15 (2001): 417-39.

11. Martin Luther, 'Two Kinds of Righteousness,' LW 31:297.

12. Luther, 'Two Kinds of Righteousness,' LW 31:299.

this alien righteousness, instilled in us without our works by grace alone—while the Father to be sure, inwardly draws us to Christ—is set opposite original sin, likewise alien, which we acquire without our works by birth alone.'[13] Here these two alien principles, righteousness and sin, come to people from without—people are born into original sin but only those who look by faith alone (*sola fide*) receive the imputed alien righteousness of Christ.

Luther explains that because of the abiding presence of sin and the weakness of faith, a believer's justified status must rest in the imputed alien righteousness of Christ. Granted, Luther does not expound the theme of imputation as clearly and ubiquitously as other theologians, such as Philip Melanchthon (1497–1560), but he clearly teaches the doctrine: 'So far as the words are concerned, this fact is easy, namely, that righteousness is not in us in a formal sense, as Aristotle maintains, but is outside us, solely in the grace of God and in His imputation.'[14] Again Luther writes: 'From this it is clear how faith justifies without works and how the imputation of righteousness is necessary nevertheless. Sins remain in us, and God hates them very much. Because of them it is necessary for us to have the imputation of righteousness, which comes to us on account of Christ, who is given to us and grasped by our faith.'[15] For Luther, the abiding presence of sin in the believer continually hampers his ability to seek justification by obedience to the law, hence only Christ's perfect righteousness can justify.[16] Luther's theology of imputed righteousness differs considerably from earlier medieval formulations. For Aquinas, imputation is the manner by which God accepts the believer's imperfect works, whereas for Luther, it is the means by which God conveys the alien righteousness of Christ.[17] This understanding of imputation informs Luther's definition of righteousness: 'It is a divine

---

13. Luther, 'Two Kinds of Righteousness,' LW 31:299.

14. Martin Luther, *Lectures on Galatians (1535)*, LW 26:234.

15. Luther, *Lectures on Galatians (1535)*, LW 26:235.

16. Luther, *Lectures on Galatians (1535)*, LW 26:230.

17. Cf. Aquinas, *Romans*, lect. 1, §335, p. 113; Luther, *Lectures on Galatians (1535)*, LW 26:230-32.

imputation or reckoning as righteousness or to a righteousness, for the sake of our faith in Christ or for the sake of Christ.'[18]

Luther's understanding of justification, and hence imputation, was revolutionary. A number of factors led to Luther's reconfiguration of justification and the introduction of imputed righteousness: (1) philosophical discussions about nominalism in contrast to realism, which caused theologians to think beyond ontological categories; (2) a return to the exegesis of the original biblical languages; (3) examining the relationship between God and man in verbal rather than exclusively ontological categories; and (4) employing the law – gospel hermeneutical distinction, which led to the establishment of two categories of righteousness, active and passive. These factors were prominent in Luther's theology as well as the broader Reformation. Luther's lieutenant, Melanchthon, was convinced of these principles and codified them in the Augsburg Confession (1530). The Confession embraces a traditional Augustinian understanding of original sin, that is, by virtue of one's birth, all people carry the contagion of sin. Like the earlier church councils, the Augsburg Confession condemns Pelagianism.[19] Correlatively, the Confession states that justification is the forgiveness of sin and, echoing the Pauline language of Romans 4:3, God imputes faith for righteousness.[20]

THE REFORMED TRADITION

The wind carried Luther's insights across Europe and into the minds of other Reformers. Juan de Valdés (1509–41) encountered Luther's writings and incorporated the idea of two kinds of righteousness into his theology of justification.[21] Valdés is significant, not only

---

18. Luther, *Lectures on Galatians (1535)*, LW 26:233.

19. Augsburg Confession §II.1-3.

20. Augsburg Confession, §IV.1-3; cf. Philip Melanchthon, *Loci Communes 1543*, trans. J. A. O. Preus (St. Louis: Concordia Publishing House, 1992), locus VII (pp. 94-95).

21. Juan de Valdés, *Commentary Upon St. Paul's Epistle to the Romans*, trans. John T. Betts (London: Trübner & Co., 1883), 42; idem, *Seventeen Opuscules*, trans. and ed. John T. Betts (London: Trübner & Co., 1882), 150-51; cf. José Nieto, *Juan de Valdés and the Origins of the Spanish and Italian Reformation*

because he imbibed Luther's writings and spread the Reformation in Spain and Italy, but because he had significant contact with Peter Martyr Vermigli (1499–1562). Vermigli had an impact upon Zacharias Ursinus (1534–83), the chief author of the Heidelberg Catechism (1563). Reformed theologians, Martin Bucer (1491–1551) and John Calvin (1509–64), reflected upon and refined the ideas of sin and righteousness. This refinement was in part fueled by a renewed interest in biblical exegesis from both Protestant and Roman Catholic theologians. Between 1532–42, for example, more than thirty-five commentaries on Romans were published.[22] From within this crowded field, Bucer offered his own observations regarding imputation in 1536.[23] Bucer defines justification as both the remission of sins and the imparting of righteousness.[24] Recent scholarship has characterized Bucer's view of forgiveness of sin as the non-imputation of sin.[25] Bucer relies upon and dialogues with Melanchthon's 1532 Romans commentary on these points.[26]

The idea that justification is the remission of sins (or non-imputation) and the imputation of righteousness appears in the later work of Calvin, who wrote his own commentary on Romans in 1539 and interacted with Bucer's commentary.[27] Calvin's explanation of

---

(Geneva: Droz, 1970), 320-21.

22. T. H. L. Parker, *Commentaries on Romans: 1532–42* (Edinburgh: T & T Clark, 1986), 1-83.

23. Martin Bucer, *Metaphrases et Enarrationes perpetuae Epistolarum … Continens metaphrasim et Enrrationem in Epistolam ad Romanos*, vol. 1 (Rihel: 1536).

24. Martin Bucer, *Common Places of Martin Bucer*, trans. and ed. David F. Wright (Appleford: Sutton Courtenay Press, 1972), 163. Note, this English edition offers a translation of Bucer's 1562 edition of the preface to his Romans commentary, which remains largely unchanged from the 1536 first edition.

25. Brian Lugioyo, *Martin Bucer's Doctrine of Justification: Reformation Theology and Early Modern Irenicism* (Oxford: Oxford University Press, 2010), 53.

26. Bucer, *Common Places*, 164; cf. Philip Melanchthon, *Commentary on Romans*, trans. Fred Kramer (1540; St. Louis: Concordia Publishing House, 1992), 110-11.

27. John Calvin, *Romans and Thessalonians*, CNTC (1960; Grand Rapids: Eerdmans, 1996), 2.

justification in his Romans commentary reflects a number of themes that appear in the works of Luther, Melanchthon, and Bucer, such as an emphasis upon promise, imputation, and the remission of sins as non-imputation: 'In order to determine the meaning of righteousness, it is necessary to understand this relation between promise and faith, for there is the same relationship between God and us as juridically exists between giver and recipient.' He goes on to note 'that those to whom righteousness is imputed are justified.'[28] Regarding the forgiveness of sins, Calvin explains that this is the non-imputation of sin.[29] Hence, in the definitive 1559 edition of his *Institutes*, Calvin defines justification as the 'remission of sins and the imputation of the righteousness of Christ.'[30]

Calvin holds to a view of original sin that has Augustinian sympathies, though he adds some unique elements. Calvin approves of Augustine's rejection of Pelagius's views, namely, that we do not sin by imitating Adam but that we are corrupted by an inborn defect from birth.[31] Calvin recognizes a dual-relationship between Adam and Christ: 'Between these two persons there is this relation, that the one ruined us by involving us in his destruction, the other by his grace has restored us to salvation.'[32] These main features echo Augustinian themes, but Calvin then makes some unique moves. Calvin notes the debate regarding the origin of the soul and sidesteps the issue, though he rejects traducianism.[33] Calvin states: 'We ought to be satisfied with this, that the Lord deposited with Adam the endowments he chose to confer on the human nature; and therefore that when he lost the favors he had received, he lost them not only for himself, but for us

---

28. Calvin, *Romans*, 84.

29. Calvin, *Romans*, 86.

30. John Calvin, *Institutes of the Christian Religion*, trans. John Allen (Grand Rapids: Eerdmans, 1949), III.xi.2.

31. Calvin, *Institutes*, II.i.5.

32. Calvin, *Institutes*, II.i.6.

33. Calvin, *Institutes*, I.xv.5.

all.'[34] Given that Adam's nature was corrupted and infected with a contagion, everyone else that originates from the root bears the mark of original sin. Calvin avers, 'The cause of the contagion is not in the substance of the body or of the soul; but because it was ordained by God, that the gifts which he conferred on the first man should by him be preserved or lost both for himself and for all his posterity.'[35]

Unlike Augustine, and other theologians leading up to the Reformation, Calvin bypasses the idea of the realistic transmission (through procreation) of original sin and instead opts for the idea of ordained transmission. There is a sense in which Calvin echoes the views of Anselm and Aquinas: namely, Adam has the Platonic ideal human nature, and as such, when he sinned he marred human nature for everyone.[36] On this point, Calvin states that God bestowed upon Adam endowments upon 'human nature' and 'therefore that when he lost the favors he had received, he lost them not only for himself, but for us all.'[37] For Calvin, the pivot point for the transmission of original sin is Adam's human nature. In this respect Adam is a representative human being because when Adam lost his God-given gifts, he lost them for all humanity, those who share in Adam's human nature.[38] This point becomes clear in Calvin's comments on John 3:6, where he writes:

> For the corruption of all mankind in the person of Adam alone did not proceed from generation but from the ordinance of God. As in one man He adorned us all, so He has also in him deprived us of His gifts. Therefore, we do not draw our individual vice and corruption

---

34. Calvin, *Institutes*, II.i.7.

35. Calvin, *Institutes*, II.i.7.

36. Cf. Aquinas, *Romans*, lect. 3, §410, p. 139.

37. Calvin, *Institutes*, II.i.7.

38. Aaron Denlinger, 'Calvin's Understanding of Adam's Relationship to His Posterity: Recent Assertions of the Reformer's "Federalism" Evaluated,' *CTJ* 44 (2009): 240-42; cf. Cornelis Venema, 'Calvin's Doctrine of the Imputation of Christ's Righteousness: Another Example of "Calvin Against the Calvinists?"' *MATJ* 20 (2009): 15-47.

from our parents but are all alike corrupted in Adam alone, because immediately after his fall God took away from human nature what He had given to it.[39]

Calvin's understanding of the transmission of original sin bears the fingerprints of Augustine, Anselm, and Aquinas, but his unique contribution lies in the fact that he bypasses all question of realistic transmission and rests it upon divine ordination. Calvin's move away from a realistic view of the transmission of sin is but one development in the Reformation. As we will see below, Reformed theologians incorporated the doctrine of the covenant in their discussions of the transmission of original sin and righteousness.

THE ROMAN CATHOLIC RESPONSE

As one might imagine, the Protestant Reformation stirred up a hornet's nest of opposition from the Roman Catholic Church. The Pope and the bishops believed that Martin Luther's teaching required an official response. And while it took significant political and theological maneuvering, the Roman Catholic Church convened an official council in the Italian city of Trent on Sunday, 13 December 1545.[40] The Council of Trent met irregularly for the next twenty years but was immediately engrossed in deliberations over the chief issue of contention between Catholics and Protestants, the doctrine of justification. The council initially devoted the lion's share of its energy to refute the Protestant doctrine of justification and especially one of its key pillars, imputed righteousness.

In what many sixteenth- and seventeenth-century theologians believed was the definitive Protestant response to Trent, Martin Chemnitz (1522–86) admitted that much of what the Council determined had been drawn from 'the writings of purer antiquity,' and was therefore 'in agreement with the Scripture.'[41] Chemnitz

---

39. John Calvin, *John 1–10*, CNTC (1960; Grand Rapids: Eerdmans, 1996), 66; Denlinger, 'Calvin's Understanding of Adam's Relationship,' 242.

40. John W. O'Malley, *Trent: What Happened at the Council* (Cambridge: Belknap Press, 2013), 75.

41. Martin Chemnitz, *Examination of the Council of Trent, Part I*, Chemnitz's

was aware, however, of the views of Anselm, who defined original sin as a deficiency of original righteousness rather than the positive presence of sin, or concupiscence.[42] Chemnitz wanted his audience to understand that original sin was not merely a privation of original righteousness but also the presence of sin.[43] Recent analysis contends that there was no dispute between Trent and Lutheranism on this particular point.[44] The same, however, cannot be said about justification and the doctrine of imputation.

There were some delegates who had sympathies for Luther's understanding of justification, such as Cardinals Reginald Pole (1500–58) and Girolamo Seripando (1493–1563).[45] Nevertheless, among the delegates at Trent, one theologian stepped forward to engage and refute the doctrine of imputation, Diego Layñez (1512–65), a Spanish Jesuit. Layñez was intent on rallying the council against the doctrine and thus, from some scribbled notes and memory, offered a three-hour speech against imputation. The speech was transcribed and eventually published with the proceedings of Trent. Despite sympathies for Luther's doctrine among some of the delegates, Layñez's speech was influential and undoubtedly led to the unanimous approval of the decree on justification.[46] Digging into Layñez's speech provides specific details as to why Trent ultimately rejected the doctrine of imputation.

Layñez began his speech with a parable that showcased three different views on how Christians are justified.[47] In this parable

---

Works, vol. 1, trans. Fred Kramer (1971; St. Louis: Concordia Publishing House, 2007), 312.

42. Chemnitz, *Examination*, 315.

43. Chemnitz, *Examination*, 337.

44. O'Malley, *Trent*, 103.

45. O'Malley, *Trent*, 104.

46. O'Malley, *Trent*, 113; Joseph H. Fichter, *James Layñez: Jesuit* (St. Louis: Herder Book Co., 1944), 61-65; Carl E. Maxcey, 'Double Justice, Diego Layñez, and the Council of Trent,' *CH* 48/3 (1979): 269.

47. For what follows, see Diego Layñez, 'Disputatio de justitia imputata,' in *Jacobi Laínez Disputationes Tridentiae*, vol. 2, ed. Hartmannus Grisar (Ratisbonae: Feliciani Rauch, 1886), 153-92. For a Spanish translation of this disputation,

Layñez presents a king who has a son, and this son is supposed to inherit all of the king's riches. This son then goes to three of his servants and offers them the chance to win the possession of a precious gem.[48] To the first servant, the son says: 'Only believe, and I, to whom all of the king's wealth has been promised, will obtain the gem and freely give it to you.'[49] The son informs the second servant that he will give him money so that he can redeem himself from servitude, purchase a horse and weapons, so that he can fight for the gem. The son frees the third servant, ensures his well-being, and gives him weapons so that he can battle and merit the gem.[50] With the first servant, Layñez explains that this was a mere imputation of the son's righteousness from the king. This view was out of the question for Layñez because it has no place for inherent righteousness.[51] Layñez associated the second servant with the views of Cardinal Seripando, who believed that Christ's imputed righteousness and inherent righteousness were both necessary for justification.[52] In his parable the third servant represented the Roman Catholic position, whereby saints merit their justification by the freely given means of the son.[53] Layñez opted for the third view because, ultimately, imputation obliterated the value of personal merit.

Beyond this initial parable, Layñez offered twelve reasons why imputation should be rejected:

1. The doctrine affirms that everyone requires imputed righteousness before the divine bar.[54]

---

see idem, 'Discurso acerca de la justicia imputada,' in *EIP. Diego Layñez*, trans. Andrés Martínez de Azagra y Beladiez (Madrid: Victorian Suárez, 1933), 331-84; cf. Maxcey, 'Double Justice,' 272-79.

48. Layñez, 'Disputatio,' I.ii (p. 154).

49. Layñez, 'Disputatio,' I.ii (p. 154): 'Tantummodo crede, et ego, qui omnes regis divitias promerui, obtinebo, ut gemma proposita tibi gratiose donetur.'

50. Layñez, 'Disputatio,' I.ii(p. 154).

51. Layñez, 'Disputatio,' I.ii (p. 154).

52. Maxcey, 'Double Justice,' 273.

53. Maxcey, 'Double Justice,' 273.

54. Layñez, 'Disputatio,' II.v (p. 160).

2. Imputed righteousness is necessary to supplement the defects of inherent righteousness.[55]

3. Imputation eliminates the merit of good works performed in love, merit that the Scriptures and doctors of the church teach.[56]

4. It eliminates the true justification and remission of sins, and consequently makes all of the New Testament's teaching false.[57]

5. Imputation excludes personal acts of satisfaction and the doctrine of purgatory.[58]

6. It is offensive to the providence of God because He has prepared the means of redemption, to Christ because it denies His merit on the Day of Judgment, and to believers, whom Christ indwells—believers are not deemed worthy for eternal life because of their good works.[59]

7. Imputation completely removes any place for inherent righteousness.[60]

8. The doctrine supplements the defects of inherent righteousness, which means there is no place for degree of reward. If all are equal, then what place is there for mansions of different sizes?[61]

9. Imputation encourages believers to abuse Christ and the grace of the law; it encourages antinomianism.[62]

---

55. Layñez, 'Disputatio,' II.vi (p. 160).
56. Layñez, 'Disputatio,' II.vi (p. 161).
57. Layñez, 'Disputatio,' II.vii (p. 161).
58. Layñez, 'Disputatio,' II.viii (p. 162).
59. Layñez, 'Disputatio,' II.viii (p. 162).
60. Layñez, 'Disputatio,' II.viii (p. 163).
61. Layñez, 'Disputatio,' II.ix (p. 163).
62. Layñez, 'Disputatio,' II.x (p. 164).

10. It foists a false and tyrannical terror upon believers because it assumes that their lives are stained and defective.[63]

11. The doctrine contains hidden venom, because those who preach it say that the reprobate cannot merit anything and that the elect do not have their sins imputed to them—such affirmations are both false and dangerous.[64]

12. Last, the doctrine is novel, and the first one to advocate it was Luther. It is also marked by obscurity and contradiction.[65]

Layñez was convinced that the doctrine of imputation was erroneous and wanted the council to recognize this.

At the core of his concerns was the idea that imputation left little room, if at all, for the believer's works in the process of justification. Layñez was willing to admit the category of imputed righteousness, but only at baptism, where a person was infused with Christ's righteousness, or through the pardoning of temporal punishment through indulgences.[66] But Layñez's fundamental objection was, 'Where we find imputation, we do not find, properly speaking, merit.'[67] In common Roman Catholic nomenclature, Layñez employs the categories of condign (full) and congruent (half or proportionate) merit; redeemed sinners are only capable of the latter. In other words, God imparts His grace to those who have been baptized, enables them to offer their congruently good works, which allows them to grow in their inherent righteousness until they can stand before the divine bar to receive their verdict of justification. Layñez, for example, appeals to Mark 10:17-28, and Christ's encounter with the rich young man to explain the place for inherent righteousness. Christ told the young man to sell all he had to show that he had not truly kept the commandments, not to

---

63. Layñez, 'Disputatio,' II.x (p. 164).

64. Layñez, 'Disputatio,' II.xi (pp. 164-65).

65. Layñez, 'Disputatio,' II.xi (p. 165).

66. Layñez, 'Disputatio,' III.xii (pp. 167-68).

67. Layñez, 'Disputatio,' III.xii (p. 167).

teach that it was impossible to keep them. It is possible to keep the commandments. 'God makes this possible,' writes Laynez, 'when he renews man so he can fulfill the commandments; which when fulfilled, saves without the necessity of imputation.'[68]

Laynez did not think that believers stood alone in their efforts to grow in righteousness. Rather, because they were in union with Christ and participants in the grace of God, saints can rest assured that their merit will not be rejected. Moreover, even in the future judgment according to works, believers can rest assured that they can plead the righteousness of Christ to mitigate whatever defects exist in their own good works.[69] Laynez repeatedly invokes the doctrine of the covenant, to argue for the acceptability of the believer's works at the final judgment.[70] In his defense, Laynez maintained the necessity of inherent righteousness because it was connected to the rest of the common Roman Catholic understanding of justification. If one rejected merit, then there was no possibility of standing before the divine bar at the final judgment. If one could not receive his final justification, then this questioned the validity and efficacy of the initial justification received in baptism. Imputation was a Trojan horse, which if admitted within the walls of the fortified city of the Roman Catholic doctrine of justification, would bring about its destruction.[71]

Due in no small part to Laynez's speech, the Council of Trent, unanimously adopted the decree on the doctrine of justification. In its canons concerning justification, Trent formally rejected the doctrine of imputation: 'If anyone says that people are justified either solely by the attribution of Christ's justice, or by the forgiveness of

---

68. Laynez, 'Disputatio,' III.xvi (p. 170): 'Deus autem id possibile reddit, dum renovat hominem ad hoc, ut mandata impleat; quibus impletis, sine imputatione salvatur.'

69. Laynez, 'Disputatio,' III.xvii (p. 171). Laynez's doctrine of the covenant likely grew out of medieval discussions (see Stephen Strehle, *Calvinism, Federalism, and Scholasticism: A Study of the Reformed Doctrine of Covenant* [New York: Peter Lang, 1988], 6-82).

70. Laynez, 'Disputatio,' III.xviii (p. 172-73).

71. Maxcey, 'Double Justice,' 277.

sins alone, to the exclusion of the grace and charity which is poured forth in their hearts by the Holy Spirit and abides in them; or even that the grace by which we are justified is only the goodwill of God: let him be anathema.'[72]

THE PROTESTANT REJOINDER

One of the initial responses to the decrees of Trent came from the pen of John Calvin. Like Chemnitz, Calvin did not have much to say regarding the council's decree on original sin. Calvin notes that the first four heads arose 'from the ancient and approved doctrine of the Church.' In fact, Calvin was bemused that Trent thundered so many anathemas in its decree on original sin when there was little disagreement between Protestants and Catholics on these issues.[73] Calvin did stipulate, however, that baptism held forth a twofold grace, the remission of sins and regeneration; by *regeneration* Calvin refers to the doctrine of sanctification. He explains that the Reformed teach that a full remission of sins is made but that regeneration has only begun and progresses throughout the course of a believer's life. 'Accordingly,' writes Calvin, 'sin truly remains in us, and is not instantly in one day extinguished by baptism, but as the guilt is effaced it is null in regard to imputation.'[74] Calvin contends, therefore, that baptism offers the removal, or non-imputation, of the guilt of sin; the Spirit progressively mitigates the pollution of sin throughout the Christian's life. Calvin also takes issue with Trent because it characterized original sin as weakness rather than depravity.[75] At this point Calvin's concern is not so much about the mechanism, i.e., the means of transmission, as the degree to which sin affects humanity.

---

72. Council of Trent, 'Session 6, 13 January 1547, Decree on Justification,' Canon 11.

73. John Calvin, 'Canons and Decrees of the Council of Trent, with the Antidote, 1547,' in *John Calvin: Tracts and Letters*, vol. 3, ed. and trans. Henry Beveridge (1851; Edinburgh: Banner of Truth, 2009), 85.

74. Calvin, 'Antidote,' 86.

75. Calvin, 'Antidote,' 109.

As to be expected, Calvin spilled a great deal of ink engaging issues related to justification and imputation. Calvin rejected the idea that justification includes sanctification, which also means he rejected a twofold justification, initial and final.[76] Calvin did not believe in the alchemy of grace and works to yield the gold of justification. Rather, justification was the remission of sins and the imputation of Christ's obedience, which was part of the larger complex of the twofold blessing of union with Christ, justification and sanctification. In other words, God renovates believers and they consequently produce good works, but He does not factor these good works in the believer's justification.[77] Calvin writes: 'The whole dispute is as to the cause of justification. The Fathers of Trent pretend that it is twofold, as if we were justified partly by forgiveness of sins and partly by spiritual regeneration; or, to express their view in other words, as if our righteousness were composed partly of imputation, partly of quality.'[78] Calvin argued against this by appealing to the apostle Paul: 'When the Apostle teaches that "by the obedience of one many were made righteous," (Rom. 5:19) he sufficiently shews, if I mistake not, that the righteousness wanting in ourselves is borrowed elsewhere.'[79] Moreover, Calvin confirmed the fears of Laýñez, who believed that imputation would eliminate personal merit in justification: 'In short, I affirm, that not by our own merit but by faith alone, are both our persons and works justified; and that the justification of the works depends on the justification of the person, as the effect on the cause. Therefore, it is necessary that the righteousness of faith alone so precede in order, and be so pre-eminent in degree, that nothing can go before it or obscure it.'[80]

In the definitive Protestant response to Trent, Martin Chemnitz offers a fuller response to the Tridentine rejection of imputation. Like

76. Calvin, 'Antidote,' 114.
77. Calvin, 'Antidote,' 115.
78. Calvin, 'Antidote,' 116.
79. Calvin, 'Antidote,' 117.
80. Calvin, 'Antidote,' 128.

Calvin before him, Chemnitz defends the doctrine of justification *sola fide*. He argues that Paul 'expressly takes justification before God to life eternal away from his works, in which he lived with a good conscience before God and man after his renewal.'[81] Instead, the only thing that believers require before the divine bar is the imputed satisfaction and obedience of Christ, received by faith alone: '[Believers] receive remission of sins, are absolved from the sentence of damnation, are received into grace, adopted as sons, and accepted to everlasting life.'[82] To refute the Tridentine rejection of imputation, Chemnitz explores a number of scriptural texts. He appeals, for example, to Galatians 3:13, where Paul states that Christ was 'made a curse for us,' and Galatians 4:4-5, namely, that Christ was born under the law. Reflecting upon 2 Corinthians 5:21, Chemnitz asks how Christ was 'made sin'? 'Certainly by imputation. And thus we are made the righteousness of God in Him.'[83] In other words, God imputes the sins of believers to Christ, and conversely imputes the satisfaction and obedience of Christ to believers. This construction represents a twofold imputation.

Chemnitz also makes appeal to Romans 8:3-4: 'For God has done what the Law, weakened by the flesh, could not do; sending His own Son in the likeness of sinful flesh and for sin, He condemned sin in the flesh, in order that the just requirement of the Law might be fulfilled in us.' According to Chemnitz, the Latin translation of Paul's statement (*de peccato damnauit peccatum*) obscures the underlying Greek (καὶ περὶ ἁμαρτίας κατέκρινεν τὴν ἁμαρτίαν). Chemnitz notes that the Septuagint repeatedly uses the phrase περὶ ἁμαρτίας ('concerning sin') in Leviticus 4 and 5 as a technical term for 'sin offering.' This means that when Paul writes, 'for sin, He condemned sin in the flesh,' he means to convey the idea that Christ died as a sin offering. Christ was condemned even though He personally owed nothing to sin. The point here is that Christ's suffering is vicarious, and He takes the legal

---

81. Chemnitz, *Examination*, 487.

82. Chemnitz, *Examination*, 500.

83. Chemnitz, *Examination*, 502.

guilt upon Himself. Christ was the sin offering and in this way fulfilled the law for believers.[84] In addition to these aforementioned texts, Chemnitz appeals to 1 Timothy 2:6, Romans, 5:9, 19, 1 Corinthians 1:30, Romans 3:24, Jeremiah 23:6, Isaiah 53:5, 6, 11, and Romans 4:23-24. By these texts Chemnitz seeks to prove that Christ perfectly fulfilled the law and is therefore the believer's righteousness: 'The Father gives that to the believers that they may be justified on account of it.'[85]

Beyond these exegetical observations, Chemnitz offers a running dialogue and polemical commentary against Diego Andrada de Payva (1528–75), a Jesuit theologian who wrote a defense of the Canons of Trent.[86] Chemnitz draws attention to Paul's regular use of the term *imputation*, an unavoidable brute fact. Andrada, however, claims that the term does not refer to the imputation of an alien righteousness, but to inherent righteousness. That is, based upon the merit of Christ, God pours love, inherent righteousness, into the regenerate. Chemnitz scoffs at such an interpretation and writes: 'It is indeed a piece of bragging impudence to keep saying such things, as if they were ruling over beasts, since never in the whole realm of nature has anyone even in a fever dreamed of such a meaning for the word "impute," for then to impute sin would be to instill iniquity into someone.'[87]

Chemnitz was not satisfied merely to appeal to the logical con-sequences of such a definition of the term *impute*. He exegetically demonstrates that *impute* is a legal-relational term, that denotes relationship between a person and accusations or rewards. In this vein Chemnitz draws attention to 2 Samuel 19:19, 'Let not the king impute iniquity to me,' and Romans 5:13, 'Where there is no law, sin is not imputed.'[88] Chemnitz notes the different ways in which

---

84. Chemnitz, *Examination*, 503.

85. Chemnitz, *Examination*, 503-04.

86. Diego Andrada, *Orthodoxarum Explicationum Libri Decem* (Coloniae: Mater-num Cholinum, 1564).

87. Chemnitz, *Examination*, 531-32.

88. Chemnitz, *Examination*, 532.

the term is used. In some cases, imputation is used when a person rightly merits compensation, such as when Paul writes: 'Now to the one who works, his wages are not reckoned as a gift but as his due' (Rom. 4:5). But in terms of justification, Chemnitz demonstrates from Romans 4 that God justifies the ungodly through imputation. 'There is in us a contrary basis,' writes Chemnitz, 'to which guilt rather than righteousness should be imputed, if God wanted to enter into judgment with us.'[89] Hence, Paul writes, 'Without works righteousness is imputed,' and God makes this imputation by gratuitous mercy. Rather than judge the believer on the basis of his own works, 'The satisfaction and obedience of Christ is the basis out of regard for which, and by reason and worthiness of which, God by grace imputes righteousness to the believers.'[90]

THE OSIANDER CONTROVERSY

Chemnitz stood firm on the doctrine of imputation and rejected the anti-Protestant pronouncements of Trent. But Reformed and Lutheran theologians did not speak with one voice—there were some dissenters. Within the Lutheran wing of the Reformation Andreas Osiander rejected the doctrine of imputation and offered his own unique explanation. Osiander was a professor at the University of Königsberg who created controversy with his doctrines of justification and union with Christ. Unlike Luther and Melanchthon, Osiander believed that justification was not a forensic declaration but instead required divine indwelling so that believers would share in Christ's personal and essential righteousness. Osiander's view was not justification by imputed but indwelt righteousness, or justification by union with Christ.[91] In other words, the believer would be

---

89. Chemnitz, *Examination*, 532.

90. Chemnitz, *Examination*, 533.

91. Timothy J. Wengert, 'Philip Melanchthon and John Calvin against Andreas Osiander: Coming to Terms with Forensic Justification,' in *Calvin and Luther: The Continuing Relationship*, ed. R. Ward Holder (Göttingen: Vandenhoeck & Ruprecht, 2013), 64; cf. Andreas Osiander, *Disputatio de Iustificatione (1550)*, in *Gesamtausgabe*, vol. 9 (Gütersloh: Gütersloher Verlagshaus, 1994), 422-47.

ontologically fused with Christ's nature in order to share in His essential righteousness. One of the initial respondents to Osiander was Melanchthon. As much as Melanchthon vigorously rejected Osiander's view, he did not reject the doctrine of union with Christ in favor of a stand-alone doctrine of justification.[92] Melanchthon writes: 'We clearly affirm the presence or indwelling of God in the reborn.'[93] Yet he carefully stipulates the relationship between indwelling and justification in the following manner: 'Although God dwelt in Moses, Elijah, David, Isaiah, Daniel, Peter, and Paul, nevertheless none of them claimed to be righteous before God on account of this indwelling or the effecting of their renewal but on account of the obedience of the Mediator and his gracious intercession, since, in this life, the remnants of sin were still in them.'[94]

Melanchthon believed Osiander's error was in shifting the ground of justification away from the imputed righteousness of Christ and moving it to the believer, which was the problem with the Roman Catholic doctrine of justification. Melanchthon writes:

> Osiander especially makes an issue of this article and contends that man is righteous on account of the indwelling of God, or on account of the indwelling of God [sic], not on account of the obedience of the Mediator, and not by the imputed righteousness of the Mediator through grace. He corrupts the proposition 'By faith we are justified' into 'By faith we are prepared that we may become just by something else,' that is, the indwelling of God. Thus in reality he is saying what the papists say: 'We are righteous by our renewal,' except that he mentions the cause where the papists mention the effect. We are just when God renews us.[95]

---

92. In his 1556 commentary on Romans, Melanchthon spends twelve columns of text in the *Corpus Reformatorum* to refute Osiander's view before he exposits the doctrine of justification (Wengert, 'Melanchthon and Calvin,' 65-66; cf. CR 15:855-67).

93. Philip Melanchthon, 'Confutation of Osiander,' in *Documents from the History of Lutheranism 1517–1750*, ed. Eric Lund (Minneapolis: Fortress, 2002), 208.

94. Melanchthon, 'Confutation of Osiander,' 208-09.

95. Melanchthon, 'Confutation of Osiander,' 209.

Melanchthon was concerned that justification by union with Christ was scarcely different from Roman Catholic views. Osiander, he believed, made justification rely upon the cause (the indwelling presence of Christ) and the Roman Catholics made justification rely upon the effect (the good works produced by the presence of Christ through the disposition of a *habitus*, infused righteousness).[96] Both views compromised the alien nature of Christ's imputed righteousness.

Melanchthon maintained the doctrine of union with Christ, but distinguished between imputed righteousness and divine indwelling so as not to move the legal ground of justification away from Christ to the believer. The Lutheran confessional tradition positively received Melanchthon's rejection of Osiander's and substantively incorporated it in the Formula of Concord (1577).[97] Moreover, the Formula of Concord also commends Luther's 1535 commentary on Galatians as a 'wonderful, magnificent exposition' of the 'lofty and sublime article on justification before God,' which means that the framers of the Formula maintained the compatibility of Melanchthon's and Luther's views on imputation, justification, and union with Christ. Osiander's views were regularly derided and rejected for years to come among Reformed theologians. Calvin wrote one of the initial responses in the final revision of the definitive 1559 edition of his *Institutes*.[98] Theodore Beza (1519–1605), for example, believed that Osiander was hallucinating when he claimed that believers received the essential righteousness of Christ and Beza thought that such a notion was an intolerable error.[99] Likewise William Whitaker (1548–1595) described Osiander as 'a man of the utmost levity and

---

96. Wengert, 'Melanchthon and Calvin,' 66.

97. See 'Solid Declaration,' art. 3, in *The Book of Concord: The Confessions of the Evangelical Lutheran Church*, ed. Robert Kolb and Timothy J. Wengert (Minneapolis: Fortress, 2000), 573; cf. Charles P. Arand, et al., *The Lutheran Confessions: History and Theology of the Book of Concord* (Minneapolis: Fortress, 2012), 217-26.

98. Calvin, *Institutes*, III.xi.8-12.

99. Theodore Beza, *Theses Theologicae* (Geneva: apud Eustathium Vignon, 1586), V.vii (p. 9).

audacity' to make his claims about essential righteousness.[100] In brief, the rejection of Osiander's views was nearly universal.

LAW AND COVENANT

Before this chapter closes, we should note one of the key developments in the doctrine of imputation, namely, the coordination of law with the doctrine of covenant. Early Reformation discussions drew a connection between imputation and Christ's fulfillment of the law. This nexus is especially evident in early Protestant uses of the law – gospel distinction. That is, Christians cannot be justified by the law but only by the gospel; Christ came to fulfill the law, which undergirds the promises of the gospel. Calvin, for example, writes: 'Paul, therefore, justly represents the righteousness of the law and that of the gospel as opposed to each other. But the gospel has not succeeded the whole law, so as to introduce a different way of salvation; but rather to confirm and ratify the promises of the law, and to connect the body with the shadows.'[101] For Calvin, the law condemns sinners and points them to Christ. Calvin argues his point from Paul's contrast between law and gospel in Romans 10:5, 'Do you perceive how he thus discriminates between the law and the gospel, that the former attributes righteousness to work, but the latter bestows it freely, without the assistance of works?'[102] In one sense, Calvin was operating with inherited theological categories—law and gospel—though he employed them in different ways than his medieval predecessors. But he was also borrowing these categories from Melanchthon who argued in terms of law and gospel.[103]

During the Reformation, however, theologians began to incorporate the doctrine of the covenant into their theology. Two notable

---

100. William Whitaker, *A Disputation on Holy Scripture* (1588; Cambridge: Cambridge University Press, 1849), 380.

101. Calvin, *Institutes*, II.ix.4.

102. Calvin, *Institutes*, III.xi.17.

103. Jordan J. Ballor, *Covenant, Causality, and Law: A Study in the Theology of Wolfgang Musculus* (Göttingen: Vandenhoeck & Ruprecht, 2012), 55.

factors deserve attention. The first arises with theologians who connected the categories of law and covenant. Wolfgang Musculus (1497–1563) was one of the first Reformed theologians to give the doctrine of the covenant its own specific *locus* in his theological system.[104] Musculus notably connects law and covenant when he states that the law is part of God's covenant.[105] By joining law and covenant, Musculus opened a new window to view imputation and Christ's law-keeping accredited to believers.[106] In the later development of the doctrine of the covenant, Edward Fisher (fl. 1627–55), author of *The Marrow of Modern Divinity*, cites Musculus on this very point and writes: 'The word which signifieth Covenant or Bargain, is put for law.'[107]

The second notable factor appears in theologians who posited a twofold covenant structure, one initial covenant with Adam and a second with Christ. In this respect, Reformed theologians developed the doctrine of the covenant in terms of the covenants of works and grace. Edward Fisher offers a classic expression: 'The law of Works is as much to say as the covenant of Works, for it is manifest (saith *Musculus*) that the word with signifieth Covenant or Bargain, is put for law, which covenant or bargain the Lord made with all mankind in *Adam* before his fall.'[108] This development, however, was not exclusively confined to the Reformed tradition. While some of the earliest and clearest statements of a twofold covenant structure appear in Reformed theologians, such as Zacharias Ursinus (1534–83), Dudley Fenner (ca. 1558–87), and Amandus Polanus (1561–1610), it appears that Roman Catholic theologians were some of the first to place Adam in covenant with God.[109]

---

104. Ballor, *Covenant, Causality, and Law*, 15.

105. Wolfgang Musculus, *Common Places of Christian Religion* (London: 1563), fol. 121v.

106. Ballor, *Covenant, Causality, and Law*, 55.

107. Edward Fisher, *The Marrow of Modern Divinity* (London: G. Calvert, 1645), 6; Ballor, *Covenant, Causality, and Law*, 217.

108. Fisher, *Marrow*, 6.

109. Zacharias Ursinus, *Larger Catechism*, q. 10, in *An Introduction to the*

The historical roots for an Adamic covenant stretch far back into the patristic era. In the Latin Vulgate, Jerome (ca. 347–420) rendered Hosea 6:7 as, *Ipsi autem sicut Adam transgressi sunt pactum* ('But they, like Adam, have transgressed the covenant'). Likewise Augustine (354–430) claimed that Adam was in covenant with God.[110] So the idea of an Adamic covenant is not peculiar to sixteenth-century Reformed theology. In fact, in 1541 Dominican theologian Ambrogio Catharinus (1483–1553) stated: 'So then, God established a covenant with Adam from the beginning.'[111] But Catharinus went beyond affirming the existence of an Adamic covenant. Augustine, for example, claimed that Adam was in covenant with God but did not construe this relationship in forensic or federal terms but in realistic and ontological ones. Sin was transmitted by generation, not by imputation. Catharinus, however, did posit a federal relationship between Adam and his progeny. Catharinus believed that all humanity was in Adam on account of the covenant.[112] God imputed Adam's action of eating the forbidden fruit to his offspring by virtue of the covenant, and it is in this manner that all humans were 'in him.'[113] Such a covenantal arrangement between God and Adam predates similar Reformed formulations by roughly forty years.[114] In his treatise on original

---

Heidelberg Catechism: Sources, History and Theology, ed. Lyle D. Bierma, et al. (Grand Rapids: Baker, 2005), 164; Dudley Fenner, *Sacra Theologia sive Veritas quae Est Secundum Pietatem* (Geneva: Eustathium Vignon, 1589), IV.i (p. 39); Amandus Polanus, *The Substance of Christian Religion* (London: 1595), 88-89.

110. Augustine, *City of God*, XVI.xxix, in NPNF¹ 2:326.

111. Ambrogio Catharinus, *De Lapsu Hominis et Peccato Originali Liber Unus*, in *Opuscula* (Lugduni: apud Mathiam Bonhomme, 1542), 189: 'Sic ergo pactum statuit Deus cum Adam ab initio.' Aaron C. Denlinger, *Omnes in Adam Ex Pacto Dei: Ambrogio Catarino's Doctrine of Covenantal Solidarity and Its Influence on Post-Reformation Reformed Theologians* (Göttingen: Vandenhoeck & Ruprecht, 2010), 11.

112. Catharinus, *Peccato Originali*, 190, 191.

113. Catharinus, *Peccato Originali*, 190; Denlinger, *Omnes in Adam*, 11.

114. Denlinger, *Omnes in Adam*, 11-13.

sin, Catharinus posits a covenant between Adam and God and a second covenant in Christ, what he calls the *novum pactum*, or new covenant.[115] In fact, other delegates to the Council of Trent advocated a twofold covenantal scheme, although they did not advocate a view of imputed guilt such as Catharinus's. Diego Layñez, for example, led the charge against the doctrine of imputation but nonetheless affirmed a twofold covenant scheme. In his famous three-hour speech against imputation Layñez mentions the 'covenant of the grace of God' (*pacti gratiae Dei*) and the 'first covenant that the Lord made with Adam' (*primo illo pacto, quod pepigit Dominus cum Adam*).[116] Later in his speech Layñez designates these two covenants as the first and second covenants (*primi et secondi pacti*).[117] Hence, there were some significant differences among advocates of this twofold covenantal scheme. Nevertheless, one should not miss the coordination of these different ideas: covenant, sin, righteousness, law, and the two Adams.

The degree to which Catharinus and Layñez laid foundational stones for the Reformed doctrine of the covenants is a fascinating question that deserves greater examination but is beyond the scope of this study.[118] Nevertheless, both Roman Catholic and Reformed theologians began to associate covenant and law, which naturally affected formulations of the doctrine of imputation. Catharinus explained his doctrine of the covenant in his treatise on original sin, and other theologians began to do the same. Zacharias Ursinus, for example, associated a covenant of creation with the law of God; he writes:

Q.   What does the divine law, or Decalogue teach?

A.   It teaches the kind of covenant that God established with mankind in creation, how he managed in keeping it, and what God requires of him after establishing a new covenant

---

115. Catharinus, *Peccato Originali*, 195.

116. Layñez, *Disputatio*, II.v (p. 159).

117. Layñez, *Disputatio*, II.xxxvii (p. 189).

118. On this question see Denglinger, *Omnes in Adam Ex Pacto*, 245-80.

of grace with him—that is, what kind of person God created, for what purpose, into what state he has fallen, and how he ought to conduct his life after being reconciled to God.[119]

By the law of God man first learned how he should act; it also showed man what God desired from him after the covenant of grace had been initiated.

Important to note, however, is that Ursinus did not associate the covenant of creation directly with Adam but instead with the broader creation.[120] He writes:

Q. What is the difference between the law and the gospel?

A. The law contains the natural covenant, established by God with humanity in creation, that is, it is known by humanity by nature, it requires our perfect obedience to God, and it promises eternal life to those who keep it and threatens eternal punishment to those who do not. The gospel, however, contains the covenant of grace, that is, although it exists, it is not known at all by nature; it shows us the fulfillment in Christ of the righteousness by Christ's Spirit; and it promises eternal life freely because of Christ to those who believe in Him.[121]

---

119. Ursinus, *Larger Catechism*, q. 10, in *Introduction to the Heidelberg Catechism*, 164.

120. David Weir, *The Origins of the Federal Theology in Sixteenth-Century Reformation Thought* (Oxford: Oxford University Press, 1990), 105. There is debate about the role Ursinus plays in the development of the covenant of creation. Weir argues that Ursinus was the first theologian to speak of a covenant of creation (*Origins of the Federal Theology*, 22). Cf. Robert Letham, 'The *Foedus Operum*: Some Factors Accounting For Its Development,' *SCJ* 14 (1983), 457-67; Peter Alan Lillback, 'Ursinus' Development of the Covenant of Creation: A Debt to Melanchthon or Calvin?' *WTJ* 43 (1981), 247. Contra Weir, Lillback, and Letham, cf. Derk Visser, 'The Covenant in Zacharias Ursinus,' *SCJ* 18 (1987), 531-44.

121. Ursinus, *Larger Catechism*, q. 36, in *An Introduction to the Heidelberg Catechism: Sources, History and Theology*, ed. Lyle D. Bierma, et al. (Grand Rapids: Baker, 2005), 168-69.

Ursinus does not speak of a covenant with Adam, but of a covenant that is engrained and embedded in the creation with the law written upon the heart of humanity, or natural law. Theologians now added a new conceptual layer to the law – gospel distinction and spoke in terms of two covenants like their Roman Catholic counterparts. The idea of covenantally imputed guilt and righteousness did not take hold in Roman Catholic theology but these ideas were fanned into a flame in Reformed theology, especially in the post-Reformation period. The upshot of this law-covenant connection is that, where early Reformed theologians spoke in terms of law and gospel, later Reformed theologians spoke in terms of the covenants of works and grace. Law and gospel were now clothed in the garb of covenant, which means that imputation would take on a slightly different appearance in the hands of post-Reformation Reformed theologians.

Conclusion

The doctrine of imputation saw significant development during the Reformation. Philosophical and exegetical windows opened new vistas upon the doctrine of imputation. The biggest developments appeared with the concept of imputed righteousness. No longer did ontological categories drive the discussion. Luther's emphasis upon the word and promise caused theologians to configure justification, and hence imputation, along legal-forensic lines. God looked upon sinners as righteous because of the imputed obedience and satisfaction of Christ. First and second generation Reformers, such as Luther and Calvin, nevertheless maintained traditional views on inherited guilt. Luther's views were similar to Augustine's and Calvin's bore the theological DNA of Anselm and Aquinas. For Luther people were sinful because they inherited original sin through procreation, and for Calvin they were sinful because Adam corrupted the Platonic ideal human nature. In these early days Protestants advocated a twofold imputation: namely, God imputes the believer's sin to Christ, and Christ's righteousness to the believer. But further developments among Roman Catholic theologians such as Ambrogio Catharinus and Reformed theologians such as Musculus and Ursinus set the stage for a threefold imputation: God imputes Adam's sin to his offspring, the believer's sin to Christ, and Christ's obedience and satisfaction to the believer.

These developments raise several questions that warrant further investigation:

1. Does the development of the doctrine of imputed righteousness constitute a theological novelty, and as such, should it be rejected as Roman Catholic theologians argued at Trent?

2. Is a twofold covenantal structure warranted? Was God in covenant with Adam?

3. Is the connection between law and covenant legitimate?

4. Should ontological or legal-forensic categories take primacy in the question of the transmission of original sin and the communication of righteousness in salvation?

5. Were Lutheran and Reformed theologians correct to reject Osiander's view of shared essential righteousness?

These issues represent, I believe, the key questions that arise from the development of the doctrine of imputation during the Reformation. But the story of the doctrine of imputation continues in the post-Reformation period. Once again debate arose among Reformed theologians regarding the precise nature of imputation. Was imputation mediate (through means) or immediate (apart from means), and were both the active and passive obedience of Christ imputed or only the passive obedience? I turn to explore and provide answers to these questions in the next chapter.

3

POST-REFORMATION

INTRODUCTION

In the wake of the Reformation one might assume that unity and agreement marked the Reformed community. After all, the Roman Catholic Church and the decrees of the Council of Trent represented a significant theological opponent to Reformed theology. In the face of a formidable foe, factions would unite to engage the challenge. Nevertheless, there was dissent and internecine debates within the walls of the Reformed fortress. In prior years it seems that the church either wrestled with questions about original sin, such as in the Pelagian controversy, or with debates over imputed righteousness, as during the Reformation. Like the pendulum on a clock, debate moved to one issue or the other, but seldom did the two issues intersect. In the post-Reformation period, however, the two issues did surface albeit in two different debates. The first debate focused upon the theology of Johannes Piscator (1546–1625), who denied the imputation of the active obedience of Christ (IAOC). Piscator believed that only the passive obedience of Christ was imputed to the believer in justification. The *active* obedience typically referred to Christ's fulfillment of the law on behalf of believers, whereas the *passive* obedience referred to Christ's suffering the penalty of the law. The second debate centered upon the claims of Josua Placaeus (Josué de la Place) (1596–1655), who was accused of denying the imputed guilt of Adam's first sin.

In order to understand these two debates, we must survey the doctrinal developments leading up to them. As noted in the previous chapter, Reformed theologians advocated a traditional doctrine of original sin whereby all humans contract the guilt of Adam's first sin. But many in the Reformed tradition discussed original sin in terms of transmission, not imputation. On the other hand, Reformed theologians advocated the doctrine of imputed righteousness in contrast to Roman Catholic claims of infused righteousness. Generally speaking, initial expressions were couched in terms of the antithesis between law and gospel, but as theologians coordinated these doctrines with the covenant concept they took on a slightly different cast. Theologians began to speak in terms of two covenants, a covenant of creation and the covenant of grace. In the post-Reformation period theologians clearly advocated a twofold covenant structure typically called the covenants of works and grace. Hence, this chapter surveys these post-Reformation developments and then segues to an examination of the imputation controversies, one over the question of the IAOC and the other over the imputed guilt of Adam's first sin.

General Developments

In the waning years of the Reformation, theologians such as Zacharias Ursinus (1534–83), author of the Heidelberg Catechism, spoke of two covenants, a natural covenant and the covenant of grace. He equated these two covenants with the categories of law and gospel respectively.[1] Theologians gradually advocated a two-covenant structure through the influence of several different sources, including Ursinus, Roman Catholic theologians such as Ambrogio Catharinus (1484–1553), and substantive claims of John Calvin (1509–64) among others. Theologians likely encountered the works of Ursinus, a well-known international contributor to Reformed theology, or through reading about the debates, works, and proceedings of the Council of Trent where Roman Catholic theologians advocated a two-fold covenantal structure, or through the works of Calvin, who contended that Adam was under legal obligations in his initial state in the garden. With these ideas percolating in the theological soil of the sixteenth-century, theologians such as Dudley Fenner (ca. 1558–87), William Perkins (1558–1602), Amandus Polanus (1561–1610), and Robert Rollock (ca. 1555–99) eventually began to advocate explicitly a two-fold covenant structure.[2] Fenner offers what is likely the earliest doctrinal use of the term *foedus operum* ('covenant of works').[3] Fenner writes: 'The covenant of works is the covenant where the condition of perfect obedience is annexed.' Whereas by contrast, 'The covenant of the free promise is the covenant, (a) concerning Christ and blessedness given forth in him, which is freely given, and (b) where the condition is: if a person receives Christ.'[4] Similar formulations appear in Perkins, Polanus, and Rollock all around the same timeframe, 1585–97.[5]

1. Zacharias Ursinus, *Larger Catechism*, q. 36, in *An Introduction to the Heidelberg Catechism: Sources, History and Theology*, ed. Lyle D. Bierma, et al. (Grand Rapids: Baker, 2005), 168-69.

2. Richard A. Muller, 'Divine Covenants, Absolute and Conditional: John Cameron and the Early Orthodox Development of Reformed Covenant Theology,' *MAJT* 17 (2006): 21.

3. Muller, 'Divine Covenants,' 21. Cf. Dudley Fenner, *Sacra Theologia sive Veritas quae est secundum Pietatem* (apud Eustathium Vignon, 1589), IV.i (p. 39).

4. Fenner, *Sacra Theologia*, IV.i (p. 39): '*Operum foedus*, est *foedus* ubi conditio annexa est perfecta obedientia ... *Foedus* gratuitae promissionis, est *foedus* (a) de *Christo* & *eulogia* in ipso extante, gratuitio promissionis, (b) ubi conditio est, si recipiatur *Christus*.'

5. William Perkins, *A Golden Chaine: or the Description of Theology*, in *The Workes*

Rollock offers a definition of the covenants of works, which bears the themes of earlier formulations of Ursinus.[6] Rollock writes:

> The covenant of God generally is a promise under some one certain condition. And it is twofold; the first is the covenant of works; the second is the covenant of grace. Paul (Gal. iv.24) expressly sets down two covenants, which in the Old Testament were shadowed by two women, as by types, to wit, Hagar, the handmaid, and Sarah, the free woman; for, saith he, *these be those two covenants*. Let us then speak something of these two covenants; and first of the covenant of works. The covenant of works, which may also be called a legal or natural covenant, is founded in nature, which by creation was pure and holy, and in the law of God, which in the first creation was engraven in man's heart.[7]

Rollock was familiar with the works of Ursinus and regularly trained his students with the Heidelberg Catechism.[8] Ursinus's fingerprints appear by virtue of fact that Rollock calls the covenant of works a 'natural covenant,' the same term Ursinus employs in his own two-fold covenant construct.[9] The main point here is twofold: (1) Rollock relies upon earlier formulations, and (2) he places law and gospel and the two Adams under the blanket of the covenant, which naturally impacted the doctrine of imputation.

Rollock explains that the fall does not abrogate the covenant of works. The promise of eternal life on the condition of perfect obedience still stands before fallen human beings.[10] Rollock writes:

---

of that Famous and Worthie Minister of Christ W. Perkins, vols. 1 (London: 1612), 31-32; Amandus Polanus, *The Substance of Christian Religion, Soundly Set Forth in Two Books* (London: 1595), 88-89; Robert Rollock, *A Treatise of God's Effectual Calling*, in *The Select Works of Robert Rollock*, ed. William Gunn, 2 vols. (Edinburgh: The Woodrow Society, 1849), II (vol. I, pp. 33-34); cf. Muller, 'Divine Covenants,' 21-26.

6. Muller, 'Divine Covenants,' 26.

7. Rollock, *Treatise on Effectual Calling*, II, in *Works*, I:34.

8. Rollock, *Works*, I:lxvi; see also Robert Letham, 'The *Foedus Operum*: Some Factors Accounting For Its Development,' *SCJ* 14 (1983): 464.

9. Ursinus, *Larger Catechism*, q. 36, in *An Introduction to the Heidelberg Catechism*, 168-69

10. Muller, 'Divine Covenants,' 26; cf. Rollock, *Effectual Calling*, IV, in *Works*, I:52.

The first and principal grace promised in this covenant [of grace] is righteousness; which must necessarily here have the first place, for after the breach of the covenant of works, that one first original justice, as they call it, was quite lost, and injustice did succeed into the place thereof. And this justice, which is here promised in the Covenant of Grace, is no inherent righteousness, as that original justice was, but is the righteousness of our Mediator Jesus Christ, which is ours by faith, and by the imputation of God.[11]

According to Rollock, believers receive eternal life through the imputation of Christ's righteousness in the covenant of grace. Rollock believed that, while one may distinguish between Christ's suffering and His law-keeping (active obedience), God imputes both to the believer by faith alone and that both constitute the righteousness of Christ.[12] But Rollock also coordinates covenant and imputation for Adam's original place in the garden.

When asked how the efficacy of the power of Adam's first sin extends to all humanity, Rollock responds:

This efficacy of that sin is by reason of that word and covenant which God made with Adam in his creation, as it were in these words; 'If man will stand and persist in that his innocency which he had by creation, he shall stand for his own good and for his progeny; but if he do not stand, but fall away, his fall shall turn as to his own damage, so to the hurt of his posterity; and whatsoever evil shall betide him, the same shall ensue to all his offspring after him.'[13]

In other words, Rollock posits a full-fledged double-imputation: God imputes Adam's guilt and Christ's righteousness to those who are respectively united to the two covenantal representatives.[14] Rollock does not talk of the transmission of original sin through

---

11. Rollock, *Effectual Calling*, III, in *Works*, I:39.

12. Rollock, *Effectual Calling*, IV, in *Works*, I:54.

13. Rollock, *Effectual Calling*, XXV, in *Works*, I:175.

14. Aaron Denlinger, *Omnes in Adam Ex Pacto Dei: Ambrogio Catarino's Doctrine of Covenantal Solidarity and Its Influence on Post-Reformation Reformed Theologians* (Göttingen: Vandenhoeck & Ruprecht, 2010), 266-67.

natural generation but 'by reason of that word and covenant which God made with Adam.' Transmission of original sin is covenantal, and hence federal, and through imputation. It is noteworthy that one of the earliest expressions of the covenantal basis for original sin appears in the Roman Catholic theologian, Ambrogio Catharinus, one whom Rollock cites in his chapter on original sin.[15] A likely scenario is that Rollock adopted Catharinus's idea of imputed guilt.[16] For Rollock, like Catharinus before him, humanity shared a covenantal solidarity with Adam, and hence God imputes guilt upon a covenantal rather than ontological basis.

Rollock was not alone in advocating a fully double-imputation. There are other noteworthy advocates including: Particular Baptist theologian Nehemiah Coxe (d. 1688), Francis Roberts (1609–75), and Westminster divine Anthony Burgess (d. 1664).[17] Coxe argues that had Adam not been in a covenant with God, then his sin would have only affected his own well being. 'It could only be upon the account of such a Covenant,' writes Coxe, 'that his Posterity should be concerned as they were, in his standing, or falling.'[18] Adam's sin impacted his posterity because he was the 'common root and Representative of all Mankind.' He did not function in a private capacity.[19] Francis Roberts comments in his massive *Mysterium & Medulla Bibliorum* on the significance of Romans 5:12 and 1 Corinthians 15:22. He answers the question as to how all people are guilty of Adam's one sin. He rejects several different options: 'Not only by *Imitation* of Adam as an evil example: for death seized on them that have not so sinned, not actually sinned, *Rom. 5.14.* Not meerly by *Propagation*, as from a corrupt Root or fountain. For the Apostle doth not parallel *Adam* and *Christ* as two common Roots only, but also as two common publike or

---

15. Rollock, *Effectual Calling*, XXV, in *Works*, I:176.

16. Denlinger, *Omnes in Adam*, 268-70.

17. For what follows, see Denlinger, *Omnes in Adam*, 273-74.

18. Nehemiah Coxe, *A Discourse of the Covenants That God made with Men Before the Law* (J. D., 1681), II.vi (p. 28).

19. Coxe, *Discourse of the Covenants*, II.v (p. 26).

universal Persons.'[20] Roberts rejects, therefore, the Pelagian and common views of the transmission of sin.

Roberts, like Coxe and Rollock, opts for covenantal solidarity and imputation. Roberts writes: 'For our immediate parents are Corrupted roots, & we corrupted by them, yet their Actual Sins are not made ours, as *Adams* is. But in *Adams* first Sin, we all became Sinners, by *Imputation*: *Adam* being an *universal Person*, and all mankind one in him by Gods covenant of works.' Roberts contends that all humanity were in Adam 'by federal *Consociation.*' He explains, 'God covenanted with *Adam*, and in him with all his Posterity: and therefore *Adams* breach of Covenant fell not only upon him, but upon all his Posterity.'[21] Anthony Burgess, one of the Westminster divines, wrote a treatise on original sin and clearly advocates the imputation of Adam's guilt to all humanity. Burgess takes a creationist view regarding the origin of the soul and then turns to answer the question as to how these newly created souls contract the contagion of original sin. Burgess writes: 'That in respect of Gods Decree and Covenant we were all present to God in *Adam.*'[22]

These different theologians might give the impression that the Reformed tradition effortlessly embraced a full-fledged double imputation without dissent or debate. But as easily as some embraced the idea of covenantal solidarity, there were most assuredly dissenting voices and considerable debate regarding the nature of this covenantal imputation. The first debate was over the precise nature of Christ's imputed righteousness. Did it consist of the active and passive obedience or merely the passive? And the second debate dealt with the nature of imputed guilt. Did it occur immediately by virtue of the covenantal bond between head and

---

20. Francis Roberts, *Mysterium & Medulla Bibliorum. The Mysterie and Marrow of the Bible. viz. God's Covenants with Man* (London: George Calvert, 1657), II.i (p. 22).

21. Roberts, *Mysterium & Medulla Bibliorum*, II.i (p. 22).

22. Anthony Burgess, *The Doctrine of Original Sin* (London: Thomas Underhill, 1659), III.xxiv.7 (p. 201).

members or mediately through the act of procreation? These are the questions that surround the Piscator and Placaeus controversies.

PISCATOR CONTROVERSY

Reformed opinions were of the same mind regarding the nature of justification. According to various Reformation-era Reformed confessions, justification consists of the forgiveness of sins and the imputation of righteousness. The First Confession of Basel (1534) claims 'all things are granted to us in Christ, who is our righteousness.'[23] The Geneva Confession (1536) states that God justifies 'through the intercession of Jesus Christ, so that by his righteousness and innocence we have remission of our sins, and by the shedding of his blood we are cleansed and purified from all our stains.'[24] The Geneva Catechism (1541/2) likewise explains that by faith alone sinners enter into the righteousness of the gospel.[25] On the surface, these statements lack a degree of specificity and do not explicitly state that God imputes Christ's righteousness to sinners. But this is the manner in which the Council of Trent read and understood Reformed and Lutheran claims about justification, evident in their condemnation of the doctrine of imputation.[26] In Reformed confessions and catechisms that appeared after the infamous Tridentine condemnation of the Protestant doctrine of justification, there was a greater degree of clarity on this issue.

The Forty-Two Articles (1553) of the Church of England state very succinctly: 'We are accounted righteous before God, only for the merit of our Lord and Savior Jesus Christ by faith, and not for our own works or deservings.'[27] The Belgic Confession (1561), for

---

23. First Confession of Basel (1534), §IX.

24. Geneva Confession (1536), §VII.

25. Geneva Catechism (1541/2), qq. 119-20.

26. See, e.g., Diego Laýñez, 'Disputatio de justitia imputata,' in *Jacobi Laínez Disputationes Tridentiae*, vol. 2, ed. Hartmannus Grisar (Ratisbonae: Feliciani Rauch, 1886), 153-92; Council of Trent, 'Session 6, 13 January 1547, Decree on Justification,' Canon 11.

27. Forty-Two Articles (1553), §XI.

example, offers the following: 'Jesus Christ is our righteousness in making available to us all his merits and all the holy works he has done for us. And faith is the instrument that keeps us in communion with him and with all his benefits.'[28] The Heidelberg Catechism (1563) asks how sinners are righteous before God and explains: 'God, without any merit of my own, out of pure grace, grants me the benefits of the perfect expiation of Christ, imputing to me his righteousness and holiness as if I had never committed a single sin or had ever been sinful, having fulfilled myself all the obedience which Christ has carried out for me, if only I accept such favor with a trusting heart.'[29] The Second Helvetic Confession (1566) offers a similar statement:

> For Christ took upon himself and bore the sins of the world, and satisfied divine justice. Therefore, solely on account of Christ's suffering and resurrection God is propitious with respect to our sins and does not impute them to us, but imputes Christ's righteousness to us as our own, so that now we are not only cleansed and purged from sins or are holy, but also, granted the righteousness of Christ, and so absolved from sin, death and condemnation, are at last righteous and heirs of eternal life. Properly speaking, therefore, God alone justifies us, and justifies only on account of Christ, not imputing sins to us but imputing his righteousness to us.[30]

In the face of the Tridentine rejection of imputed righteousness, Reformed theologians became much more explicit in advocating the doctrine.

In spite of the large-scale support for the doctrine of imputed righteousness, some theologians promoted a different version of the concept. The most notable standout was Johannes Piscator. Piscator believed that justification solely entailed the forgiveness of sins and not the imputation of Christ's righteousness. Based upon his reading of Acts 13:38-39, Piscator maintained: 'The apostle in this

---

28. Belgic Confession (1561), §XXII.
29. Heidelberg Catechism (1563), q. 60.
30. Second Helvetic Confession (1566), XV.iii.

place defines justification by forgiveness of sins only, is manifest, partly by the consequence of sentences, whereof one is added to another, as explaining the same partly by the very phrase, *to be justified from sins*: which is no other thing, than to be absolved from sins committed, and by consequence, to obtain forgiveness of sins.'[31] In his *Aphorismes of Christian Religion*, Piscator explains the place of Christ's obedience within the matrix of christology and soteriology. According to Piscator Christ had to be perfectly obedient in order to qualify Himself to serve as mediator; if He was not personally holy, He would have been incapable of pleasing God. But Piscator does not take the next step and claim that God then imputes Christ's obedience to believers by faith alone. Rather, he maintains that Christ's obedience is ultimately 'tasting death for us, and so in paying the punishment we did owe for the breach of the law.'[32] Noteworthy is the fact that Piscator's statement comes from his abridgement of Calvin's *Institutes of the Christian Religion*, which means that he understood that the famous Genevan reformer was a proponent of his view.

In one of the more succinct and clear presentations of Piscator's doctrine, David Pareus (1548–1622) offers a taxonomy and defense in a letter written to Count Ludwig Wittgenstein. In his letter Pareus explains that participants on each side of the debate agree on many points, such as the definition of the term *to justify*, that justification is by faith alone, that Christ's righteousness is not infused in sinners, and that the alien righteousness that justifies is the merit of Christ alone. But he also notes the key point of contention between the warring parties, namely, the precise nature of Christ's merit. Pareus outlines four different positions that involve the imputation of Christ's (1) essential or divine righteousness, (2) human, or original, righteousness, (3) active law-keeping, and (4)

---

31. Johannes Piscator, *A Learned and Profitable Treatise on Man's Justification* (London: 1599), 20.

32. Johannes Piscator, *Aphorismes of Christian Religion: or, A Verie Compendious Abridgement of M. I. Calvins Institutions* (London: Richard Field, 1596), XIII.vii (p. 68).

passive obedience. Among these views Pareus explains that they differed in terms of a single to fourfold imputation. Pareus also notes that, as best as he can recall, the question never arose prior to 1570 and does not appear in the works of Luther, Melanchthon, Zwingli, Calvin, Martyr, Musculus, or Hyperius.[33]

Beyond the four views listed above, Pareus further divides his taxonomy according to the following four different views, which vary in terms of a single to fourfold imputations:

- Single: passive

- Double: active and passive

- Triple: active, passive, and habitual holiness

- Quadruple: divine, human, active, and passive.[34]

Pareus then engages the three erroneous views and explains his own. He rejects quadruple imputation because it requires accrediting the essential righteousness of Christ. Pareus associates this view with the similar notion of Andreas Osiander (1498–1552), who argued that Christ indwells believers with His essential righteousness, something Pareus characterizes as 'madness.'[35]

Pareus rejects double and triple imputation for nine different reasons:

1. Promoters confound Christ's personal righteousness with His merit, or more technically, they confound the efficient and material causes of justification.

2. Advocates impose false dilemmas upon the theological question by employing binary categories of unrighteous and righteous, transgressing and fulfilling the law, dead and alive.

---

33. David Pareus, 'The Epistle of D. *David Parie* to the Illustrious and Noble Count, Lord *Ludovick Witgensteinius* Concerning *Christs Active and Passive Justice*,' in Zacharias Ursinus, *Certain Learned and Excellent Discourses*, ed. David Pareus (London: H. L., 1613), 792-93.

34. Pareus, 'Concerning Christ's Active and Passive Justice,' 793.

35. Pareus, 'Concerning Christ's Active and Passive Justice,' 795.

3. Why is Christ's passive obedience insufficient for justification?

4. If the forgiveness of sins is not the whole of our justification, then how can Romans 4 be true, 'Blessed are they whose sins are forgiven'?

5. If believers are not forgiven for their failure to obey the law through the passive obedience of Christ because such sins require the active obedience, how can it be true, 'The blood of Christ purges us from all sin'?

6. If we are justified by the active obedience of Christ, then what need was there for His death and suffering? His passive obedience is superfluous.

7. The division of Christ's righteousness into two or three parts derogates Christ's death and God's righteousness.

8. To seek our justification in different parts of Christ's work distracts our faith and robs us of comfort.

9. Nowhere does Scripture divide Christ's righteousness into two or three parts, and nowhere does it mention the imputation of Christ's holiness.[36]

In the wake of his nine reasons against the imputation of Christ's active obedience, Pareus explores the confessional and catechetical testimony to support his view. He maintains that though the Heidelberg Catechism mentions the imputation of the satisfaction, righteousness, and holiness of Christ, the author never intended to teach anything more than the imputation of the passive righteousness of Christ.[37] In addition to the Catechism, Pareus appeals to Melanchthon, Calvin, and the French Confession (1559) and claims that they only speak of justification as the forgiveness of sins.[38] With respect to Calvin and his famous definition of

---

36. Pareus, 'Concerning Christ's Active and Passive Justice,' 795-96.

37. Pareus, 'Concerning Christ's Active and Passive Justice,' 798, 804-05.

38. Pareus, 'Concerning Christ's Active and Passive Justice,' 799.

justification, Pareus argues that the Genevan only intended to advocate the passive obedience of Christ. Calvin's definition from his *Institutes* reads as follows: 'Thus we simply explain justification to be an acceptance, by which God receives us into his favor, and esteems us as righteous persons; and we say that it consists in the remission of sins and the imputation of the righteousness of Christ.'[39] Pareus interprets the last phrase, 'and the imputation of the righteousness of Christ,' as explanatory of the phrase 'remission of sins.' In other words, Calvin's statement should read, 'We say that justification consists in the remission of sins, which is the imputation of the righteousness of Christ.'[40]

To say the least, Piscator's rejection of the IAOC created a firestorm of controversy.[41] The Synod of Gap (1603) censured Piscator for his denial of the IAOC and wrote a letter to him so that he would no longer trouble the churches with his 'new-fangled Opinions.' The Synod also wrote letters to the universities of England, Scotland, Leiden, Geneva, Heidelberg, Basel, and Herborn and requested that they join them in their censure of Piscator. Local synods and consistories were also urged to 'have a careful Eye on those persons who be tainted with that Error, be they Ministers or private Christians, and … silence them; and in case of a willful stubborn persistency in their Error, to depose them, if they have a Pastoral Charge in the Church, from the Ministry.'[42] The Synod quickly rejected Piscator's views because they believed that the Protestant churches taught the IAOC.

---

39. John Calvin, *Institutes of the Christian Religion*, trans. John Allen (Grand Rapids: Eerdmans, 1949), III.xi.2.

40. Pareus, 'Concerning Christ's Active and Passive Justice,' 800.

41. For what follows, see Heber Carlos de Campos Jr., 'Johannes Piscator (1546-1625) and the Consequent Development of the Doctrine of the Imputation of Christ's Active Obedience,' (Ph.d diss., Calvin Theological Seminary, 2009), 13-18.

42. John Quick, ed., 'The Acts and Decisions and Decrees of the XVII National Synod of the Reformed Churches of France, Held in the Town of Gap, and Providence of Dolphiny, in *Synodicon in Gallia Reformata*,' 2 vols. (London: Thomas Parkhurst, 1692), I:227.

The Formula of Concord (1577), for example, maintains that the obedience of Christ 'consists not only in His suffering and death but also in the fact that He freely put himself in our place under the law and fulfilled the law with this obedience and reckoned it to us as righteousness.' The Formula calls this twofold obedience, Christ's 'total obedience,' which is something that Christ 'performed on our behalf for God in his deeds and suffering.' Through this total obedience 'God forgives our sin, considers us upright and righteous, and grants us eternal salvation.'[43] Calvin argued that justification consisted in the forgiveness of sins *and* the imputation of righteousness.[44] Luther argued for the need of an alien righteousness for justification.[45] Theodore Beza (1519–1605) was explicit on the need for IAOC.[46] In fact, recent research has pointed to Beza's views on threefold imputation (active, passive, and habitual holiness) as a likely source for the Heidelberg Catechism's language of God crediting the 'perfect satisfaction, righteousness, and holiness of Christ' to believers in justification.[47] Along these lines, Beza writes: 'For our sinnes are defaced by the blood of Christ, and the guiltines of our corruption itself (which the Apostle calleth sinfull sinne) is healed in us by litle and litle, by the gift of sanctification, but yet lacketh besides that, an other remedie, to wit, the perfect sanctification of Christs [*sic*] owne flesh, which also is to us imputed.'[48]

The Synod of Gap's reproof did not quell the fires of controversy. Delegates at the Synod of Dort (1618–19) debated the matter. Efforts by the Synod's President, Johannes Bogerman (1576–1637),

---

43. Formula of Concord, Solid Declaration, III:15, in *The Book of Concord: The Confessions of the Evangelical Lutheran Church*, ed. Robert Kolb and Timothy J. Wengert (Minneapolis: Fortress, 2000), 564.

44. Calvin, *Institutes*, III.xi.2.

45. Martin Luther, 'Two Kinds of Righteousness,' in LW 31:297-306.

46. Campos, Jr., 'Johannes Piscator,' 89-98.

47. Heidelberg Catechism, q. 60; cf. Campos, Jr., 'Johannes Piscator,' 92-98.

48. Theodore Beza, *The New Testament of our Lord Jesus Christ*, trans. I. Tomson (London: Christopher Barker, 1586), comm. Rom. 8:2 (fol. 221v); Campos, Jr., 'Johannes Piscator,' 97 n. 121.

to amend the Belgic Confession in such a way to accommodate both parties failed. Article XXIV of the Confession stated: 'Jesus Christ is our righteousness in making available to us all his merits and all the holy works he has done for us.' Bogerman tried to replace these words with the phrase, 'Christ's obedience,' but the measure was nearly universally defeated when brought to a vote with only two delegates in favor of the change. In opposition to the effort to remove language that implied the IAOC, the Synod elected to add an explanatory phrase, which is here underscored: 'Jesus Christ is our righteousness in making available to us all his merits and all the holy works he has done for us <u>and in our place</u>.' This emendation was recommended by the Synod as the authoritative confession of the Reformed Churches in the Netherlands and only had two delegates vote against the change.[49] This modfication represents a significant ecclesial rejection of Piscator's views.

The Irish Articles (1615) rejected Piscator's views. Written under the guidance and input of James Ussher (1581–1656), the Archbishop of Armagh and eventual Primate over Ireland, the Articles specifically state that the Father provided the merits of His Son to pay the ransom for the elect, fulfill the law on their behalf, and satisfy God's justice. Article XXXV states: 'He, for them, fulfilled the law in his life; that now, in him, and by him, every true Christ man may be called a fulfiller of the law.' The Irish Articles leave no room for Piscator's views and Ussher was personally explicit in his affirmation of the IAOC.[50] But the confessional statements of Dort and the Irish Articles still did not settle the dispute.

The issue was debated with some intensity at the Westminster Assembly when it took up its initial work of revising the Thirty-Nine Articles. The debates over the IAOC were reflective of earlier controversies that involved some of the assembly's members.[51] There

---

49. Nicolaas H. Gootjes, *The Belgic Confession: Its History and Sources* (Grand Rapids: Baker, 2007), 151-52.

50. Richard Snoddy, *The Soteriology of James Ussher: The Acts and Object of Saving Faith* (Oxford: Oxford University Press, 2014), 116-20.

51. Campos, Jr., 'Johannes Piscator,' 215-38.

was a twofold outcome from the assembly's wrangling over the question of the IAOC. First, when the assembly revised article XI on justification, they included reference to the phrase, the 'whole obedience' of Christ to denote the imputation of His active and passive obedience.[52] Second, much has been made of the fact that the divines did not include the phrase 'whole obedience' in the final edition of the Westminster Confession, which has been interpreted as a conciliatory move towards opponents of the IAOC.[53] Rather than the phrase, 'whole obedience,' the Westminster Confession instead states that the believers receive the imputed 'obedience and satisfaction of Christ.'[54]

Based upon a holistic reading of the Westminster Standards (Confession, Larger and Shorter Catechisms), a number of historians believe that the divines affirm the necessity of the IAOC, and their case is correct for several reasons.[55] First, the following paragraph in chapter XI states: 'Christ by his obedience, and death, did fully discharge the debt of all those that are thus justified, and

---

52. *The Proceedings of the Assembly of Divines Upon the Thirty-Nine Articles of the Church of England*, appended to *The Humble Advice of the Assembly of Divines, Now by Authority of Parliament Sitting at Westminster* (London: Company of Stationers, 1647), 8-9. For analysis of the original debates over the revision of article 11 and the IAOC, see J. V. Fesko, *The Theology of the Westminster Standards: Historical Context and Theological Insights* (Wheaton: Crossway, 2014), 209-17.

53. So Chad Van Dixhoorn, 'Reforming the Reformation: Theological Debate at the Westminster Assembly 1643–52,' 7 vols. (Ph.d. diss. University of Cambridge, 2004), I:326-30; J. R. Daniel Kirk, 'The Sufficiency of the Cross, pt. I: The Crucifixion as Jesus' Act of Obedience,' *SBET* 24/1 (2006): 37.

54. Westminster Confession, XI.i. I draw the following analysis from Fesko, *Westminster Standards*, 224-28.

55. Strange, 'Imputation of the Active Obedience,' 50-51; Jeffrey K. Jue, 'The Active Obedience of Christ and the Theology of the Westminster Standards: A Historical Investigation,' in *Justified in Christ: God's Plan for us in Justification*, ed. K. Scott Oliphint (Fearn: Christian Focus, 2007), 99-130; Carl R. Trueman, 'The Harvest of Reformation Mythology? Patrick Gillespie and the Covenant of Redemption,' in *Scholasticism Reformed: Essays in Honour of Willem J. van Asselt*, ed. Maarten Wisse, Marcel Sarot, and Willemien Otten (Leiden: Brill, 2010), 212.

did make a proper, reall, and full satisfaction to his Fathers Justice in their behalf' (XI.iii).[56] At first glance this might not seem all that significant, but subsequent editions of the Confession remove a crucial piece of grammar that obscures the point the divines made. In the Scottish Free Presbyterian edition of the Standards, which is supposed to be a reprint of the original Critical Text produced by S. W. Carruthers, a comma has been removed:[57]

Scottish Free Presbyterian Carruthers' edition	Christ, by His obedience and death, did fully discharge the debt of all those that are thus justified …
Original 1647	Christ by his obedience, and death, did fully discharge the debt of all those that are thus justified …

The difference is barely noticeable but significant because in the original two separate aspects of Christ's work are distinguished by a comma, which in later editions has been removed. This combines what was once separate and reflected the passive *and* active obedience. This is a fact that past historians, pro or con, have not previously noted.

Second, in the broader context of the Standards, the series of Larger Catechism questions on the humiliation of Christ (qq. 46-50) explain that Christ perfectly fulfilled the law (q. 48), which is distinguished from His death (qq. 49-50). And when qq. 70-71 on justification are held together with qq. 46-50, taken as a whole, they impress upon the reader the necessity of the active obedience of Christ. This is especially true against the backdrop of the dual-covenant structure of works and grace; the law demands obedience to obtain eternal life. In this respect, Leviticus 18:5 was a common

---

56. *The Humble Advice of the Assembly of Divines, Now by Authority of Parliament sitting at Westminster, Concerning a Confession of Faith* (London: 1647).

57. *Westminster Confession of Faith* (1646; Glasgow: Free Presbyterian Publications, 1995).

proof text for the covenant of works, which according to Reformed theologians places a cause and effect relationship between obedience and eternal life.[58]

Third, there are a number of indicators from speeches for the IAOC that few commentators take into account.[59] When the assembly was initially revising the Thirty-Nine Articles and its statement on justification, one of the proponents of the IAOC, Daniel Featly (1582–1645), saw two liabilities to the phrase 'whole obedience' for three reasons, namely 'redundancie, deficiencie, and noveltie.' Featly believed that the word *whole* was redundant because

---

58. See, e.g., WCF VII.i (cites Rom 10:5; Gal 3:12); William Pemble, *Vindiciae fidei, or A Treatise of Justification by Faith* (1625; Oxford: John Adams, Edw. and John Forrest, 1659), II.i (p. 159); John Preston, *The new covenant or the saints portion* (London: Nicolas Bourne, 1639), 314; idem, *The brest-plate of faith and love* (London: Nicolas Bourne, 1630), 38; Thomas Hooker, *The unbeleevers preparing for Christ* (London: Andrew Crooke, 1638), 59; Edward Fisher, *The Marrow of Modern Divinity: Touching both the Covenant of Works, and the Covenant of Grace* (London: G. Calvert, 1645), 48; Samuel Rutherford, *The Covenant of Life Opened: Or, a Treatise of the Covenant of Grace* (Edinburgh: Robert Brown, 1654), I.xiii (p. 89); Rollock, *Effectual Calling*, III, in *Works* I:34; Francis Turretin, *Institutes of Enlenctic Theology*, trans. George Musgrave Giger, ed. James T. Dennison, Jr. (Phillipsburg: P & R, 1992–97), VIII.vi.4; Wilhelmus á Brakel, *The Christian's Reasonable Service*, 4 vols., trans. Bartel Elshout (Morgan: Soli Deo Gloria, 1992), XII (vol. I, p. 360); Benedict Pictet, *Christian Theology*, trans. Frederick Reyroux (London: R. B. Seeley and W. Burnside, 1834), III.vii (p. 155); James Ussher, *A Body of Divinitie, or The Summe and Substance of Christian Religion* (London: Tho. Downes and Geo: Badger, 1645), 125; David Dickson, *Truths Victory Over Error* (Edinburgh: John Reed, 1634), XIX (pp. 137-38); Patrick Gillespie, *The Ark of the Testament Opened* (London: R. C., 1681), I.v (pp. 180-81); Edward Leigh, *Body of Divinity* (London: William Lee, 1662), IV.i (p. 306); Herman Witsius, *Conciliatory, or Irenical Animadversions*, trans. Thomas Bell (Glasgow: W. Lang, 1807), VIII.i-ii (pp. 86-87); Jeremias Bastingius, *An Exposition or Commentarie Upon the Catechisme of Christian Religion Which Is Taught in the Scholes and Churches Both of the Lowe Countries and of the Dominions of the Countie Palatinate* (Cambridge: John Legatt, 1593), fol. 122; cf. William Whitaker, *An Answer to the Ten Reasons of Edmund Campian* (London: Felix Kyngston, 1606), 252-53; John Downame, *The Christian Warfare against the devil world and flesh* (London: William Stansby, 1634), II.viii (p. 103).

59. Cf. Van Dixhoorn, 'Reforming the Reformation,' I:328.

this would entail, in his mind, Christ's obedience to the ceremonial law, something for which believers were not responsible. He thought that the word *obedience* was deficient because it did not accurately convey what was imputed to believers; not even the terms *active* and *passive* obedience were accurate in Featley's mind. He believed that the sinner's malady and therefore remedy was threefold: [60]

Malady	Remedy
Original sin	Christ's original righteousness
Sins of omission	Christ's active obedience
Sins of commission	Christ's passive obedience

Featley, consequently, was aware of the possible weaknesses of the phrase, 'whole obedience.' While it is circumstantial evidence, Featley's criticisms likely indicate why the phrase was not used in the later composition of the Confession and catechisms. It should be noted, however, that the phrase, 'whole obedience,' is used by some Reformed theologians to refer to the active and passive obedience of Christ.[61] For example, John Davenant (1572–1641) explains: 'With

---

60. Daniel Featley, *Dippers Dipt, or The Anabaptists Duck'd and Plung'd Over Head and Ears* (London: 1647), 204-05; fellow divine Edward Leigh also adopts this same threefold understanding of Christ's imputed righteousness and specifically cites Featley's speech from the assembly (*Body of Divinity*, VII.vi [p. 517]).

61. Cf. Thomas Cranmer, *An Answer To A Crafty and Sophistical Cavillation Devised by Stephen Gardiner* (1555; Cambridge: Cambridge University Press, 1844), 86; Lucas Trelcatius, *Briefe Institution of Common Places of Sacred Divinitie* (London: Francis Burton, 1610), II.ix (p. 261); George Walker, *Socinianisme in the Fundamentall Point of Justification Discovered, and Confuted* (London: John Bartlet, 1641), dedicatory epistle, 73, 139; Petrus de Witte, *Catechizing upon the Heidelbergh Catechisme, of the Reformed Christian Religion* (Amsterdam: Printed by Gillis Joosten Saeghman, 1664), q. 37 (p. 13); Roberts, *Mysterium & medulla bibliorum*, II.i, (p. 31); Richard Baxter, *The life of faith. In three parts*, in *The practical works of the late reverend and pious Mr. Richard Baxter*, 4 vols. (1660; London: Thomas Parkhurst, Jonathan Robinson, and John Lawrence, 1707), III.viii (p. 598); John Owen,

respect to the explanation of the terms, when we speak of *the death of Christ*, we comprehend in it the whole obedience of Christ, active and passive, the completion of which, and as it were the last act, was effect in his death; on which account Divines are accustomed by synecdoche to attribute to his death what relates to his entire obedience.'[62]

Fourth, one element that no one to date has explored is how the phrase 'obedience and satisfaction' has been used in the literature of the period. The bulk of the analysis on the question of the confession and the IAOC has centered upon the assembly's debate, the revisions of the Thirty-Nine Articles, chapter XI of the Confession, and the missing word *whole*, from 'whole obedience.' No one, to my knowledge, has asked whether the phrase 'obedience and satisfaction' means anything other than the active and passive obedience of Christ. In works that predate the assembly, such as John Downame's *The Christian Warfare* (1634), the phrase denotes the active and passive obedience of Christ: 'We obtained the remission of our sins, not for our workes or inherent righteousness, or any virtue that is in our selves, but by and for the alone merits, obedience, and full satisfaction of Christ,' which in context is referred to as 'the obedience and satisfaction of Christ.'[63] This phrase also appears

---

The doctrine of justification by faith through the imputation of the righteousness of Christ, explained, confirmed, & vindicated (London: R. Boulter, 1677), 295.

62. John Davenant, *An Exposition of The Epistle of St. Paul To the Colossians* (1627; London: Hamilton, Adams, and Co., 1831), 341. Some theologians, such as Thomas Watson, divided Christ's satisfaction into two parts and do not refer to the 'obedience of Christ.' Watson writes: 'His SATISFACTION, and this consists of two: 1. *His Active Obedience* … 2. *His Passive Obedience*' (*A Body of Practical Divinity* [London: Thomas Parkhurst, 1692], q. XXXV [p. 100]).

63. Downame, *Christian warfare*, II.li (p. 274); cf. William Perkins, *A clowd of faithfull witnesses, leading to the heavenly Canaan: Or, a commentarie upon the 11. Chapter to the Hebrewes*, in *The workes of that famous and worthy ministery of Christ, in the Universitie of Cambridge, Mr. William Perkins* (London: Cantrell Legge, 1618), verse 2 (p. 5); Francis Cheynell, *The rise, growth, and danger of Socinianisme, together with a plaine discovery of a desperate designe of corrupting the Protestant religion* (London: Samuel Gellibrand, 1643), IV (p. 41).

in George Walker's (ca. 1581–1651) defense of the doctrine of justification; this is significant because Walker offered 24 speeches, second only to Johsua Hoyle's (d. 1654) 25 speeches, in favor of the IAOC.[64]

Another appearance of the phrase occurs in James Ussher's *Body of Divinity* where he asks: 'What then are the parts of Christ's Obedience and Satisfaction?' Ussher then answers:

> His *Sufferings* and his *Righteousness*, *Phil. 2.5, 6, 7, 8.* 1 *Pet. 2.23*; For it was requisite, that he should *first* pay all our Debt, and satisfy God's Justice, (*Esa. 53.5, 6. Job 33.24*) by a price of infinite Value. (1 *Tim. 2.6*) Secondly, Purchase and merit for us God's Favour, (*Ephes. 1.6*) and Kingdom, by a most absolute and perfect Obedience, (*Rom. 5.19*). By his suffering he was to merit unto us the Forgiveness of our sins; and by his fulfilling the Law he was to merit unto us Righteousness: Both which are necessarily required for our Justification.[65]

Ussher's work was published in 1645, which was well in advance of the assembly's debates over chapters XI and XII on justification and adoption in session 678 on 23 July 1646.[66] The employment of the phrase before and during the assembly, therefore, indicates that it was reflective of both the active and passive obedience of Christ. The same can also be said for works that employ the phrase released after the publication of the Confession, or those that interpret the Standards' use of the phrase.[67] Hence, these four reasons (the

---

64. Walker, *Socinianisme*, 139, 232.

65. Ussher, *Body of Divinitie*, 171.

66. Strange, 'Imputation of the Active Obedience of Christ,' 44; Alex F. Mitchell and John Struthers, eds, *Minutes of the Sessions of the Westminster Assembly of Divines* (Edinburgh: Blackwood and Sons, 1874), 258-59.

67. Giovanni Diodati, *Pious and learned annotation upon the Holy Bible: plainly expounding the most difficult places thereof* (London: Nicholas Fussell, 1651), comm. 1 Cor. 6.11; Roberts, *Mysterium & bibliorum*, 609; John Wallis, *A Brief and Easie Explanation of the Shorter Catechism* (London: Peter Parker, 1662), n. p.; Baxter, *Life of faith*, III.vii (p. 598); Samuel Annesley, *The Morning Exercises at Cripplegate*, vol. 6 (1675; London: Thomas Tegg, 1844), 558-59; Owen, *Doctrine of Justification*, 190, 339; John Brown, *The Life of Justification Opened* (Utrecht: 1695), VI (p. 47).

grammar of the 1648 original, the broader context of the Standards, the perceived deficiencies of the term *whole obedience*, and the contextual meaning of *obedience and satisfaction* before, during, and after the assembly) indicate that the divines did not accommodate the minority views of those opposed to the IAOC.

The Westminster Confession was received beyond the assembly when Reformed Congregationalists and Particular Baptists adopted the confession in modified form. In these revised editions the framers added a few clarifying words to make the necessity of the IAOC explicit. The Savoy Declaration, the Congregational version of the Westminster Confession, for example, states that justification includes the imputation of 'Christs [*sic*] active obedience unto the whole Law, and passive obedience in his death, for their whole and sole righteousness.'[68] The inclusion of the terms *active* and *passive* righteousness is largely due to the influence of Thomas Goodwin (1600–80) and John Owen (1616–83).[69] The Second London Confession (1689), the Particular Baptist version of the Westminster Confession, employs the same language found in the Savoy revisions.[70]

One of the last salvos in the debates over the IAOC comes from the pens of Francis Turretin (1623–87) and Johannes Heidegger (1633–98), authors of the Formula Consensus Helvetica (1675). Turretin and Heidegger wrote the Formula to deal with the increasingly popular views of Moises Amyraut (1596–1664) and the Academy of Saumur.[71] Amyraut was infamously known for his

---

68. *A Declaration of the Faith and Order Owned and Practiced in the Congregational Churches in England* (London: John Field, 1659), XI.i. Hereafter referred to as Savoy Declaration.

69. Carl R. Trueman, *John Owen: Reformed Catholic, Renaissance Man* (Aldershot: Ashgate, 2007), 107-08.

70. *A Confession of Faith, Put forth by the Elders and Brethren of Many Congregations of Christians (Baptized upon Profession of their Faith) in London and the Country* (London: John Harris, 1688), XI.i. Hereafter referred to as Second London Confession.

71. Martin I. Klauber, 'The Helvetic Formula Consensus (1675): An Introduction and Translation,' *TJ* 11NS (1990): 103.

views on hypothetical universalism, but he was also an opponent of the IAOC.[72] In response to Amyraut, the Formula states:

> But by the obedience of his death Christ, in the place of the elect, so satisfied God the Father, that in the estimate of his vicarious righteousness and of that obedience, all of that which he rendered to the law, as its just servant, during his entire life, whether by doing or by suffering, ought to be called obedience. For Christ's life, according to the Apostle's testimony (Phil 1:8), was nothing but submission, humiliation and continuous emptying of self, descending step by step to the lowest extreme, even to the point of death on the Cross; and the Spirit of God plainly declares that Christ in our stead satisfied the law and divine justice by his most holy life, and makes that ransom with which God has redeemed us to consist not in his suffering only, but in his whole life conformed to the law. The Spirit, however, ascribes our redemption to the death, or the blood, of Christ, in no other sense than that it was consummated by suffering; and from that last definitive and noblest act derives a name indeed, but not in such a way as to separate the life preceding from his death.[73]

The formula wraps Christ's obedience to the law together with His suffering, and argues that these two elements commonly appear under the biblical language of the 'blood of Christ.' In the following canon, the Formula specifically engages the denial of the IAOC: 'Finally, they so separate the active and passive righteousness of Christ, as to assert that he claims his active righteousness as his own, but gives and imputes only his passive righteousness to the elect.' Turretin and Heidegger believed that such a move rent the obedience of Christ asunder and diminished the significance of the merit of Christ.[74]

On the whole, the majority of Reformed theologians during the late sixteenth and seventeenth century affirmed the IAOC,

---

72. Campos, Jr., 'Johannes Piscator,' 208-09.

73. Formula Consensus, canon XV, trans. Klauber, 'Helvetic Formula Consensus,' 119.

74. Formula Consensus, canon XVI, trans. Klauber, 'Helvetic Formula Consensus,' 119.

though there were notable detractors. Beyond those mentioned above, explicit proponents of the IAOC include William Perkins, Johannes Cocceius (1603–69), Pierre DuMoulin (1568–1658), Thomas Boston (1676–1732), John Bunyan (1628–1688), Samuel Rutherford (1600–61), and Gisbert Voetius (1589–1676). In addition to Piscator, Pareus, and Amyraut, opponents of the IAOC include Sibrandus Lubbertus (ca. 1555–1625), John Goodwin (1594–1665), Richard Baxter (1615–91), and Josua Placaeus.[75] It is the last name, Placaeus, that is of interest for the other major debate regarding the doctrine of imputation in the seventeenth century, namely, the nature of imputed guilt.

Placaeus Controversy

The controversy over meditate imputation finds its origins in the writings of Josua Placaeus, a theologian who served at the Academy of Saumur.[76] A spark of controversy erupted at the Synod of Charenton (1644–45), where ministers accused Placaeus of denying the doctrine of imputed guilt: 'There was a Report made in the Synod of a certain Writing, both Printed and Manuscript, holding for this Doctrin [sic], that the whole Nature of Original Sin consisted only in that Corruption, which is Hereditary to all *Adam's* Posterity, and residing originally in all Men, and denieth the Imputation of his first Sin.'[77] The Synod quickly reacted to this report and condemned Placaeus:

> The Synod condemneth the said Doctrin [sic] as far as it restraineth the Nature of Original Sin to the sole Hereditary Corruption of *Adam's* Posterity, to the excluding of the Imputation of that first Sin by which he fell, and interdicteth on pain of all Church-Censures all Pastors,

---

75. For references to relevant works, see Campos, Jr., 'Johannes Piscator,' 197, 199, 207, 216-17, 220, 227, 234-35, 238-46, 280-81.

76. For what follows, see John Murray, *The Imputation of Adam's Sin* (Phillipsburg: P & R, 1959), 42-47.

77. 'The Synod of Charenton, Synod XXVIII 1644–45,' in John Quick, ed., *Synodicon in Gallia Reformata*, 2 vols. (London: Thomas Parkhurst, 1692), II:473.

Professors, and others, who shall treat of this Question, to depart from the common received Opinion of the Protestant Churches, who (over and besides that Corruption) have all acknowledged the Imputation of *Adam's* first Sin unto his Posterity.[78]

The entry for the Synod's actions does not indicate how thoroughly these matters were investigated, but merely states that Placaeus was heterodox in his denial of the imputation of Adam's sin.

In reply to the Synod's condemnation, Placaeus countered that he affirmed the imputation of Adam's sin, though he introduced the distinction between *mediate* and *immediate* imputation. Placaeus explained that the subject under discussion was not Adam's sins in general but his first actual transgression. Concerning Adam's first sin, Placaeus distinguishes between immediate imputation, which is antecedent, or mediate imputation, which is consequent. In immediate imputation the universal guilt for Adam's sin according to the order of nature (*ordo naturae*) precedes inherent corruption present in the human race. The opposite is true with mediate imputation, where according to the order of nature inherent corruption precedes guilt.[79] In other words, do people sin because they are guilty (immediate) or are they guilty because they sin (mediate)? Placaeus made a shrewd move by embracing the term *imputation* in his own view, which gave the impression that he was in some sense in favor of the doctrine. But elsewhere in his writings he explicitly rejected imputation and argues original sin comes only through natural generation.[80]

In the ensuing debate a number of theologians engaged Placaeus's claims, most notably Andre Rivet (1572–1651) and Francis Turretin. Rivet wrote a large treatise refuting Placaeus, which

78. 'Synod of Charenton,' in *Synodicon*, II:473; see also, F. P. Van Stam, *The Controversy Over the Theology of Saumur, 1635–1650: Disrupting Debates Among the Huguenots in Complicated Circumstances* (Amsterdam: APA-Holland University Press, 1988), 183, 209-12.

79. Josua Placaeus, *De Imputatione Primi Peccati Adami Josue Placaei in Academia Salmuriensi S. s. Theologiae Professoris Disputatio* (Saumur: Ioannem Lesnerium, 1661), 18.

80. Placaeus, *De Imputatione Primi Peccati*, 425.

consisted of a collection of quotations from Reformation confessions, catechisms, and theologians to prove that Placaeus's appeal to various authorities was to no avail.[81] Placaeus claimed that the doctrine of immediate imputation was foreign to the Reformed churches.[82] Placaeus also appealed to Calvin, Luther, Melanchthon, Zanchi, Vermigli and others to support his own view.[83] In some respects, however, Rivet's treatise seems to miss the mark because he cites multiple sources that do not directly address the question of immediate imputation.

Placaeus offered a number of different exegetical arguments in support of his views. In support of his position, for example, Placaeus appealed to Romans 5:12-13, namely, that sin entered the world through one man and that it was in the world before the law was given. Placaeus willingly conceded that Paul spoke of the entrance and spread of sin into the world, but he nevertheless believed that Paul spoke of inherent sin, not imputed guilt. The sin that entered the world, contends Placaeus, is not Adam's first actual sin. [84] To support his claim, Placaeus points to the fact that Paul states: 'But sin is not counted where there is no law.' According to Placaeus, the Mosaic law is anachronistic to Adam's state in the garden, hence Paul cannot be speaking of the imputation of Adam's sin.[85] Placaeus maintained, therefore, that the means by which Adam's offspring inherited his guilt was through procreation.[86]

---

81. Murray provides the following bibliographic data, Andre Rivet, *Decretum Synodi Nationalis Ecclesiarum Reformatarum Galliae Initio Anni 1645 de Imputatione Primi Peccati Omnibus Adami Posteris*, in *Opera Theologica*, vol. 3 (Rotterdam: 1660), 798-823. I was only able to access this work via the English translation made by Charles Hodge: Andre Rivet, 'On Imputation,' in *Theological Essays: Reprinted from the Princeton Review* (New York: Wiley & Putnam, 1846), 196-217.

82. Placaeus, *De Imputatione Primi Peccati*, 426.

83. Placaeus, *De Imputatione Primi Peccati*, 453-77.

84. Placaeus, *De Imputatione Primi Peccati*, 358.

85. Placaeus, *De Imputatione Primi Peccati*, 363.

86. Placaeus, *De Imputatione Primi Peccati*, 366; see also Van Stam, *Controversy*, 180.

Francis Turretin offered a very different explanation of Romans 5:12. An important presupposition to Turretin's defense of immediate imputation is that he believed the category of mediate imputation was non-existent. He believed that Placaeus raised a smokescreen and sought cover beneath the term *imputation* all the while he denied the substance of the doctrine.[87] For Turretin, in the order of nature imputation must be antecedent to inherent corruption because of the nature of Adam's role as the covenantal head of humanity.[88] With this understanding Turretin approaches Romans 5:12 with a different set of theological assumptions than Placaeus. Turretin points out that Romans 5 falls within the broader context of Paul's arguments in support of the doctrine of justification. In particular, Paul argues for the imputation of Christ's righteousness, and he does so by demonstrating the parallel between Adam and Christ. Through their respective actions, Adam and Christ legally and forensically affect those they represent.[89] Turretin pointedly asks the question, If Paul does not have imputed but inherent guilt in view, then why are sinners only held accountable for Adam's first sin? Should they not incur the liability for all of Adam's sins? To rebut Placaeus, Turretin appeals to the fact that Paul says that Adam's one trespass brought condemnation, and conversely Christ's one act of righteousness brought justification (Rom. 5:19). Turretin succinctly explains: 'We are constituted sinners in Adam in the same way in which we are constituted righteous in Christ.'[90]

These competing interpretations of Romans 5:12-13 offer a brief glimpse into the debate but nevertheless reveal the differences between the two positions. At the end of the day, Placaeus was unable to sway a majority of his peers. Although Placaeus denied that the Synod of Charenton accurately condemned his views, Turretin's analysis does appear to strike a clean blow despite Placaeus's objections. Namely, in truth, Placaeus did not advocate

---

87. Turretin, *Institutes*, IX.ix.6.

88. Turretin, *Institutes*, IX.ix.11.

89. Turretin, *Institutes*, IX.ix.16.

90. Turretin, *Institutes*, IX.ix.16.

a doctrine of imputation. Imputation, by definition, involves the forensic or declarative assignment of a status by the action of another, either condemnation or justification, according to common Reformed usage of the term.[91] While it is true and uncontested that all humanity inherits a corrupt nature from Adam, a point only disputed by Pelagians, the ground of humanity's condemnation lies in Adam's sin, not through inherent corruption according to Rollock or Beza. Rollock, for example, attached the communication of sin to the terms of the covenant, not to the shared ontological connection between Adam and his offspring: 'This efficacy of that sin is by reason of that word and covenant which God made with Adam in his creation.'[92] Likewise, in his explanation of Romans 5:12, Beza writes: 'The guilt which precedes corruption, is by the imputation of Adam's disobedience; as the remission of sins and the abolition of guilt, is by the imputation of the obedience of Christ. Nothing can be plainer.'[93] Similar statements appear in Bartholomäus Keckerman (ca. 1571–1608), Leonhard Rijssen (ca. 1636–1700), and Petrus van Mastricht (1630–1706).[94]

Given the perceived biblical warrant, widespread acceptance of the doctrine of imputed guilt, and confidence of conviction, Turretin and Heidegger proscribed Placaeus's views in the Formula Consensus.[95] In one sense, these two stalwarts of orthodoxy were not adding anything new because the Swiss churches had already rejected Placaeus's views in 1645.[96] Nevertheless, it seems

---

91. E.g., Heidegger, *Corpus Theologiae*, X.xxxii (p. 340).

92. Rollock, *Effectual Calling*, XXV, in *Works*, I:175.

93. Theodore Beza, 'Note Rom. 5:12,' as cited in Rivet, 'On Imputation,' 203.

94. Bartholomäus Keckerman, *Systema S. S. Theologiae Tribus Libris* (Hanovia: Guilielmum Antonium, 1610), II.v (p. 253); Leonhard Rijssen, *Summa Theologiae Elencticae Completa* (Bern: Danielem Tschisselii, 1703), IX.xxxv (p. 246); Petrus van Mastricht, *Theoretica-Practica Theologia*, 9th ed. (Rhenum: W. van de Water, 1724), IV.ii.10 (p. 444).

95. Cf. Heidegger, *Corpus Theologiae*, X.xxxiii (pp. 340-41).

96. Antoine Garrissoles, *Decreti Synodici Carentoniensis De Imputatione Primi Peccati Adae Explicatio et Defensio* (Montalbani: Petrum & Phlippum Braconerios, 1648), 1-4; Van Stam, *Contoversy*, 320, 361.

that Turretin and Heidegger wanted comprehensively to reject theological views associated with the Academy of Saumur. Based upon the structure of the covenant of works, the Formula maintains that Adam could have secured either blessing or curse because he was the head and root of all humanity: 'We hold therefore, that the sin of Adam is imputed by the mysterious and just judgment of God to all his posterity. For the Apostle testifies that "in Adam all sinned, by one man's disobedience many were made sinners" (Rom. 5:12, 19) and "in Adam all die" (1 Cor. 15:21-22).'[97] In a nutshell, the Formula contends that people sin because they are guilty of Adam's sin; they are not guilty merely because they sin. This does not mean that Turretin and Heidegger reject any connection between inherent corruption and penal liability. They admit both are a reality but that imputed guilt takes priority: 'Therefore, man, because of sin, is by nature, and hence from his birth, before committing any actual sin, exposed to God's wrath and curse.'[98] And lest there be any doubt, the Formula explicitly states the necessity of affirming the doctrine of immediate imputation: 'Accordingly, we can not, without harm to the Divine truth, agree with those who deny that Adam represented his posterity by God's intention, and that his sin is imputed, therefore, immediately to his posterity.' Turretin and Heidegger believed that to deny immediate imputation destroyed the very concept.[99] To affirm mediate imputation was to deny imputation altogether.

As strong as the Formula's proscription of mediate imputation was, there were still those who adhered to the doctrine and there appears to be some confessional room for it in other quarters of the Reformed church. The Westminster Confession of Faith, for example, was published in 1648, just some three years after the

---

97. Formula Consensus Helvetica, canon X, trans. Klauber, 'Helvetic Formula Consensus,' 117-18.

98. Formula Consensus Helvetica, canon XI, trans. Klauber, 'Helvetic Formula Consensus,' 118.

99. Formula Consensus Helvetica, canon XII, trans. Klauber, 'Helvetic Formula Consensus,' 118.

condemnations against Placaeus's views by the Synod of Charenton in 1645. There was little time for the Westminster assembly to determine whether Placaeus and mediate imputation were within the pale of orthodoxy.[100] Nevertheless, the Confession does advocate the doctrine of immediate imputation without proscribing mediate imputation.[101] The Confession states: 'They [Adam and Eve] being the root of all man-kinde, the guilt of this sin was imputed, and the same death in sin and corrupted nature, conveied to all their posterity descending from them by ordinary generation' (VI.iii; cf. LC q. 22; SC q. 16). Placaeus would never say that God imputed the guilt of Adam's first sin to all humanity.

Beyond the proceedings at Westminster, once again Congregational and Particular Baptist theologians offered clarifying refinements to the Confession. The Savoy Declaration, unlike the Westminster Confession, for example, explicitly invokes the covenant of works in its opening statement on the fall of man.[102] The Declaration then goes on to state: 'They [Adam and Eve] being the Root, and by Gods appointment standing in the room and stead of all mankinde, the guilt of this sin was imputed, and corrupted nature conveyed to all their posterity descending from them by

---

100. Donald McLeod, 'Original Sin in Reformed Theology,' in *Adam, the Fall, and Original Sin*, ed. Hans Madueme and Michael Reeves (Grand Rapids: Baker, 2014), 140-41.

101. A number of different historians have reached this conclusion. See Henry Boynton Smith, *System of Christian Theology*, 2nd ed. (New York: A. C. Armstrong and Son, 1884), 283; Henry Clay Sheldon, *History of Christian Doctrine*, 2 vols. (New York: Harper & Brothers, 1886), II:127; Robert Shaw, *An Exposition of the Westminster Confession of Faith* (1845; Fearn: Christian Focus, 1998), 117-18; William Cunningham, *The Reformers and the Theology of the Reformation*, in *The Collected Works of the Rev. William Cunningham*, vol. 1 (Edinburgh: T & T Clark, 1862), 382-83. Others maintain that the Confession is undecided on the issue (George Park Fisher, *History of Christian Doctrine* [New York: Charles Scribner's Sons, 1911], 359-60). And still yet others maintain that the Confession teaches both views (see James Leo Garrett, *Systematic Theology*, 2 vols. [Grand Rapids: Eerdmans, 1990], I:564).

102. Cf. Westminster Confession, VI.i; Savoy Declaration, VI.i.

ordinary generation.'[103] Like the Westminster Confession, the Savoy Declaration does not proscribe mediate imputation, but it is quite explicit regarding immediate imputation. The Second London Confession does not introduce the covenant of works, but it nevertheless offers very similar language in its statement on imputed guilt, which echoes the Savoy Declaration: 'They being the root, and *God's* appointment, standing in the room, and stead of all Mankind; the guilt of the *Sin* was imputed, and *corrupted* Nature conveyed, to all their Posterity, descending from them by ordinary generation, being now conceived in *Sin*, and by nature children of Wrath, and servants of *Sin*, the subjects of *Death*, and all other miseries, spiritual, temporal and eternal, unless the *Lord Jesus* set them free.'[104] Once again, the confession is silent regarding mediate imputation but explicit in its promotion of imputed guilt.

Despite the strong ecclesiastical endorsement of immediate imputation, and in some cases outright rejection of mediate imputation, a number of theologians became advocates of the latter, including Campegius Vitringa (1659–1722), Hermann Venema (1697–1787), Johann Friedrich Stapfer (1708–1775), and Daniel Wyttenbach (1706–79).[105] There is a case to be made that proponents of mediate imputation advocated a more traditional catholic view of inherited guilt.[106] There were others on the European scene, however, who openly rejected the imputation of Adam's sin in any

---

103. Savoy Declaration, VI.iii.

104. Second London Confession, VI.iii.

105. Murray, *Imputation*, 47; cf. Campegius Vitringa, *Doctrina Christianae Religionis per Aphorismos Summatim Descripta*, 4th ed (Francker: Fransiscum Halmam, 1702), 171; Johannes Friederich Stapfer, *Institutiones Theologiae Polemicae Universae*, vol. 1 (Zurich: Heideggerum et Socios, 1757), III.x.857-58 (pp. 236-37); Herman Venema, *Institutes of Theology*, trans. Alex W. Brown (Edinburgh: T & T Clark, 1854), 518-32; Daniel Wyttenbach, *Tentamen Theologiae Dogmaticae Methodo Scientifica Pertractata*, vol. 1 (Frankfurt: Andreae et Hort, 1747), VII.806-08 (pp. 608-10).

106. See, e.g., Johannes Polyander, et al., *Synopsis Purioris Theologiae*, vol. 1, ed. Dolft te Velde, trans. Riemer A. Faber (Leiden: Brill, 2014), XV.ix-xii (pp. 356-61).

form, such as Socinian theologians and Remonstrants like Phillip van Limborch (1633–1712).[107] Van Limborch argued that human beings are born with the habit of sin, a propensity towards sin, not with original sin, the guilt of Adam's first transgression.[108]

CONCLUSION

Looking over the scene of post-Reformation Reformed theology, one might have the impression that it was marked by bickering and in-fighting over pedantic questions regarding issues that the early Reformers never engaged. Without doubt, theologians in the late sixteenth and seventeenth century engaged the doctrine of imputation with much greater precision in comparison with the earliest formulations of Luther, Melanchthon, or Calvin. But with the march of time, increased polemics with Roman Catholicism and the declarations of Trent, as well as new questions, theologians desired to explain the nature of imputation with greater precision. Second and third generation reformers sought to employ the doctrine of the covenant because they believed it offered a more biblical account of both the transmission of sin and the imputation of righteousness. Naturally, there were dissenting voices and ensuing debates, which created greater precision, clarified terminology, and confessionally codified boundaries. The seventeenth century witnessed the confessional enshrinement of a covenantal double imputation: God imputes Adam's sin and Christ's righteousness because they are the respective federal heads of the covenants of works and grace. While it may be a slight exaggeration, in the centuries to follow the doctrine of imputation sees little development. Rather, theologians identify with one of the many different views espoused in the previous eighteen centuries. And despite the efforts of Roman Catholic, Reformed, and Lutheran

---

107. Faustus Socinus, *De Jesu Christo Servatore*, III.iii, in Alan W. Gomes, 'Faustus Socinus' *De Jesu Christo Servatore*, Part III: Historical Introductions, Translation and Critical Notes' (Ph.D. diss, Fuller Theological Seminary, 1990), 253.

108. Philip van Limborch, *A Compleat System, or Body of Divinity*, vol. 1 (1702), III.i.3-4 (pp. 191-205).

theologians to bury Pelagius beneath a heap of condemnations and anathemas, the decrepit hand juts forth from its grave and Pelagianism reappears in the modern period.

4

The American Modern Period

Introduction

Earlier generations debated the propriety of imputed righteousness, argued over mediate versus immediate imputation of sin, and disputed about the imputed active obedience of Christ. In the ensuing unfolding of the Enlightenment, philosophers such as Immanuel Kant (1724–1804) rejected and derided any notion of inherited guilt, sin, or corruption. Kant, for example, writes:

> For this is no *transmissible* liability which can be made over to another like a financial indebtedness (where it is all one to the creditor whether the debtor himself pays the debt or whether some one else pays it for him); rather is it *the most personal of all debts*, namely a debt of sins, which only the culprit can bear and which no innocent person can

assume even though he be magnanimous enough to wish to take it upon himself for the sake of another.[1]

Post-Enlightenment thought isolated individuals from corporate existence and hence excluded any notion of solidarity. But just because the waves of opposition sought to sweep away biblical doctrines such as imputation, there were nevertheless theological rocks along the shore of history that withstood the imposing tides that eroded belief elsewhere in the broader church.

The American rocks that withstood the shifting tides were Jonathan Edwards (1703–58) in the eighteenth century, and notably Charles Hodge (1797–1878), W. G. T. Shedd (1820–94), Samuel J. Baird (1834–92), James Henley Thornwell (1812–62), Henry Boynton Smith (1815–77), and Robert L. Dabney (1820–98) in the nineteenth century. But although these theologians continued to embrace the doctrine of imputation in the face of waning faith they were not all agreed. Edwards offered his own unique views on imputation that were largely and almost universally rejected by subsequent nineteenth-century theologians. And despite the fact that all of the aforementioned nineteenth-century theologians were all Reformed Presbyterians who adhered to the Westminster Standards, this did not guarantee uniformity of conviction.

This chapter, therefore, surveys the development and reception of the doctrine of imputation in the eighteenth and nineteenth centuries from the vantage point of the American theological scene in the eighteenth and nineteenth centuries. This geographic and historical timeframe provides examples of numerous different views on imputation. This chapter first focuses upon Edwards, though he by no means was the only theologian who maintained a doctrine of imputation. But many others subsequently engaged his views positively and negatively. The chapter then shifts to survey the nineteenth century and the significant debates over the precise nature of imputation. Unlike previous centuries where disagreement was about establishing the legitimacy of imputed righteousness or

---

1. Immanuel Kant, *Religion Within the Limits of Reason Alone*, trans. Theodore M. Greene & Hoyt H. Hudson (New York: Harper & Row, 1960), II.i (p. 66).

debating the distinction between the active and passive obedience of Christ, the nineteenth-century discussion focused upon the specific question of the imputation of Adam's sin to his posterity. Theologians certainly drew connections to imputed righteousness, but they clashed over whether Adam's sin was imputed mediately, immediately, realistically, or whether it was imputed at all. Albert Barnes (1798–1870), for example, denied the doctrine of imputation altogether. Some even rejected all opinions and advocated an informed agnosticism on the whole question. Hence, the chapter surveys the five main schools of thought: Pelagian imitation (Barnes), immediate imputation (Hodge), mediate imputation (Smith), realistic imputation (Shedd, Baird, and Thornwell), and informed agnosticism (Dabney). The chapter then concludes with some general observations about the reception and development of the doctrine of imputation.

EIGHTEENTH CENTURY

Jonathan Edwards is one of the most notable figures in American eighteenth-century history, and for this reason present-day theologians herald him as a symbol of Reformed orthodoxy. Yet there are many conflicting opinions about his theology in general; and analyses are all over the board concerning his doctrine of imputation.[2] Paul Helm believes that Edwards did not advocate a federal doctrine of imputed original sin.[3] Charles Hodge believed that Edwards's doctrine was inconsistent because he incorporated mediate imputation in his doctrine of original sin, but Hodge characterized this as an 'excrescence,' a peculiarity that did not affect the rest of his theology.[4] B. B. Warfield classified Edwards as a thoroughgoing federalist.[5]

2. Oliver D. Crisp, *Retrieving Doctrine: Essays in Reformed Theology* (Downers Grove: InterVarsity Press, 2010), 47, 56-57.

3. Paul Helm, *Faith and Understanding* (Grand Rapids: Eerdmans, 1997), 152-76.

4. Charles Hodge, *Systematic Theology*, 3 vols. (rep.; Grand Rapids: Eerdmans, 1993), II:207.

5. B. B. Warfield, 'Edwards and the New England Theology,' in *The Works of Benjamin B. Warfield*, 10 vols. (rep.; Grand Rapids: Baker, 1989), IX:513-38.

Robert Dabney objected to Edwards's doctrine of original sin on the grounds that, according to Edwards, God supposedly constituted humanity's federal oneness with Adam merely by divine fiat in the same way God establishes our personal identity. Dabney also objected to Edwards's inclusion of the doctrine of continual creation in his understanding of original sin. Just as God continually moment-by-moment destroys and creates and upholds our personal identity merely by His will, so God maintains humanity's federal unity with Adam. Dabney characterized Edwards's view as worthless speculation and hence 'repudiated' it.[6] William Cunningham argued that Edwards adopted the views of Johann Friedrich Stapfer (1708–75), who employed the terminology of both mediate and immediate imputation. Cunningham dismissed Edwards's conclusions on the grounds that the New England theologian never carefully studied the doctrine of imputation. Edwards, in Cunningham's estimation, was ignorant of the various debates concerning original sin.[7] Other nineteenth-century theologians, such as W. G. T. Shedd, acknowledged that Edwards closely followed Stapfer.[8] How, then, do we assess Edwards's doctrine of original sin and his broader doctrine of imputation if theologians have identified his view as fully federal, inconsistently federal, non-federal, speculative, ignorant, or one that embraces both mediate and immediate concepts?

The answer lies, I believe, in Oliver Crisp's thesis that Edwards did not repristinate earlier views but rather wedded traditional Reformed theology to Enlightenment philosophical comitments. Space prohibits a thorough examination of the evidence for

---

6. Robert L. Dabney, *Syllabus and Notes of the Course of Systematic and Polemic Theology*, 2nd ed. (St. Louis: Presbyterian Publishing Co., 1878), 338.

7. William Cunningham, *The Reformers and the Theology of the Reformation*, in *The Collected Works of the Rev. William* Cunningham, vol. 1 (Edinburgh: T & T Clark, 1862), 384.

8. W. G. T. Shedd, *A History of Christian Doctrine*, 2 vols. (New York: Charles Scribner's Sons, 1909), II:163-64; also Z. M. Humphrey, 'Review of *Henry Boynton Smith: His Life and Work* (1881),' *The Presbyterian Review* 2 (1881): 489.

the various opinions, nevertheless we can first briefly examine Edwards's key statement of the doctrine and then identify its unique elements. First, Edwards believed that Adam and his offspring were federally united: 'God, in each step of his proceeding with Adam, in relation to the covenant or constitution established with him, looked on his posterity as being one with him.'[9] Edwards places both Adam and his offspring within a covenantal context. Second, Edwards ties the transmission of guilt and depravity of heart to Adam's sin; just as they both came upon Adam, they also came upon his offspring 'as if he and they had all coexisted.'[10] Edwards clearly articulates a federal view of imputed sin.[11]

Third, Edwards does seem to endorse a view of immediate imputation, but in other places seems to articulate a doctrine of mediate imputation.[12] Nevertheless, Edwards carefully distinguishes between an inherited corrupt nature and the exercise of that nature as a 'confirmed principle':

> The depraved disposition of Adam's heart is to be considered two ways. (1) As the first rising of an evil inclination in his heart, exerted in his first act of sin, and the ground of the complete transgression. (2) An evil disposition of heart continuing afterwards, as a confirmed principle, that came by God's forsaking him; which was a punishment for his first transgression. This confirmed corruption, by its remaining and continued operation, brought additional guilt upon his soul.[13]

Adam, therefore, has a double-guilt: his evil disposition, and the outworking of that disposition as a confirmed principle.[14] Even though the fruit chronologically follows the existence of the evil

---

9. Jonathan Edwards, *Original Sin*, Works of Jonathan Edwards, vol. 3 (New Haven: Yale University Press, 1970), 389.

10. Edwards, *Original Sin*, 389.

11. Crisp, *Retrieving Doctrine*, 60-61.

12. Edwards, *Original Sin*, 348, 390; Crisp, *Retrieving Doctrine*, 61.

13. Edwards, *Original Sin*, 390.

14. Crisp, *Retrieving Doctrine*, 62.

disposition, God treats them as one sinful unit.[15] And as such, when God imputes this sin to Adam's offspring, it bears this same twofold structure. Adam's progeny first possess the evil disposition but they only become truly guilty once the disposition becomes a confirmed principle. Adam's offspring become guilty, therefore, both through the imputation of Adam's sin (as disposition and confirmed principle), and through their own sinful actions accrue additional guilt.[16]

The question arises, How is this different from earlier Reformed views? At one level, Edwards's doctrine sounds quite similar to earlier formulations. This most likely accounts for the wide array of opinions about where, precisely, Edwards's view falls. At this point, however, one must factor not only Edwards's doctrine of imputed sin but also his doctrine of continual creation. In contrast to earlier Reformed views that rested upon a catholic doctrine of creation, Edwards's occasionalism required that God destroyed and recreated the creation moment by moment. Crisp likens Edwards's view to a strip of film where each frame represents a destruction and *ex nihilo* re-creation of the cosmos.[17] Given his occasionalism, Edwards believed that there were no secondary causes in the creation— God was the chief actor, and hence He had to re-create the world moment by moment. Given his doctrine of continual creation, there had to be a way to connect Adam to his progeny both forensically and ontologically. Hence, Edwards borrowed from realism the idea that there had to be an ontological foundation behind Adam's unity with his offspring. And from federalism he appropriated the idea that God treats Adam and his offspring as one unit.[18]

But to these traditional elements Edwards added his doctrine of continual creation. This is the unique philosophical element in his otherwise traditional doctrine that explains its peculiarities and why theologians struggle to categorize his view. Within an occasionalist

---

15. Crisp, *Retrieving Doctrine*, 63.

16. Crisp, *Retrieving Doctrine*, 63.

17. Crisp, *Retrieving Doctrine*, 66; idem, *Jonathan Edwards on God and Creation* (Oxford: Oxford University Press, 2012), 32-34.

18. Crisp, *Retrieving Doctrine*, 67.

framework, one action cannot stand alone because the human agent is unable to carry the action to the next moment of time. God must therefore destroy and recreate the human agent to carry the action forward. Hence, original sin can only exist as a disposition and a confirmed principle. They are chronologically distinct but forensically united. God imputes this disposition-confirmed principle to Adam's posterity, and the same pattern unfolds. This structure explains the immediate and mediate elements in Edward's covenantal doctrine of imputation. Edwards's occasionalism, therefore, impacts his doctrine of imputation, and it also impacts his doctrine of imputed righteousness. God imputes righteousness to people by faith alone, but they are not genuinely justified until faith issues forth in good works. Once again, the disposition-confirmed principle colors his doctrine of justification and imputed righteousness.[19]

NINETEENTH CENTURY

Edwards sought to articulate traditional Reformed theology within an Enlightenment framework, but subsequent Reformed theologians were content with the previously established categories of mediate and immediate imputation. In the nineteenth century theologians principally rotated around these two positions. There were five main views in nineteenth-century Reformed theology: Pelagian imitation (Barnes), immediate imputation (Hodge), mediate imputation (Smith), realistic transmission (Shedd, Baird, Thornwell), and agnosticism (Dabney).[20]

PELAGIAN IMITATION (BARNES)

Augustine, church councils, and numerous theologians buried Pelagius but his spirit lived on. His ghost inhabited seventeenth-century Socinian theology and also settled in a sermon series

---

19. For further analysis, bibliography, and documentation, see J. V. Fesko, *The Covenant of Redemption: Origins, Development, and Reception* (Göttingen: Vandenhoeck & Ruprecht, 2015), 122-42.

20. This typology originates from George P. Hutchinson, *The Problem of Original Sin in American Presbyterian Theology* (Phillipsburg: P & R, 1972), 15.

by Presbyterian minister Albert Barnes. Barnes's sermons were eventually published as an expositional commentary on Romans in 1835. In his comments on Romans 5:19,* 'For as by the one man's disobedience the many were constituted sinners, so by the one man's obedience the many will be constituted righteous,' Barnes rejects the idea that Paul refers to imputation. Rather, when Paul says that many were constituted sinners, Barnes maintains that Paul merely intends to say that it was a fact that people were sinful. If this verse means, as some maintain, that people were held accountable for Adam's sin, then the converse would also be true. Namely, that all humanity would be constituted righteous by Christ. Barnes rejects this idea. Moreover, in his understanding, if people were condemned on account of Adam's sin, they would nevertheless be innocent of any actual wrongdoing. In the divine economy of things, God condemns only those truly guilty of sin.[21]

In his rejection of imputation, Barnes was specific about what Paul did and did not affirm in Romans 5:19 and the surrounding context; he gives four reasons. First, Paul mentions nothing about representation; he does not designate Adam as a representative for humanity, nor does this concept appear anywhere else in Scripture. Second, Paul mentions nothing of the doctrine of covenant, nor does this appear anywhere else in Scripture. Third, Paul only addresses the fact that Adam sinned, which ensured that the rest of humanity would be sinners. To argue for anything more is 'mere philosophical speculation.' And, fourth, the fact of sin guarantees that others will be sinful, just as a drunkard guarantees that his family will be reduced to poverty.[22] In Barnes's analysis, neither Scripture nor the apostle Paul ever explain how Adam plunged the human race into sin.[23]

Given that Barnes rejected imputed guilt, it should come as no surprise that he rejected imputed righteousness in his doctrine of

---

21. Albert Barnes, *Notes, Explanatory and Practical, On the Epistle of Romans* (New York: Leavitt, Lord, and Co., 1834), 127.

22. Barnes, *Romans*, 128.

23. Barnes, *Romans*, 129.

justification. In his explanation of Romans 4:3, 'Abraham believed God, and it was counted to him as righteousness,' Barnes notes that 'it,' refers to Abraham's faith, not to the righteousness of another, whether God's or the Messiah's. In some sense Abraham's faith was counted as righteousness. But what, according to Barnes, does Paul mean by *righteousness*? Barnes believes that righteousness is a status of friendship: 'One who was admitted to the favor and friendship of God.'[24] In summary, 'In being justified by faith, it is meant, therefore, that we are treated as righteous; that we are forgiven; that we are admitted to the favor of God, and treated as his friends.'[25] In other words, justification is merely the forgiveness of sins, and to be righteous means to have the status of 'friend of God.'

For his views Barnes merited an ecclesiastical trial before the Presbyterian Synod of Philadelphia in 1835 where he was charged with the heresy of Pelagianism. Rev. George Junkin (1790–1868) initially brought nine charges against Barnes principally drawn from his commentary on Romans, but the presbytery cleared him of the charges. Junkin believed that in the course of the trial debate shifted from imputation to the bigger question of whether Barnes was guilty of heresy. And heresy was something for which people historically burned at the stake, and presbyters shuddered at such gruesome thoughts.[26] Junkin, of course, was discouraged and believed the presbytery failed to deal with the issues.[27] Moreover, Junkin was distraught that presbyters refused to employ the Westminster Standards as a benchmark to determine Barnes's guilt or innocence.[28]

So Junkin appealed to synod; the charges were that Mr. Barnes:

---

24. Barnes, *Romans*, 95.

25. Barnes, *Romans*, 95.

26. George Junkin, *The Vindication, Containing A History of the Trial of the Rev. Albert Barnes by the Second Presbytery and the by the Synod of Philadelphia* (Philadelphia: Wm. S. Martien, 1836), xxi.

27. Junkin, *The Vindication*, xxiii.

28. Junkin, *The Vindication*, xxiv.

1. Teaches 'that all sin consists in voluntary action.'[29]

2. Teaches 'that Adam (before and after his fall) was ignorant of his moral relations to such a degree, that he did not know the consequence of his sin would or should reach any further than to natural death.'[30]

3. Teaches 'That unregenerate men are able to keep the commandments and convert themselves to God.'[31]

4. Asserts that 'faith is an act of the mind, and not a principle, and is itself imputed for righteousness.'[32]

5. Denies 'that God entered into covenant with Adam constituting him a federal or covenant head, and representative to all his natural descendants.'[33]

6. Denies 'that the first sin of Adam is imputed to his posterity.'

7. Denies 'that mankind are guilty, i.e., liable to punishment on account of the sin of Adam.'

8. Denies 'that Christ suffered the proper penalty of the law, as the vicarious substitute of his people, and thus took away legally their sins and purchased pardon.'

9. Denies 'that the righteousness, i.e., the active obedience of Christ to the law, is imputed to his people for their justification; so that they are righteous in the eye of the law, and therefore justified.'[34]

---

29. A. J. Stansbury, *Trial of the Rev. Albert Barnes, Before the Synod of Philadelphia, in Session at York, October 1835, On a Charge of Heresy, Preferred Against Him by the Rev. George Junkin* (New York: 1836), 105.

30. Stansbury, *Trial*, 108.

31. Stansbury, *Trial*, 110.

32. Stansbury, *Trial*, 119.

33. Stansbury, *Trial*, 126.

34. Stansbury, *Trial*, 128.

The trial record rambles in good Presbyterian fashion where numerous speeches waltzed back and forth upon the floor of the synod with the outcome of Barnes's conviction and suspension from office.[35]

The Synod sustained Junkin's appeal on the grounds that Barnes was guilty of fundamental errors that were contrary to the system of doctrine contained in the word of God and summarized in the Westminster Standards.[36] Barnes, however, ultimately appealed to the General Assembly, which overturned his conviction. This trial was only smoke from a larger fire that burned within the Presbyterian Church. The trial was a microcosm of larger theological disagreements between new school and old school parties within the church. New school theologians drew inspiration from the New England doctrines that originated from Jonathan Edwards, whereas old school theologians saw themselves as adhering to traditional Reformed doctrines.[37] The Barnes trial was therefore one of the straws that eventually broke the back of the Presbyterian Church and led to a new school-old school split in 1837.[38]

IMMEDIATE IMPUTATION (HODGE)

Charles Hodge was the tip of the spear and led the charge against new school, which naturally means that his doctrine of imputation was quite different from Barnes's. There are three main works where Hodge expounds his doctrine of imputation: two articles in the *Princeton Review*, his commentary on Romans, and in his *Systematic Theology*.[39] Hodge begins his doctrine of imputation by noting the

---

35. Stansbury, *Trial*, 285.

36. Junkin, *The Vindication*, xxvi.

37. See, e.g., Douglas A. Sweeney, *Nathaniel Taylor, New Haven Theology, and the Legacy of Jonathan Edwards* (Oxford: Oxford University Press, 2003).

38. D. G. Hart & John R. Muether, *Seeking a Better Country: 300 Years of American Presbyterianism* (Phillipsburg: P & R, 2007), 119-20.

39. Charles Hodge, 'Inquiries Respecting the Doctrine of Imputation,' *The Biblical Repertory and Theological Review* vol. 2 / no. 3 (1830): 425-72; idem, 'The Christian Spectator on the Doctrine of Imputation,' *The Biblical Repertory and Theological Review* 3/3 (1831): 407-43; cf. *The Biblical Repertory*

natural union that exists between Adam and his offspring; he indicates that this union is the ground of the imputation of Adam's sin, though he stipulates that this union is both natural and federal.[40] Adam was the natural head of the human race by virtue of his relationship to them, namely, between parent and child. But beyond this natural union there was also a special relationship whereby God constituted Adam the federal head and representative of all humanity.[41] Hodge surveys the Scriptures to demonstrate the representative principle, whether in Achan's sin whereby his family suffered for his actions, the imprecations that the Jews called down upon their own heads and those of their children when they crucified Christ, or God's covenant with Abraham.[42] Hodge argues that the doctrine of imputation is pervasive and also evident in the Day of Atonement, for example, when the priest placed his hands upon the head of the sacrificial animal to signify the transfer of guilt (Lev. 16).[43]

Hodge links imputation both to original sin, the vicarious sufferings of Christ, and the doctrine of justification. The doctrine of imputation runs through them all:

> This is the idea inculcated in every part of the Bible. And this is what the Scriptures teach concerning the atonement of Christ. He bore our sins; He was made a curse for us; He suffered the penalty of the law in our stead. All this proceeds on the ground that the sins of one man can be justly, on some adequate ground, imputed to another. In justification the same radical idea is included. ... There is a logical connection, therefore, between the denial of the imputation of Adam's sin, and the denial of the Scriptural doctrines of atonement and justification.[44]

---

and *Princeton Review, Index Volume* (1825–68): 209; Charles Hodge, *A Commentary on the Epistle to the Romans* (New York: Robert Carter & Brothers, 1880).

40. Hodge, *Systematic Theology*, II:196.

41. Hodge, *Systematic Theology*, II:196-97.

42. Hodge, *Systematic Theology*, II: 198-99.

43. Hodge, *Systematic Theology*, II:201.

44. Hodge, *Systematic Theology*, II:201.

For Hodge, Romans 5:12-19 serves as the chief fulcrum for imputed sin and righteousness. Imputation explains the respective actions of the two Adams. The judicial ground for the condemnation of all humanity lies in Adam's one sin; conversely, the judicial ground for justification lies in the representative obedience of Christ for all those who are in Him.[45] One man's sin constitutes the many as sinners and one man's obedience constitutes many as righteous. In short, 'Union with Adam is the cause of death; union with Christ is the cause of life.'[46] When we get into the particulars of Hodge's doctrine, there are several noteworthy points. First, Hodge was keenly aware of his doctrinal context—he wanted to refute New England theology and the claims of Albert Barnes. In his commentary on Romans, Hodge rejected a number of common errors and opinions. The doctrine of imputation does not:

- Include the idea of a mysterious identity of Adam (contra Edwards).

- Involve the transfer of the moral turpitude of Adam's sin to his offspring.

- Teach that his offence was personally or properly the sin of all men, or that his act was mysterious.

- Imply that Christ's righteousness becomes ours personally and inherently, or that Christ transfers His moral excellence to us.

Instead, Hodge maintained: 'In virtue of the union, representative and natural, between Adam and his posterity, his sin is the ground of their condemnation, that is, of their subjection to penal evils; and that, in virtue of the union between Christ and his people, his righteousness is the ground of their justification.'[47] For Hodge, imputation is an immediate forensic act.

---

45. Hodge, *Systematic Theology*, II:202.

46. Hodge, *Systematic Theology*, II:203.

47. Hodge, *Romans*, 135.

Second, Hodge believed that when God imputed Adam's sin to humanity, He only imputed the penalty, not Adam's guilt or moral corruption. Hodge explains: 'To impute sin, in Scriptural and theological language, is to impute *the guilt of sin*. And by guilt is meant not criminality or moral ill-desert, or demerit, much less moral pollution, but the *judicial obligation to satisfy justice*.'[48] In technical terms, Hodge maintains that Adam's imputed sin is not his guilt (*reatus culpae*), nor the *demeritum* (demerit), but the penalty (*reatus poenae*).[49] Hodge's opinion diverges from the majority report within the tradition; namely, theologians argued that God imputed both guilt (*reatus culpae*) and penalty (*reatus poenae*).[50] In his lectures on the Heidelberg Catechism Zacharias Ursinus (1534–83) writes: 'By the death of Christ, who is the second Adam, we obtain a twofold grace: we mean justification and regeneration. It follows, therefore, that we must all have derived from the first Adam the twofold evil of guilt [*reatus*] and corruption of nature [*depravatio naturae*], otherwise there had been no necessity for a twofold grace and remedy.'[51] Others such as Girolamo Zanchi (1516–90), John Calvin (1509–64), and Francis Turretin (1623–87) make the same

---

48. Hodge, *Systematic Theology*, II:194, emphasis added.

49. John Murray, *The Imputation of Adam's Sin* (1959; Phillipsburg: P & R, n. d.), 74.

50. Medieval theologians distinguished between liability to penalty (*reatus poenae*) and liability to guilt (*reatus culpae*). They maintained that Christ removed guilt (*culpa*) through baptism but that the believer still had to account for penalty (*poena*) through temporal satisfactions, i.e., penance (cf. Richard A. Muller, *Dictionary of Latin and Greek Theological Terms: Drawn Principally from Protestant Scholastic Theology* [Grand Rapids: Baker, 1986], s. v. *reatus*; Thomas Aquinas, *Summa Theologica* [rep.; Allen: Christian Classics, 1948], IIIa q. 86 art. 4; IaIIae q. 87 art. 1; Heinrich Denzinger, *Compendium of Creeds, Definitions, and Declarations on Matters of Faith and Morals*, 43rd ed. [San Francisco: Ignatius press, 2012], §§1689-92, §§1712-15). Reformed orthodox theologians generally refused to distinguish *poena* and *culpa* and simply discussed the *reatus* of sin. Hodge, of course, employs the distinction for different reasons than medieval theologians.

51. Zacharias Ursinus, *The Commentary of Dr. Zacharias Ursinus on the Heidelberg Catechism*, trans. G. W. Williard (1852; Phillipsburg: P & R, n. d.), 40; idem, *Corpus Doctrinae Christianae* (Hanoviae: Jonas Rosae, 1651), 43.

point.[52] There were notable exceptions to this pattern, however, such as John Owen (1616–83): 'For nothing is intended by the imputation of sin unto any, but the rendering them justly obnoxious unto the punishment due unto that sin; as the not imputing of sin is the freeing of men from being subject or liable unto punishment.'[53]

Hodge argued that God imputed Adam's sin to his offspring, which only entailed the liability to penalty (*reatus poenae*), not Adam's guilt (*reatus culpae*). He argued this because of the parallel between imputed sin and righteousness and the representative actions of the two Adams. Hodge explains: 'The scope of the passage is to illustrate the doctrine of justification on the ground of the righteousness of Christ, by a reference to the condemnation of men for the sin of Adam. The analogy is destroyed, and the point of the comparison fails, if any thing in us be assumed as the ground of the infliction of the penal evils of which the apostle is here speaking. That we have corrupt natures and are personally sinners, and therefore liable to other and further inflictions is indeed true, but nothing to the point.'[54] Hodge does not deny that humanity inherits a corrupt nature from Adam; he affirms this reality.[55]

In the bigger picture, his penalty-only imputation view may represent a minority within the tradition, but Hodge influenced a distinguished line of Reformed theologians who adopted his view, including his son, A. A. Hodge (1823–86), B. B. Warfield, Caspar Wistar Hodge, Jr. (1870–1937), and J. Gresham Machen (1881–1937).[56] Machen, for example, writes: 'When the Bible

---

52. Girolamo Zanchi, *Omnium Operum Theologicorum*, vol. 4 (Geneva: Ioannis Tornaesij, 1649), I.iv (col. 38); John Calvin, *Institutes of the Christian Religion*, trans. John Allen (Grand Rapids: Eerdmans, 1948), II.i.8; idem, *Institutio Christianae Religionis* (Geneva: Roberti Stephani, 1559); Francis Turretin, *Institutes of Elenctic Theology* (Phillipsburg: P & R, 1992-97), IX.iii.1-7.

53. John Owen, *The Doctrine of Justification by Faith*, in *The Works of John Owen*, vol. 5, ed. William H. Goold (1850-53; Edinburgh: Banner of Truth, 1998), 324.

54. Hodge, *Romans*, 119.

55. Hodge, *Romans*, 118.

56. A. A. Hodge, *Outlines of Theology* (1860; Edinburgh: Banner of Truth,

teaches that Adam's first transgression was imputed to his descendants, that does not mean that those descendants had actually committed that first transgression. But the penalty which God pronounced upon that sin of Adam rested upon them.'[57] The chain was not broken until John Murray (1898–1975) defended a view of immediate imputation, but unlike Hodge, maintained that imputation brought both guilt (*reatus culpae*) and penalty (*reatus poenae*).[58]

MEDIATE IMPUTATION (SMITH)

In spite of Hodge's influence in nineteenth-century American Presbyterian theology, there were other significant voices. One such voice came from new school Presbyterian theologian Henry Boynton Smith.[59] Boynton was opposed to the theory of immediate imputation:

1. Romans 5:12 does not directly address the question of whether imputation is mediate or immediate.

2. It presents sin in merely a forensic manner.

3. It rests on an un-philosophical view of Adam's relationship to his offspring and employs the doctrine of the covenants in an unbiblical manner. It loses the moral organic unity of the human race.

4. In addition to imputation, the view must still concede the presence of corruption through natural descent, which it

---

1991), 348-66, esp. 357-58; B. B. Warfield, 'Review of *God's Image in Man* by James Orr,' in *The Works of B. B. Warfield*, 10 vols. (1932; Grand Rapids: Baker, 1981), 140; idem, 'Imputation,' in *Works*, IX:301-08; Caspar Wistar Hodge, 'Imputation,' in *International Standard Bible Encyclopedia*, vol. 3, ed. James Orr (1939; Grand Rapids: Eerdmans, 1974), 1462-66; J. Gresham Machen, *The Christian View of Man* (1937; Edinburgh: Banner of Truth, 1999), 11, 208-19, esp. 216; Hutchinson, *Original Sin*, 82-83.

57. Machen, *Christian View of Man*, 216.

58. Murray, *Imputation of Adam's Sin*, 74-75.

59. Hart and Muether, *Seeking a Better Country*, 136-37.

characterizes as punishment. This punishment does not have any ground in the individual.

5. It does not explain in what way God is just in allowing Adam to serve as the representative of the human race.

6. It erroneously argues for a parallel between imputed righteousness and guilt. Just because Christ's righteousness is imputed gratuitously does not mean God imputes sin in the same manner.

7. Historically, few have advocated immediate imputation.[60]

Smith rejects a number of other views in addition to immediate imputation.

Smith dismisses the view of Samuel Hopkins (1721–1803), a disciple of Jonathan Edwards, which he describes as a theory of divine constitution.[61] Under this theory man was placed under a divine constitution, or a covenant, which comprehended all humanity. By this constitution Adam's sin became the sin of all humanity.[62] But according to Hopkins, Adam's offspring are not sinners before they exist. Rather, they only become guilty once they are born and begin to act as moral agents.[63] Smith objects to the idea that people are sinners before they exist because it: is unnatural, neglects the unity of the human race, ignores the existence of man's sinful nature prior to sinful acts, and does not answer the question of how to classify infants who die before they commit sin.[64] Smith also rejects a similar constitutional theory that was sometimes aligned with Hopkins's theory, a view

---

60. Henry Boynton Smith, *System of Christian Theology*, 2nd ed. (New York: A. C. Armstrong & Son, 1884), 306-08.

61. Smith, *System of Theology*, 308.

62. Samuel Hopkins, *The System of Doctrines Contained in Divine Revelation*, 2 vols. (Boston: Isaiah Thomas, 1793), I:289, 292, 309-10, 315.

63. Hopkins, *System of Doctrines*, 325.

64. Smith, *System of Theology*, 309.

that he describes as physical depravity. Because of Adam's sin his offspring are born with a constitutional derangement. Even though both views employ the word *constitution*, Smith notes that the former refers to a divine arrangement (covenant) and the latter denotes man's physical constitution, a condition devoid of moral character.[65] This was the view of Nathaniel William Taylor (1786–1858), another disciple of Jonathan Edwards.[66] Smith objected to this view on the grounds that it virtually eliminated the doctrine of original sin and turned it into an amoral physical ailment.[67] Smith likewise brushed aside the Pelagian view of original sin and the theory that humanity becomes guilty of sin through the pre-existence of the soul.[68]

In his mind, the only credible view was the theory of mediate imputation, which he summarizes in six points:

1. The human race is not a collection of individuals but an organic, physical, moral unity.

2. Adam was divinely appointed as head of the human race, and therefore all humanity were virtually, potentially, and even seminally, in him. They were not in Adam as individuals, but were present like acorns nestled in a tree.

3. Through the fall Adam lost his original righteousness and corrupted his nature, and all people inherit this corruption by natural descent. The corruption is manifest in two ways: (a) negatively in the absence of holiness, and (b) positively in the presence of moral evil.

4. Given humanity's innate depravity, all people are liable to evil, suffering, and death unless God intervenes with the grace of redemption.

---

65. Smith, *System of Theology*, 310.

66. Sweeney, *Nathaniel Taylor*, 1-68.

67. Smith, *System of Theology*, 310.

68. Smith, *System of Theology*, 312-13.

5. People possess both a depraved nature and bear guilt due to Adam's sin.

6. The guilt of humanity's native corruption is due, therefore, to the guilt of Adam's sin; God imputes this guilt to the whole human race by means of humanity's natural descent from Adam. Every branch in the tree is corrupt because they all grow from the same Adamic root.[69]

The difference between mediate and immediate imputation can be summarized in the following manner. With immediate imputation God directly and covenantally imputes the guilt of sin to Adam's posterity; in mediate imputation God transmits Adam's guilt through natural descent. In the former guilt precedes existence; in the latter existence precedes guilt. In other words, with immediate imputation Adam's posterity is corrupt because they are guilty; whereas with mediate imputation they are guilty because they are corrupt.[70]

REALISTIC TRANSMISSION (SHEDD, BAIRD, AND THORNWELL)

If Barnes represented a revived Pelagian view of original sin, then W. G. T. Shedd stands out as one of the best-known advocates of a revived Augustinian realistic theory of the transmission of sin. Shedd's articulation and defense of his view appears in an essay on original sin, his commentary on Romans, and in his *Dogmatic Theology*.[71] But Shedd rests his book of original sin upon a different shelf of Scripture. Unlike most of his contemporaries who immediately appealed to Romans 5, among other passages, Shedd instead first appealed to Ephesians 2:3, which states that we were

---

69. Smith, *System of Theology*, 313-17.

70. Crisp, *Retrieving Doctrine*, 56.

71. W. G. T. Shedd, 'Original Sin,' in *Discourses and Essays* (Andover: W. F. Draper, 1856), 218-71; idem, *Dogmatic Theology*, 3 vols. (1888; Grand Rapids: Zondervan, 1969), II:168-260; idem, *A Critical and Doctrinal Commentary upon the Epistle of St. Paul to the Romans* (New York: Charles Scribner's Sons, 1879); cf. Hutchinson, *Original Sin*, 36-45.

by *nature* children of wrath.[72] We know that we posses a sinful nature, but how do we move from having a sinful nature to being children of wrath? In other words, how does one account for guilt? In Shedd's opinion, the only way someone can be guilty is if they voluntarily will something. Hence, guilt arises from a voluntary action of the will.[73] Without going into the details, Shedd links all individuals under Adam's representation based upon Romans 5. As Shedd understands it, the Westminster assembly drew the connection between Adam and his offspring based upon this passage, but he nevertheless admits that this is 'one of the darkest points of speculative theology.'[74] And hence, the Westminster Confession does not exhaustively explain the precise nature of imputed sin. Rather, 'They locate the individual in Adam, and make him, in some mysterious but real manner, a responsible partaker of Adam's sin—a guilty sharer, and, in some solid sense of the word, *co-agent* in a common apostasy.'[75]

Despite the darkness that shrouds the subject, Shedd argues this co-agency rests in a natural or substantial union between Adam and his posterity:

> Adam and his posterity existed together, and sinned together, as a unity. The posterity were not vicariously represented in the first sin, because representation implies the absence of the party represented; but they sinned the first sin being seminally existent and present; and this first sin is deservedly imputed to them, because in this generic manner it was committed by them.[76]

Theories of mediate and immediate imputation assume the absence of Adam's posterity and hence rest the imputation of sin upon Adam's function as a vicarious representative. But in Shedd's

---

72. Shedd, 'Original Sin,' 226.

73. Shedd, 'Original Sin,' 237, 243-44.

74. Shedd, 'Original Sin,' 250.

75. Shedd, 'Original Sin,' 260-61.

76. Shedd, *Dogmatic Theology*, II:14.

scheme there is no need for representation because Adam's off-spring are seminally present and hence co-agents in Adam's sin. Additionally, in contrast to Hodge's penalty-only imputation, Shedd maintains that Adam's sin brings both corruption and penalty: 'The guilt of the first sin, both as culpability (*culpa*) and obligation to the penalty of eternal death (*reatus poenae*), is chargeable upon Adam and his posterity upon the common principle that sin is chargeable upon the actor and author of it.'[77] Shedd also anticipates an objection regarding the parallel between the respective imputations arising from the (dis)obedience of the two Adams. Rather than posit a strict parallel as Hodge, Shedd instead opts for an antithetical parallelism: 'The imputation of Adam's sin, upon this theory, differs from the imputation of Christ's righteousness, in being deserved, not undeserved or gratuitous.'[78]

For Hodge, the ground for the imputation is federal, or covenantal, but for Shedd it is ontological. Shedd writes: 'The doctrine of the imputation of the first sin to all men, and of their punishment therefor, rests upon the doctrine of the *natural* and *substantial unity* of Adam and his posterity in the first act of sin.'[79] Once again, Shedd's position acknowledges a discontinuity between the work of the two Adams. Humanity receives the imputed guilt and corruption by virtue of their natural union with Adam, but the redeemed receive the imputed righteousness of Christ by virtue of their representative union with Him. The union between Christ and believers is 'not natural and substantial but moral, spiritual, and mystical; not generic and universal, but individual and by election; not caused by the creative act of God but by his regenerating act.'[80]

In further contrast to Hodge, Shedd argued that one could not maintain both a representative and natural union between Adam and his posterity. But Shedd was aware that to pit these two

---

77. Shedd, *Dogmatic Theology*, II:14.

78. Shedd, *Dogmatic Theology*, II:14.

79. Shedd, *Romans*, 127.

80. Shedd, *Romans*, 141.

unions against one another potentially created a tension between affirming the natural union as the basis for the transmission of sin and at the same time maintaining the doctrine of the covenant of works, which lies at the heart of a representative union. Shedd believed that the natural union was the exclusive basis of the transmission of sin, which was compatible with the covenant of works. But was such a view compatible with the Westminster Standards? Shedd recognized that the Larger Catechism (q. 22) characterized Adam as a public person. If the divines meant that Adam and his posterity constituted a unity, one that acted directly rather than representatively, then the covenant of works was not antithetical to a natural-union based transmission of sin. Shedd stipulates, 'It must be observed, that it was not the covenant of works that *made* the union of Adam and his posterity. The union of Adam and his posterity, be it representative or natural, was prior to the covenant, and is supposed in order to it.'

In other words, Shedd believed that God created Adam and the metaphysical infrastructure for the transmission of sin prior to His covenant with Adam. The covenant is not the mechanism for the imputation of sin, but rather the shared natural union is. 'Hence, the so-called "federal union",' writes Shedd, 'does not mean a union constituted *by* the foedus or covenant of works. It is rather a *status*, or *relation*, than a union proper.'[81] But Shedd does not believe the covenant of works is purely superfluous, but rather secondary to the natural union.[82] An underlying element within Shedd's formulation is the adherence to traducianism, which maintains that human beings create souls through the act of procreation. This view stands in contrast to creationism, which maintains that God directly creates souls. In Shedd's analysis, traducians would naturally hold to a realistic theory of imputation and creationists a representative theory.[83]

---

81. Shedd, *Dogmatic Theology*, II:39-40.
82. Shedd, *Dogmatic Theology*, II:41.
83. Shedd, *Dogmatic Theology*, II:41.

Other nineteenth-century Presbyterian theologians also fell under the spell of Realism including Samuel J. Baird (1817–93) and James Henley Thornwell (1812–62).[84] But Baird and Thornwell did not replicate Shedd's formulations. Like Shedd, Baird held to traducianism and hence advocated a realistic theory wedded to the covenant of works.[85] But unlike Shedd, who prioritized creation and natural union to the covenantal representative union forged in the covenant of works, Baird argued that Adam was created in covenant. Baird explains: 'For we are not held accountable for Adam's breech of the covenant, in consequence of the transaction respecting the tree; but because of the inscription of the covenant in Adam's nature, and our being-in-him, in whose nature it was inscribed.'[86]

If Shedd prioritized the natural to the federal union, and Hodge prioritized the federal to the natural, then Baird held both in equilibrium:

> The point which we now propose to establish, is that we were federally in Adam by virtue of his investiture with our common nature, with the covenant inscribed in it;—that the covenant being written on his nature, and provision made, in the parental relation, for the transmission to us of that nature, thus bound in covenant,—the necessary effect of the whole arrangement was, to constitute Adam our federal head, by virtue of the parental relation thus characterized.[87]

Baird believed he was standing on worn orthodox ground, evidenced by his citation of Petrus Van Mastricht (1630–1706) in support of his argument. Van Mastricht writes:

> The covenant of nature is so called, because it not only enforces obedience to that law, which as to its chief features was inscribed in

---

84. Hutchinson, *Original Sin*, 45-59.

85. Samuel Baird, *The First Adam and the Second: The Elohim Revealed in the Creation and Redemption of Man* (Philadelphia: Lindsay & Blakiston, 1860), 256, 288; cf. Turretin, *Institutes*, VIII.iii.5.

86. Baird, *First Adam*, 311.

87. Baird, *First Adam*, 311; Hutchinson, 50.

man's nature, but also because it attached to the universal nature of man, even of those who were yet to have existence by the order of generation.[88]

Baird wed his realistic theory to a doctrine of humanity's creation *in* covenant, a covenant inscribed upon human nature, and hence Adam's sin fell upon his posterity because they were both seminally and covenantally in Adam by virtue of the coterminous natural and federal unions.

Thornwell was critical of Baird's realistic theory on the ground that it would make Adam's posterity guilty for his first and all of his subsequent sins given their natural union with him.[89] Thornwell also believed that Baird's creation *in* covenant was contrary to the Westminster Standards because, according to Thornwell, the Standards teach that Adam entered into the covenant after his creation. To prove his point Thornwell appeals to the Latin translation of the Shorter Catechism (q. 12), which reads: 'When God had created man (*postquam Deus hominem condidisset*) he entered into a covenant of life with him.'[90] The Latin term *postquam* means *after*. Like Shedd, he believed that the natural union was the ground of the federal union, but despite the prioritization, Thornwell advocated the necessity of both unions because the natural could not bear the weight of original sin alone.[91] And in fact, Thornwell arguably placed a significant amount of weight upon the federal union—more so than Shedd.

Thornwell, for example, expressed his disagreement with the views of old school stalwart Robert J. Breckinridge (1800–71) because the latter argued that man's fallen character was determined

---

88. Baird, *First Adam*, 311; cf. Petrus Van Mastricht, *Theoretico-Practica Theologia*, 9th ed., vol. 1 (Trajecti ad Rhenum: apud W. van der Water, 1724), III.xii.8 (p. 416).

89. James H. Thornwell, 'Nature of Our Interest in the Sin of Adam, Being a Review of Baird's Elohim Revealed,' in *Collected Writings*, vol. 1, ed. John B. Adger (Richmond: Presbyterian Committee of Publication, 1871), 515-68.

90. Thornwell, 'Sin of Adam,' 551; Hutchinson, *Original Sin*, 53.

91. Thornwell, 'Sin of Adam,' 553; Hutchinson, *Original Sin*, 53.

by the natural rather than federal union.[92] Instead, Thornwell argued that the federal union determined the moral character of the human race, not the natural union. Humanity's depravity was the judicial penalty, not the formal ground of the imputed sin. The natural union simply determined the extent of Adam's federal representation. The natural union answered the question of who, precisely, is in the covenant.[93]

At this point, Thornwell sounds much like Hodge.[94] In fact, in his criticism of Breckinridge, Thornwell concedes that the latter's position is Calvin's and that the Westminster Confession may be interpreted in such a manner, but he then stipulates that the catechisms present a different picture: 'There the imputation of guilt is direct and immediate, and the true explanation of the degraded condition of the human race.'[95] Nevertheless, as critical as he was of Shedd's realism, Thornwell eventually but reluctantly conceded the necessity of a realistic basis for the transmission of sin. Thornwell writes: 'I am free to confess that I cannot escape from the doctrine, however, mysterious, of a *generic unity* in man as the true basis of the representative economy in the covenant of works. The human race is not an aggregate of separate and independent atoms, but constitutes an organic whole, with a common life springing from a common ground.'[96] Thornwell believed that there was a common nature in man, but this nature was not merely a logical category but a 'substantive reality.'[97] So Thornwell advocated a

---

92. James H. Thornwell, 'Theology, Its Proper Method and Its Central Principle Being a Review of Breckinridge's Knowledge of God Objectively Considered,' in *Collected Writings*, vol. 1, ed. John B. Adger (Richmond: Presbyterian Committee of Publication, 1871), 477; cf. Robert J. Breckinridge, *The Knowledge of God Objectively Considered Being the First Part of Theology Considered as a Science of Positive Truth, Both Inductive and Deductive* (New York: Robert Carter & Brothers, 1858), 487-88.

93. Thornwell, 'Sin of Adam,' 478-79.

94. Hutchinson, *Original Sin*, 53.

95. Thornwell, 'Sin of Adam,' 479.

96. Thornwell, 'Original Sin,' 349.

97. Thornwell, 'Original Sin,' 350. There are those, such as Morton Smith, who

realistic doctrine of transmitted sin, but was closer to Baird than Shedd, who rejected the principle of representation.[98] In the end, however, Thornwell held his views loosely, as he admitted he was unequal to the task of offering a definitive opinion on the precise nature of imputed sin: 'If required to specify precisely what that is which constitutes the unity, the nature and kind of relationship, we frankly confess that we are not competent to solve the problem.'[99]

AGNOSTIC (DABNEY)

As with many challenging issues, people often line up either for or against a proposition, but a small minority often refuse to take sides—they maintain a degree of detachment as they peer over the different opinions nestled in a perch of neutrality. One such theologian was Robert L. Dabney. Dabney entered the fray of the nineteenth-century debates over imputation through a review of Robert W. Landis's (fl. 1826–83) book on original sin.[100] In his book Landis expressed grave concerns over the dangerous views of Hodge, which led the Princetonian into 'mortifying and fatal inconsistencies and contradictions.'[101] Not only did Landis believe that Hodge's views were contrary to Scripture, but he inveighed that the Pope of Presbyterianism had introduced Pelagian, Socinian, Arminian, and German Rationalism.[102] Dabney sympathetically took up Landis's book and his criticisms against Hodge, but nevertheless offered a more sober analysis.

---

believe that Thornwell was not a realist, but that he nonetheless presented a novel view (Morton Smith, *Studies In Southern Presbyterian Theology* [Phillipsburg: P & R, 1987], 152-54; cf. Hutchinson, *Original Sin*, 58 n. 66).

98. Hutchinson, *Original Sin*, 59.

99. Thornwell, 'Adam's Sin,' 553; Hutchinson, *Original Sin*, 59.

100. Robert L. Dabney, 'The Doctrine of Original Sin,' in *Discussions: Theological and Evangelical*, vol. 1 (1890; Edinburgh: Banner of Truth, n. d.), 143-68; Robert W. Landis, *The Doctrine of Original Sin as Received and Taught by the Churches of the Reformation* (Richmond: Whittet & Shepperson, 1884).

101. Landis, *Original Sin*, 30; Hutchinson, *Original Sin*, 61.

102. Landis, *Original Sin*, 219; Hutchinson, *Original Sin*, 66.

Dabney opined that Hodge had 'an extreme view' and he pushed 'the consequences in the hardiest manner' and asserted with the 'sternest dogmatism' that his view was the Calvinistic norm.[103] Nevertheless, unlike Landis, Dabney willingly acknowledged that there was historical precedent in the tradition for Hodge's view. Dabney specifically mentions Bernaruds de Moor (ca. 1710–65) and Francis Turretin in this vein. He concedes that virtually everything that Hodge argues appears in Turretin's locus on original sin.[104] But although Dabney labels Hodge's views as extreme, he still followed him at a number of points. In his definition of imputation, Dabney defines it in a very similar manner as Hodge: 'This much misunderstood doctrine does not teach that Adam's act was actually made ours.' Rather, 'I would define, that it is not Adam's sin which is imputed to us, but the guilt (obligation to punishment) of his first sin.'[105] But in contrast to Hodge, Dabney prioritizes the natural over the federal unions: 'The grounds of this legal union we hold to be two; 1st the natural union with him as the root of all mankind; 2nd the federal relation instituted by him, by God's covenant with him.'[106] Moreover, like Hodge Dabney acknowledges that the respective imputations of the two Adams stand in parallel.[107]

But when Dabney delves into the specifics of the doctrine, he runs through the various opinions and ultimately dismisses them all. He engages the question of the nature of imputation from the standpoint of two common Pelagian objections: How can God impute Adam's sin to my account if I did not consent to his role as my federal representative? Under such a divinely imposed arrangement, am I not held accountable for another man's deed?[108] Dabney then turns to five different answers to these questions but finds them

---

103. Dabney, 'Original Sin,' 144-45.

104. Dabney, 'Original Sin,' 165.

105. Robert L. Dabney, *Syllabus and Notes of the Course of Systematic and Polemic Theology*, 2nd ed. (St. Louis: Presbyterian Publishing Company, 1878), 329.

106. Dabney, *Syllabus*, 329.

107. Dabney, *Syllabus*, 332.

108. Dabney, *Syllabus*, 338.

all unsatisfactory. Wesleyans say this arrangement would be unjust were it not for the remedy of the second Adam. Edwards asserts that the connection between Adam and his posterity by divine fiat and his theory of personal identity address the objections. Baird offers his realistic theory. And Dabney also mentions mediate and immediate imputation as two other offered solutions.[109] None of these views adequately answer the Pelagian objections.

Dabney was acutely aware of the importance of the doctrine, as it addresses questions surrounding the nature of imputation, the transmission of Adam's guilt, justification, union with Christ, and God's providential oversight of the creation.[110] So Dabney engages the issue by first rejecting, what is in his mind, the false dichotomy between mediate and immediate imputation. He says that this debate needlessly aggravated the difficulties of the awful and mysterious doctrine of original sin. Advocates of immediate imputation misrepresent the doctrines of spiritual union and justification.[111] Dabney admits that both covenants (works and grace) rest upon a principle of imputation, nevertheless there is a significant discontinuity between the two: 'The imputation of Adam's sin was a transaction of strict, judicial righteousness; the other transaction was one of glorious, free grace.'[112]

Dabney also admits that the imputation of Adam's guilt is partly grounded in his nature, but which nature precisely, his fallen or un-fallen nature?[113] When the debate shifts from Adam to Christ, all agree that the federal union with Christ accounts for the imputation of His righteousness. But what specific aspect of union with Christ accounts for the transfer of righteousness? Dabeny answers, the spiritual union. This precludes a strict parallel between the two imputations because Adam's sin is immediate and antecedent to actual sin, whereas Christ's imputed righteousness comes after one's

109. Dabney, *Syllabus*, 338-42.

110. Dabney, *Syllabus*, 342.

111. Dabney, *Syllabus*, 342.

112. Dabney, *Syllabus*, 343.

113. Dabney, *Syllabus*, 344.

spiritual union with Him—it is not immediate and antecedent.[114] Dabney deals with other objections but ultimately paints himself into a corner. He objects to elements of every theory. Where does that leave Dabney? He stands on a small patch of ground of highly informed agnosticism. Dabney writes:

> This dispensation of God, then, remains unique, without any parallel in any human jurisprudence. It is solemn, mysterious, awful; but it is placed where it is impossible to convict it of injustice on God's part. That His exercise of His sovereignty in this strange dispensation is holy, righteous, benevolent, and wise, we have this sufficient proof; that He has given His own Son, in free grace, to repair the mischiefs which human sin causes under the case. Let us remember, that the covenant of paradise was liberal, equitable, and splendidly beneficent in its own character. Its failure was exclusively man's and Satan's fault. God has not been the efficient of any man's sin or depravation, but only the permissive Disposer.[115]

In short, Dabney stood opposed to all other explanations and planted his flag firmly on the mountain of mystery.[116]

CONCLUSION

In World War II scores of aircraft engaged in aerial combat at the same time. Planes crisscrossed the sky and shot at each other but had to keep a watchful eye to avoid colliding with other aircraft. Fighter pilots referred to such engagements as the *fur ball* because it resembled a pack of wild dogs nipping, biting, and tearing at one another—in other words, it was a dogfight. *Fur ball* adequately describes the modern period in the eighteenth and nineteenth centuries, especially in the American Presbyterian scene. Despite the towering nature of Edwards's presence in the contemporary scene, few today seem to be aware that his doctrines of original sin and imputation were deemed novel and erroneous. Whatever

---

114. Dabney, *Syllabus*, 345.

115. Dabney, *Syllabus*, 350.

116. Hutchinson, *Original Sin*, 81.

disagreements nineteenth-century theologians had among themselves, they agreed in their rejection of Edwards's views. But the nineteenth-century fur ball demonstrates, first, that they were fundamentally in agreement over the principal scriptural teachings that humanity inherits Adam's guilt and corruption, and that believers receive Christ's righteousness—all of this occurs through imputation. Yet, they disagreed over the precise mechanisms and how to prioritize the natural and federal unions. Did the natural union support the federal union, or did the federal undergird the natural? Was Adam created and then subsequently entered into a covenant with God, or did God create Adam in covenant? Does God impute both guilt and corruption, or only guilt? Is the ground of the imputation real, forensic, or both? All of these questions swirl about the fur ball and certainly deserve attention and require answers.

5

THE PRESENT DAY

INTRODUCTION

Revolutions disrupt commonly held assumptions and attitudes and force people to reconsider their most basic assumptions. In the foregoing history of the development of the doctrine of imputation the participants, regardless of their view, held one thing in common—the normative authority of the Scriptures for doctrinal formulation. Exegetes and theologians undoubtedly came to different positions, but they all argued from the biblical text. In the present day, two different revolutions have dramatically re-shaped the discussion: (1) the higher-critical movement, and (2) the relationship between general and special revelation, or more specifically, the relationship between science and theology.

The first revolution began in the opening days of the Enlightenment. Theologians no longer trusted the *Deus dixit* ('God says') of Scripture but instead looked within to the *Cogito ergo sum* ('I think therefore I am') as the foundation of all knowledge. This was one of the pivotal moments in history that led to the rise of higher criticism.[1] Theologians questioned the inspiration and authority of the Scriptures. They applied Darwinian evolutionary theory to different academic disciplines, including biblical studies. Scholars questioned, therefore, the Mosaic authorship of the Pentateuch and applied Julius Wellhausen's (1844–1918) Documentary Hypothesis to account for the origins of the first five books of the Bible.[2] Biblical scholars questioned the divine source of revelation and instead attributed it to a human evolutionary process. Adam eventually ceased to be historical and became a mythical figure that the biblical authors supposedly used to explain the universal human sinful condition.

The second revolution also involved the evolutionary theories of Charles Darwin (1809–82) and his *Origin of Species* (1859). As theologians investigated the world around them they questioned the compatibility between the facts of science and the biblical creation narrative. Nineteenth-century theologians, such as Charles Hodge (1797–1898) and B. B. Warfield (1851–1921), sought to harmonize science and the Bible; the former argued that the days of creation were actually long geologic periods and the latter made the case for a purified theistic evolution.[3] Neo-Darwinian evolutionary theory has now claimed that the scientific facts and the biblical narrative are incompatible. Scientists and theologians

1. Michael C. Legaspi, *The Death of Scripture and the Rise of Biblical Studies* (Oxford: Oxford University Press, 2010).

2. Julius Wellhausen, *Prolegomena to the History of Israel* (Edinburgh: Adam & Charles Black, 1875), 1-16; cf. Kenneth A. Kitchen, *On the Reliability of the Old Testament* (Grand Rapids: Eerdmans, 2003), 486-92.

3. Charles Hodge, *Systematic Theology*, 3 vols. (rep.; Grand Rapids: Eerdmans, 1993), I:570-74; B. B. Warfield, *Evolution, Science, and Scripture: Selected Writings*, ed. Mark A. Noll and David Livingstone (Grand Rapids: Baker, 2000).

contend that recent genetic research has overturned the erroneous view that all of humanity descended from one human couple, Adam and Eve.

Higher criticism and the relationship between science and theology are dense and complicated subjects that each have oceans of literature. I do not, therefore, want to engage these subjects per se, as they would take the investigation far afield.[4] Rather, I raise them insofar as these developments intersect with the doctrine of imputation. Higher criticism has led theologians to question the historicity of the biblical creation account as well as Adam's existence. This naturally impacts the doctrine of imputation. Can God impute sin if there was no actual covenant head and if there was no actual historical transgression to impute? Relatedly, how does one account for the universal depravity if humanity's descent from Adam is a scientific impossibility? Theologians answer these questions differently depending upon their particular concerns or convictions.

This chapter, therefore, covers the development of the doctrine of imputation in contemporary theology. The chapter first briefly explores the views of Friedrich Schleiermacher (1768–1843), Karl Barth (1886–1968), and Rudolf Bultmann (1884–1976). All three theologians radically reconceived the doctrine of imputation due to the inroads of higher criticism. The second section examines the views of N. T. Wright and Peter Enns. Both Wright and Enns are members of the biblical studies guild and recast the doctrine of imputation on exegetical grounds. The third and

---

4. Cf., e.g., Hans Madueme and Michael Reeves, eds., *Adam, the Fall, and Original Sin: Theological, Biblical, and Scientific Perspectives* (Grand Rapids: Baker, 2014), 53-84, 225-50; C. John Collins, *Did Adam and Eve Really Exist? Who They Were and Why You Should Care* (Wheaton: Crossway, 2011); Matthew Barrett and Ardel B. Caneday, eds., *Four Views on the Historical Adam* (Grand Rapids: Zondervan, 2013); William VanDoodewaard, *The Quest for the Historical Adam: Genesis, Hermeneutics, and Human Origins* (Grand Rapids: Reformation Heritage Books, 2015); Vern Poythress, 'Adam versus Claims from Genetics,' *WTJ* 75/1 (2013): 65-82; J. P. Versteeg, *Adam in the New Testament: Mere Teaching Model or First Historical Man?* 2nd ed. (1977; Phillipsburg: P & R, 2012).

final section explores a small selection of scholars who primarily engage the subject of original sin from a scientific perspective. In the past, theologians always believed that the church had to interpret general revelation in the light of special revelation. Theology was the queen of the sciences, and thus special revelation trumps general revelation. Given the erosion of biblical authority, Scripture no longer has a normative function. Rather, for many, general revelation and scientific claims about it must govern one's understanding of Scripture and theology. If science says that Adam and Eve were not the sole progenitors of the human race, then the biblical doctrines of creation and original sin must be modified accordingly. The chapter concludes with some general observations about these present-day developments.

Modern Theology

Schleiermacher

Friedrich Schleiermacher has been hailed as the father of modern liberal theology. Given his radical departure from commonly established doctrinal norms, he has justly merited the title. Schleiermacher reconstructed theology around subjective, existential, rather than objective categories. The chief principle in his theology is the necessity for believers to have the feeling of absolute dependence, or God consciousness.[5] Sin, therefore, is not the willful transgression of the objective moral standard of God's law but the inability to achieve the feeling of absolute dependence. Conversely, this means that Christ stands as the one true human being—the chief example of supreme God-consciousness.[6] Schleiermacher's subjectively driven theology excises legal-forensic categories. Hence, he does not have a doctrine of imputation for a number of reasons.

---

5. Friedrich Schleiermacher, *The Christian Faith* (London: T & T Clark, 1999), IV.iii (pp. 15-16); cf. Carl Trueman, 'Original Sin in Modern Theology,' in *Adam, the Fall, and Original Sin: Theological, Biblical, and Scientific Perspectives*, ed. Hans Madueme and Michael Reeves (Grand Rapids: Baker, 2014), 169.

6. Trueman, 'Original Sin,' 170.

First, Schleiermacher severed doctrinal formulation from Scripture. It was immaterial, therefore, whether the biblical narratives were historical or allegorical.[7] As reluctant as he was in using Scripture, Schleiermacher believed he could nevertheless appeal to the story of the fall to illustrate the origin and rise of universal sinfulness.[8] Schleiermacher recognized Paul's point in the Adam-Christ parallel in Romans 5:12-21 and 1 Corinthians 15:21-22—to show how Adam introduced sin into the world and conversely how Christ had removed it.[9] But Schleiermacher nevertheless avers: 'We can thus readily dispense with all those artificial theories which for the most part tend only to lay stress upon the divine justice in imputing Adam's sin to, and exacting its penalty from, his posterity.' Schleiermacher dispensed with imputation because, in his mind, the doctrine rested upon a specific theory of the origin of souls, a subject that was beyond anyone's ability to know such things.[10]

Second, arguing for the existence of a covenant between Adam and God, which served as the legal basis upon which his sin was imputed to his posterity, represented an arbitrary interpretation of God's command and made Adam and God's relationship entirely external and legal. Such a construction had a detrimental effect upon the doctrine of redemption.[11]

Third, in what way does the biblical narrative illustrate humanity's sinfulness? Eve serves as a representation of sensuality, an attitude that turns one away from God-consciousness. And Adam represents how easily people imitate the sinful conduct they observe.[12] Schleiermacher applies this Adamic paradigm to

7. Schleiermacher, *Christian Faith*, LXXII.v (pp. 301-03); Trueman, 'Original Sin,' 170.

8. Schleiermacher, *Christian Faith*, LXXII.v (p. 303).

9. Schleiermacher, *Christian Faith*, LXXII.iv (p. 300).

10. Schleiermacher, *Christian Faith*, LXXII.iv (p. 300-01).

11. Schleiermacher, *Christian Faith*, LXXII.iv (p. 301).

12. Schleiermacher, *Christian Faith*, LXXII.v (p. 303); Trueman, 'Original Sin,' 170-71.

humanity, which illustrates how the good and the bad develop side by side and ultimately represents the fall of each individual.[13] Schleiermacher eliminates legal, moral, and forensic categories and replaces them with the subjective God-consciousness. Adam and Eve are negative examples, which should not be followed, and Christ serves as the positive example—the perfect example of God consciousness. Schleiermacher wears the garb of Enlightenment categories, higher critical views of Scripture, and existentialism, but he represents a renaissance of Pelagian doctrines of original sin and salvation. If his doctrine has no legal or covenantal categories, then of course Schleiermacher does not have a doctrine of imputation.

BARTH

In many respects Barth saw himself as the antithesis to Schleiermacher. If Schleiermacher placed the doctrine of the Trinity in appendix to his systematic theology then Barth placed the doctrine at the very outset of his *Church Dogmatics*.[14] If Schleiermacher believed that exegesis was not the primary task of dogmatics, then Barth placed the word in a prominent place in his system.[15] But in spite of whatever antitheses there might be between the two theologians, Barth's doctrine of original sin never truly escaped the clutches of Schleiermacher's liberalism. Barth was aware of the great divergence between classic Reformed orthodoxy and Schleiermacher's formulations. Barth praised Reformed orthodoxy because it turned away from a realistic explanation of the origin of sin and turned to imputation. In this vein Barth approvingly cites Johannes Heinrich Heidegger (1633–98): 'Just as Christ's perfect righteousness is imputed by the grace of God unto justification of life, so it is necessary that Adam's sin is imputed to his posterity through the judgment of God unto condemnation.' But even then,

---

13. Schleiermacher, *Christian Faith*, LXXII.v (p. 303); Trueman, 'Original Sin,' 171.

14. Karl Barth, *Church Dogmatics*, 14 vols. (Edinburgh: T & T Clark, 1936-68), I/1:295-490; cf. Schleiermacher, *Christian Faith*, 738-51.

15. E.g., Barth, *Church Dogmatics*, I/1:311, 334.

Barth was dissatisfied because he believed that the Reformed orthodox did not 'draw all of the necessary deductions.'[16] What, in Barth's mind, was necessary to align the doctrine of original sin with the biblical text?

In Barth's estimation the first necessary task was rightly recognizing the genre of the creation narrative. In his view the Genesis narrative is not history (*Historie*) but *Geschichte*, saga.[17] Barth argues that when the Bible reports the creation of the heavens and earth and especially Adam,

> It is not history but only saga which can tell us that he came into being in this way and existed as the one who came into being in this way—the first man. We miss the unprecedented and incomparable thing which the Genesis passages tell us of the coming into being and existence of Adam if we try to read and understand it as history, relating it either favorably or unfavorably to scientific paleontology, or to what we now know with some historical certainty concerning the oldest and most primitive forms of human life.[18]

History and saga stand apart as genres, and as such, saga cannot be historically verified.[19]

Second, Barth operates with the assumption that higher-critical theories of the origins of the Pentateuch are correct; he accepts the Documentary Hypothesis. He does not believe that Genesis 3 and 2:2-3 should be exegetically combined because they originate from different sources, J (Jahwist) and P (Priestly), respectively. He believes that the priestly editor unskillfully juxtaposed the events of the seventh day with the fall, a day of joy, peace, and freedom followed by a day of pride and sin. Barth questions, therefore, the historicity of these events given the clumsy report.[20] Third, Adam

---

16. Barth, *Church Dogmatics*, IV/1:511; Johannes Heidegger, *Medulla Theologiae Christianae: Corporis Theologiae Praevia Epitome*, 2nd ed. (Tiguri: Henrici Bodmeri, 1713), X.xix (p. 214).

17. Trueman, 'Original Sin,' 176.

18. Barth, *Church Dogmatics*, IV/1:508.

19. Barth, *Church Dogmatics*, IV/1:508.

20. Barth, *Church Dogmatics*, IV/1:508.

was not a historical person but the term *adam* instead refers to every person: 'But it is the name of Adam the transgressor which God gives to world-history as a whole. The name of Adam sums up this history as the history of the mankind which God has given up, given up to its pride on account of its pride.'[21] Fourth, Barth does not believe there was a time in history where the creation was un-fallen: '[History] constantly re-enacts the little scene in the garden of Eden. There never was a golden age. There is no point in looking back to one. The first man was immediately the first sinner.'[22]

At this point, one might expect Barth to dispense with the doctrine of imputation, especially given that his doctrines of creation and anthropology bear striking resemblances to Schleiermacher's.[23] But Barth does have traces of Reformed orthodox convictions about redemption, although he does not merely repristinate earlier views. Unlike the standard Adam-Christ parallel to explain imputed guilt and righteousness, Barth capsizes the relationship and argues for a Christ-Adam parallel. Barth writes, 'Man's essential and original nature is to be found, therefore, not in Adam but in Christ.'[24] Hence, 'our relationship to Christ has an essential priority and superiority over our relationship to Adam.'[25] This inverted understanding of humanity's relationship to Adam has implications for his doctrine of original sin:

> If we could regard Adam and our participation in his sin and condemnation as an isolated and self-centered whole, then it would be impossible to find there any connection with Christ and our participation in His grace and life. But so to regard Adam is impossible. Paul does not go to Adam to see how he is connected with Christ; but goes to Christ to see how *He* [Christ] is connected with Adam.[26]

---

21. Barth, *Church Dogmatics*, IV/1:508.

22. Barth, *Church Dogmatics*, IV/1:508.

23. Trueman, 'Original Sin,' 178.

24. Karl Barth, *Christ and Adam: Man and Humanity in Romans 5* (1956; Eugene: Wipf & Stock, 2004), 17.

25. Barth, *Christ and Adam*, 23.

26. Barth, *Christ and Adam*, 34-35.

Romans 5, therefore, explains Christ's work, it does not reveal the origins of sin. Barth makes this point abundantly clear when he writes: 'Our unity with Adam is less essential and less significant than our true unity with Christ.'[27] Barth rends humanity's historical connection to Adam and instead tries to anchor it exclusively to Christ. This pattern becomes evident in another Barthian inversion. Historically Reformed theologians spoke in terms of law and gospel, or the covenants of works and grace.[28] But Barth rejects the concept of the covenant of works and instead speaks in terms of gospel and law. Christ is all-determinative and His history, therefore, becomes our history.[29] Believers ultimately participate in Christ by means of their election in Him. By being in Christ, we participate in the covenant of grace. Christ is the one elected and rejected man and embraces both judgment and salvation. Hence, Barth does not employ the language of imputation, as there is no need for it within his system. God does not impute Adam's sin to humanity because Adam is ultimately an illustration of all humanity. All humanity is sinful but God has already entered into a covenant with sinful humanity in Christ. Hence there is no need for the positive imputation of righteousness. In Barth's theology election accomplishes what imputation did in Reformed orthodoxy.[30]

Barth undoubtedly differs from Schleiermacher at key points. For Schleiermacher Christ is simply a moral example—a forerunner and trailblazer, but certainly not a redeemer. Barth presents Christ as redeemer—indeed Christ stands tall in Barth's system. But Barth's understanding of Adam still bears the marks of Schleiermacher's

27. Barth, *Christ and Adam*, 46, also 74.

28. Westminster Confession of Faith, VII; cf. Andrew A. Woolsey, *Unity and Continuity in Covenantal Thought: A Study in the Reformed Tradition to the Westminster Assembly* (Grand Rapids: Reformation Heritage Books, 2012).

29. Barth, *Church Dogmatics*, IV/1:458.

30. Bruce L. McCormack, '*Justitia aliena*: Karl Barth in Conversation with the Evangelical Doctrine of Imputed Righteousness,' in *Justification in Perspective: Historical Developments and Contemporary Challenges*, ed. Bruce L. McCormack (Grand Rapids: Baker, 2006), 190-93.

liberalism.[31] Adam is not historical but a mythical figure that merely explains humanity's condition. Hence, for Barth, there is no need for imputed sin to explain the universality of sin, and given humanity's election in Christ, there is no need for imputed righteousness. Election takes the place of imputed righteousness. The Christ of eternity engulfs history—Adam is ultimately, in Barth's view, historically superfluous.

BULTMANN

The a-historical trend continues in another theological figure of the twentieth century in Rudolph Bultmann. His own understanding of original sin arises from his view on the relationship between mythology and the New Testament.[32] Bultmann famously opined that the New Testament was rife with mythical and gnostic elements. How can modern people who use electricity, technology, and take advantage of medical and surgical advances nevertheless embrace a three-tiered world inhabited by angels and demons?[33] All of these mythological elements should be excised and one must instead determine what elements of the New Testament are necessarily relevant to modern man. Within this framework Bultmann argues that death as the punishment for sin is abhorrent to modern man because he views death simply as a natural postulate of existence. Bultmann writes: 'Human beings are subject to death even before they have committed any sin. And to attribute human mortality to the fall of Adam is sheer nonsense, for guilt implies personal responsibility, and the idea of original sin as an inherited infection is sub-ethical, irrational, and absurd.'[34] Bultmann, like Pelagius, rejects the idea that man was

---

31. Trueman, 'Original Sin,' 178.

32. Trueman, 'Original Sin,' 179-80.

33. Rudolph Bultmann, 'New Testament and Mythology: The Mythological Element in the Message of the New Testament and the Problem of Its Reinterpretation,' in *Kerygma and Myth*, ed. Hans Werner Bartsch (New York: Harper & Row, 1961), 5.

34. Bultmann, 'New Testament and Mythology,' 7.

created in an immortal state and that death and mortality was the consequence of sin. Hence, he rejects inherited, transmitted, or imputed guilt and punishment.

Conversely, Bultmann also rejects the idea of vicarious suffering: 'How can the guilt of one man be expiated by the death of another who is sinless—if indeed one may speak of a sinless man at all? What primitive notions of guilt and righteousness does this imply?'[35] To make such claims necessitates making sin a legal matter: 'It would be no more than an external transgression of a commandment, and it would make nonsense of all our ethical standards.'[36] If the church wants the New Testament to be meaningful, then it must excise these mythical elements—the fall, inherited guilt and sin, and vicarious suffering, and hence imputed righteousness, are irrelevant to modern man.

What, then, is the point in Romans 5:12-21? In concert with the Old Testament views of his day, Bultmann argued that *Paul* believed there was a connection between sin and death.[37] In Romans 5:12-21 he was therefore expounding the idea of original sin—the Adamic curse that rests upon humanity. But in Bultmann's view, 'Paul is unquestionably under the influence of Gnostic myth.'[38] Regardless of its gnostic origins, Bultmann explains Paul's specific point: 'It cannot be denied that in Rom. 5:12ff. the sin of humanity after Adam is attributed to Adam's sin and that it therefore appears as the consequence of a curse for which mankind is not itself responsible. At the most, men sinning under the curse of Adam's sin could be regarded as guilty only in a legal sense, inasmuch as law deals only with the guilty deed.'[39]

Despite Paul's clarity, Bultmann concludes the apostle is mistaken. In the modern world, Romans 5:12-21 cannot be about the

---

35. Bultmann, 'New Testament and Mythology,' 7.

36. Bultmann, 'New Testament and Mythology,' 8.

37. Rudolf Bultmann, *Theology of the New Testament: Complete in One Volume* (New York: Charles Scribner's Sons, 1951, 1955), I:249.

38. Bultmann, *Theology of the New Testament*, I:251.

39. Bultmann, *Theology of the New Testament*, I:251.

origins of sin but rather is about the origin of death.[40] In terms evocative of Schleiermacher, Bultmann presents the true nature of the Adam-Christ parallel:

> Through Christ, that is, there was brought about no more than the *possibility* of life, which, however, in men of faith becomes certain reality. That suggests, then, that one should assume by analogy that through Adam there was brought about for Adamitic mankind the *possibility* of sin and death—a possibility that does not become reality until individuals become guilty by their own responsible action. Whether that may be regarded as Paul's real thought must, to be sure, remain a question.[41]

Bultmann is a thoroughgoing child of the Enlightenment, and as such, he promotes the heroic individual divorced from any corporate identity. Individuals are only connected to Adam or Christ insofar as they choose to embrace death or life. Such is the message of the New Testament, one clouded by gnostic and mythical elements of inherited sin and guilt and vicarious representation and suffering. Bultmann's doctrine is Pelagian to the core and hence has no place for the doctrine of imputation.

BIBLICAL STUDIES

The forgoing treatments of imputation largely originated outside of conservative evangelical theology. Schleiermacher and Bultmann carried no brief for traditional theological categories, let alone Reformed orthodoxy. Barth was more conservative than both Schleiermacher and Bultmann, but then again the *neo* in Neo-orthodoxy meant that he was not shy of departing from traditional beliefs such as the historicity of Adam, law and gospel, the covenant of works, and the doctrine of imputation. But in the twentieth century within the biblical studies guild two scholars who have self-identified as evangelicals and being committed to Reformed theology have departed from traditional views related

---

40. Bultmann, *Theology of the New Testament*, I:252.

41. Bultmann, *Theology of the New Testament*, I:252-53.

to the doctrine of imputation. N. T. Wright has made it no secret that he rejects the doctrine of imputation, and Peter Enns has made significant departures from the Reformed tradition even though he taught for fourteen years at Westminster Theological Seminary in Philadelphia. Westminster was, of course, the seminary founded by J. Gresham Machen (1881–1937), an institution initially committed to the old school Reformed theology of Hodge and Warfield.

N. T. WRIGHT

With the onset of the Enlightenment a radical individualism took hold in philosophy and theology. Barth rejected Schleiermacher's and Bultmann's emphasis upon the individual and offered his own corporate emphasis by election in Christ as well as through participation, or union with Christ.[42] Within the New Testament guild, N. T. Wright has leveled critiques of Bultmann and the perceived connections between individualism and classic Reformation formulas of justification.[43] In this vein Wright rejects the idea of imputation and argues that it is a minor sidelight within the Pauline corpus, and has received undue attention in the hands of Reformed theologians. Wright therefore rejects the doctrine of imputation: 'It makes no sense that the judge imputes, imparts, bequeaths, conveys or otherwise transfers his righteousness to either the plaintiff or the defendant. Righteousness is not an object, a substance or gas that can be passed across the courtroom.'[44]

Rather than advocate what Martin Luther (1483–1546) and John Calvin (1509–64) called the 'glorious exchange,' where God imputes the sins of the elect to Christ and His obedience to the elect by faith alone, Wright makes the case that union with Christ is the true Pauline category.[45] Other New Testament scholars such

42. Adam Neder, *Participation in Christ: An Entry into Karl Barth's Church Dogmatics* (Louisville: Westminster John Knox, 2009).

43. E.g., N. T. Wright, *What Saint Paul Really Said: Was Paul of Tarsus the Real Founder of Christianity?* (Grand Rapids: Eerdmans, 1997), 14-15,113-34.

44. Wright, *What Saint Paul Really Said*, 98.

45. N. T. Wright, *Justification: God's Plan and Paul's Vision* (Downers Grove:

as James D. G. Dunn have argued that justification, and hence imputation, is but one of the many multifaceted but nevertheless interchangeable metaphors that Paul employs. Consequently, justification should not be given too much influence in the formulation of a biblical soteriology, which should instead center upon union with Christ.[46] Other New Testament scholars sympathetic to Wright and Dunn argue similarly for 'incorporated righteousness' rather than imputed righteousness.[47]

One of the key exegetical features in Wright's rejection of imputation is his understanding and definition of *righteousness* (δικαιοσύνη). Traditional Reformed theology defines righteousness as moral equity—adhering to a moral or legal standard.[48] Hence, imputed righteousness ultimately refers to Christ's imputed, or accredited, obedience. Christ obeys the law and God imputes His law-keeping to those who are in union with Him. According to Wright, righteousness does not denote moral equity but rather two different things: for God it denotes His covenant faithfulness and for human beings it denotes covenant membership.[49] When Paul writes,

---

InterVarsity Press, 2009), 135-36, 157-58, 232-33; cf., e.g., Martin Luther, *Lectures on Galatians*, in LW 26:132-33, 167-68; John Calvin, *Institutes of the Christian Religion*, trans. John Allen (Grand Rapids: Eerdmans, 1949), IV.xvii.2.

46. James D. G. Dunn, *The Theology of Paul the Apostle* (Grand Rapids: Eerdmans, 1998), 231.

47. Michael F. Bird, 'Incorporated Righteousness: A Response to Recent Evangelical Discussion Concerning the Imputation of Christ's Righteousness in Justification,' *JETS* 47/2 (2004): 253-75; idem, 'Justification as Forensic Declaration and Covenant Membership: A *Via Media* Between Reformed and Revisionist Readings of Paul,' *TynB* 57/1 (2006): 109-30; idem, *The Saving Righteousness of God: Studies on Paul, Justification, and the New Perspective* (Milton Keyes: Paternoster, 2007), 60-87, 113-54; idem, 'Progressive Reformed View,' in *Justification: Five Views*, ed. James K. Beilby and Paul Rhodes Eddy (Downers Grove: InterVarsity Press, 2011), 145-52.

48. Westminster Confession of Faith, XI.i, XIX.ii; John Calvin, *Romans & Thessalonians*, CNTC (1960; Grand Rapids: Eerdmans, 1996), comm. Rom. 4:4 (pp. 84-85); Francis Turretin, *Institutes of Elenctic Theology*, 3 vols. (Phillipsburg: P & R, 1992-97), XVI.ii.1-27.

49. N. T. Wright, 'Romans and the Theology of Paul,' in *Pauline Theology*, ed.

therefore, that God credited righteousness to Abraham (Rom. 4:3), the text means that God counted Abraham a member of the covenant. Hence Wright has no concept of imputed righteousness. A similar pattern holds true for Wright's doctrine of original sin. Wright acknowledges that Paul addresses the subject of original sin in Romans 5:12-21. But Wright is cagey in his exegesis of the text. He admits, for example, '*Paul clearly believed* that there had been a single first pair, whose male, Adam, had been given a commandment and had broken it.'[50] Wright does not specifically state, however, whether Adam actually existed. He throws a blanket of 'complexity' over matters of science and theology on this point to explain his reticence about Adam and original sin. In the end, Wright argues: 'Paul's meaning must be both an entail of sinfulness has spread throughout the human race from its first beginnings and that each individual has contributed their own share to it. Paul offers no further clue as to how the first of these actually works or how the two interrelate.'[51]

In the balance, Wright represents a significant shift within present-day theology, a move that has turned back to the exegesis of the Scriptures and dispensed with prejudice against anti-supernaturalism and radical individualism. But Wright has not entirely escaped the grip of the anti-historical trends that characterize contemporary understandings of original sin. Wright embraces the historicity of Christ and the resurrection, for example, which stands in stark contradiction to Bultmann.[52] For Bultmann, the resurrection is another ahistorical myth of the New Testament.[53] But when it comes to the historicity of Adam, Wright

---

David M. Hay & E. Elizabeth Johnson (Minneapolis: Fortress, 1995), 38-39; idem, *Paul and the Faithfulness of God* (Minneapolis: Fortress, 2013), 774-1042.

50. N. T. Wright, *Romans*, NIB, vol. 10 (Nashville: Abingdon, 2002), 526, emphasis added.

51. Wright, *Romans*, 527.

52. N. T. Wright, *The Resurrection of the Son of God* (Minneapolis: Fortress, 2003).

53. Bultmann, 'New Testament and Mythology,' 8.

seems unwilling to acknowledge explicitly his existence. In his commentary on Romans, Wright merely says that *Paul* believed that Adam was a historical person. Such a statement makes one wonder whether *Wright* believes that Adam was a historical person. In a recent book Wright seems to allow for the possibility of a historical Adam and Eve, though he does not press the point: 'Just as God chose Israel from the rest of humankind for a special, strange, demanding vocation, so perhaps what Genesis is telling us is that *God chose one pair from the rest of early hominids for a special, strange, demanding vocation.* This pair (call them Adam and Eve if you like) were to be the representatives of the whole human race.'[54] By qualifying his remarks with the word, 'perhaps,' it does not appear that a historical Adam and Eve are essential to Wright's understanding of inherited guilt and sin.

PETER ENNS

Peter Enns styled himself as one who was teaching with the ethos and spirit of old school Princeton seminary. Yet, very shortly after he departed Westminster Seminary in 2008, he published a book that transgressed boundaries that no old Princeton theologian would have ever crossed.[55] Unlike his Princeton forbearers who made every effort to harmonize Scripture with the claims of science, Enns argues that the two are ultimately incompatible when it comes to the creation account: 'The scientific data do not allow it.'[56] Enns's presupposition of antithesis between science and the biblical creation account naturally drives him to reconstruct the doctrines of creation, man, original sin, and imputation. Enns argues most of his case from the twin foci of the Genesis creation account and Paul's

54. N. T. Wright, *Surprised by Scripture: Engaging Contemporary Issues* (San Francisco: Harper One, 2014), 37. I am grateful to Malcolm Maclean for alerting me to this source.

55. John J. Yeo, *Plundering the Egyptians: The Old Testament and Historical Criticism at Westminster Theological Seminary (1929–98)* (Lanham: University Press of America, 2010).

56. Peter Enns, *The Evolution of Adam: What the Bible Does and Doesn't Say about Human Origins* (Grand Rapids: Brazos, 2012), 79.

epistle to Rome. He claims that Paul's epistle is not a treatise on systematic theology but instead a letter that aims to prove that Jews and Gentiles form the one people of God.[57] This, in Enns's mind, sets Paul's epistle on a different trajectory, a path that does not arrive at traditional evangelical, let alone Reformed conclusions.

First, when Paul appeals to Adam in Romans 5:12-21, 'Adam read as the "first human," *supports* Paul's argument about the universal plight and remedy of humanity, but it is not a *necessary* component for that argument. In other words, attributing the cause of universal sin and death to a historical Adam is not necessary for the gospel of Jesus Christ to be a fully historical solution to that problem.'[58] Enns does not invoke the names, but he likely refers to the opinions of erstwhile Westminster faculty John Murray (1898– 1975) and Cornelius Van Til (1895–1987), who both argued that Barth's rejection of Adam's historicity imperiled the gospel.[59] As a former professor at Westminster, Enns was likely aware of these claims. According to Enns, one might read Romans 5:12-21 and conclude that Adam did not truly exist although *Paul* believed he did. But according to Enns, to deny Adam's historical existence does not destroy the gospel contra Murray and Van Til.

Second, in his judgment, as important as Adam is to Pauline theology, Enns counters that Adam actually hardly appears outside of the creation narrative (Gen. 1–3). 'If Adam's disobedience lies at the root of universal sin and death, why does the Old Testament never once refer to Adam in this way?'[60] In his analysis, Adam's name only appears one time in the Old Testament after Genesis 5:3 (cf. 1 Chron. 1:1).[61] This proves the Old Testament has little interest, if at all, in Adam's purported role in the introduction of sin

---

57. Enns, *Evolution of Adam*, 81.

58. Enns, *Evolution of Adam*, 82.

59. John Murray, *Romans*, NICNT, 2 vols. (Grand Rapids: Eerdmans, 1959, 1965), I:384-90; Cornelius Van Til, *An Introduction to Systematic Theology* (Phillipsburg: P & R, 1974), 29.

60. Enns, *Evolution of Adam*, 82.

61. Enns, *Evolution of Adam*, 83.

into the world: 'The Old Testament does not seem to be interested in the causal question, why do Israelites or others do what they do? And it certainly does not explain the sinful choices of others by appealing to Adam. If Adam's causal role were such a central teaching of the Old Testament, we wonder why the Old Testament writers do not return to this point again and again, given Israel's profound capacity to disobey.'[62]

Third, Enns claims that Paul did not exegete Genesis 1–3 according to its original intent and meaning: 'Paul's use of the Old Testament, here or elsewhere, does not determine how that passage functions in its original setting.' Enns stipulates that Paul's claims about the universality of sin are true, but he has gone beyond what the Old Testament claims about Adam generally or Genesis specifically.[63] In short, it is difficult to avoid the conclusion that Enns believes that Paul misused Old Testament texts; Paul misused them for good reasons and even under divine inspiration, but he nevertheless misused them.[64] In his own words, Enns states: 'Paul's Adam is not a result of a "straight" reading of Genesis or the Old Testament.'[65]

So Romans 5:12-21 does not necessitate a historical Adam, the Old Testament is uninterested in Adam's causal role in the introduction of sin into the world, and Paul did not employ the Genesis narratives as they were originally understood. Given these three points and his contention that Christians must accept the latest scientific research, Enns believes that we must considerably revise our understanding of Adam and original sin. Enns explains that after the virtual silence of the Old Testament, Adam makes a dramatic appearance in Paul's epistles to showcase the Adam-Christ

---

62. Enns, *Evolution of Adam*, 86.

63. Enns, *Evolution of Adam*, 87.

64. Peter Enns, *Inspiration and Incarnation: Evangelicals and the Problem of the Old Testament* (Grand Rapids: Baker, 2005), 113-66; cf. G. K. Beale, *The Erosion of Inerrancy in Evangelicalism: Responding to New Challenges to Biblical Authority* (Wheaton: Crossway, 2008).

65. Enns, *Evolution of Adam*, 80.

parallel and the respective consequences of their (dis)obedience. But Enns cautions:

> For Paul's analogy to have any force, it seems that both Adam and Jesus must be actual historical figures. Not all Christian traditions will necessarily see it that way, but this is clearly a commonly held assumption today and the root reason why Christian and evolution are in such tension for many, in my opinion. A historical Adam has been the dominant Christian view for two thousand years. We must add, however, that the general consensus was formed before the advent of evolutionary theory. To appeal to this older consensus as a way of keeping the challenge of evolution at bay is not a viable option for readers today.[66]

Enns, therefore, rejects the traditional view and leaves the historicity of Adam as an open question. He wants to rethink Genesis as Ancient Near Eastern myth, which serves to explain Israel's place in the world, but Genesis 1–3 is not a literal or historical account of Adam's creation. He also wants to rethink Paul and recognize that he was a pre-scientific man with erroneous assumptions about his world and about Adam's existence.[67]

Like Barth, Enns willingly recognizes the reality of universal sin and death, but admitting these truths does not demand a historical Adam.[68] In fact, he explicitly states: 'By saying that Paul's Adam is not the historical first man, we are leaving behind Paul's understanding of the *cause* of the universal plight of sin and death.'[69] Hence, Enns does not explicitly make the statement, but he rejects the Adamic origins of sin and consequently has no place for imputed guilt. He acknowledges the historicity of Jesus, but this admission does not mean he believes in the doctrine of imputed righteousness.

In his explanation of Paul's exegesis of Genesis 15:6, 'Abraham believed God and it was credited to him as righteousness,' Enns

---

66. Enns, *Evolution of Adam*, xvi, 120.

67. Enns, *Evolution of Adam*, xviii.

68. Enns, *Evolution of Adam*, 123.

69. Enns, *Evolution of Adam*, 123.

provides further clues regarding his rejection of imputation. Standard Reformed explanations of Romans 4:3 (Gen. 15:6) claim that Abraham believed God's promise to give him numerous offspring, and God imputed the righteousness of Christ through faith to Abraham. Enns offers a different interpretation of Romans 4:3. Enns claims that in its original context, 'Genesis 15:6 does not refer to the act of faith that makes one righteous before God.' Enns offers two chief reasons for this conclusion. First, the point of Genesis 15 is not Abraham's initial act of faith; his conversion occurred in Genesis 12:1, not Genesis 15:6. Second, Abraham's act of faith (trust) had a concrete object—it concerned God's promise to give him numerous offspring. Hence, Paul misreads the text: 'For Paul to extrapolate from that some general sense of a sinner being justified before God apart from the law does not seem to be consistent with the context. Abraham is simply saying that he trusts God to deliver on his promise of offspring, and God counts that as an act of righteousness towards him.'[70]

Hence, Genesis 15:6 is not about imputed righteousness but rather covenant fidelity—obedience: 'Here, God says to Abraham, "I promise I will give you children." Abraham responds, "I trust you to do that." God says, "In this act of trust, you have done well [you are righteous]." This seems to be the heart of the exchange; if it were not for Paul, readers would pass this verse with hardly a pause.'[71] Enns fully believes that Paul's eisegesis is a creative, authoritative, and Christ-driven exercise but is a reading that does not accord with the original intent or understanding of the Genesis 15:6.[72] Enns, therefore, never comes out and explicitly states, 'I reject imputed guilt and righteousness,' but given his exegesis of one of the classic proof texts for the doctrine, he sidelines the doctrine. In fact, he embraces the polar opposite interpretation of this famous text: Reformed theologians have historically argued that the text is about the imputed righteousness of Christ, an alien righteousness,

---

70. Enns, *Evolution of Adam*, 112.

71. Enns, *Evolution of Adam*, 112.

72. Enns, *Evolution of Adam*, 112.

and Enns contends that it is about Abraham's covenant faithfulness, his obedience.

In the end, Enns wants to preserve the integrity of Christ's redemptive work even if it means dispensing with Adam's historicity. Enns recognizes that his interpretation of Paul may lead readers to conclude he has a low view of Scripture, but on the contrary, he believes his explanation shows how Paul elevates Christ. 'Paul invests Adam with capital he does not have either in the Genesis story, the Old Testament as a whole, or the interpretations of his contemporary Jews,' writes Enns. Paul's reading of the Old Testament was driven, nevertheless, by his encounter with the risen Christ. Enns concludes with a Barthian observation, namely, 'Christians who take Paul's *theology* with utmost seriousness are not also bound to accept Paul's view of Adam *historically*.'[73] In other words, Enns believes Paul's letters are infallible but not inerrant. For Enns, sin and death are a reality, but we do not know specifically how this universal problem arose. Christ, nevertheless, provides redemption—He opens a platform for believers, like Abraham, to offer their covenant fidelity. Enns ultimately casts aside the categories of imputed guilt and righteousness.

SCIENTIFIC CHALLENGERS

The most recent scientific findings motivate theologians like Enns to alter their doctrine but they still feel constrained by scriptural elements at certain points. Others, however, have heard the siren call of science and have cast off their scriptural inhibitions and completely recast the doctrine of original sin. One such example comes from Daryl Domning and Monika Hellwig in their recent book *Original Selfishness*.[74] Domning is an evolutionary biologist and Hellwig is a theologian; both are Roman Catholics. Domning and Hellwig seek to prove the compatibility between evolution and the claims of the Bible, but they admit that one of the chief obstacles

---

73. Enns, *Evolution of Adam*, 135.

74. Daryl P. Domning and Monika K. Hellwig, *Original Selfishness: Original Sin and Evil in the Light of Evolution* (Aldershot: Ashgate, 2006).

is the doctrine of original sin.[75] They both note that historically the Roman Catholic Church (RCC) rejected evolution as 'completely contrary to scripture and faith' in 1860, just one year after the publication of Darwin's *Origin of Species*. In 1950 Pope Pius XII (1876–1958) issued an encyclical that accepted the principle of organic evolution of the human body. Then in 1980 through the Pontifical Academy of Sciences and statements by Pope John Paul II (1920–2005) the RCC officially accepted the fact of human evolution.[76]

Domning and Hellwig note the inherent tensions with such developments, as they observe that the official Roman Catholic catechism 'seems to adhere to belief in a literal Adam, Eve, and Garden of Eden.'[77] But even then, they note that the catechism ultimately claims ignorance as to how, precisely, original sin is transmitted: 'The transmission of original sin is a mystery that we cannot fully understand.'[78] Nevertheless, Domning and Hellwig find a resolution to these tensions in the work of individual Roman Catholic scholars. Despite the RCC's purported belief in a literal Adam and Eve, Carmelite scholar Carlos Mesters (b. 1931) has suggested that the Genesis account is an allegorical projection—it points back to the future—the narrative is not a literal account of historical events but a prophetic vision of the future projected into the past.[79]

If there is no Adam and Eve, then how do we account for the transmission of original sin? Domning and Hellwig opt for the insights of Jesuit theologian, Piet Schoonenberg (1911–99), who

---

75. Domning and Hellwig, *Original Selfishness*, ix.

76. Domning and Hellwig, *Original Selfishness*, 2-3; Pius XII, 'Encyclical *Humani generis*, 12 August 1950,' in Heinrich Denzinger, *Compendium of Creeds, Definitions, and Declarations on Matters of Faith and Morals*, 43rd ed., ed. Peter Hünermann (San Francisco: Ignatius Press, 2012), §§3875-899 (pp. 799-807).

77. Domning and Hellwig, *Original Selfishness*, 4.

78. Domning and Hellwig, *Original Selfishness*, 4; *Catechism of the Catholic Church* (Ligouri: Ligouri Publications, 1994), §404 (p. 102).

79. Domning and Hellwig, *Original Selfishness*, 5.

argues that sin is transmitted culturally.[80] But Domning and Hellwig are aware that a cultural transmission view of original sin conflicts with the RCC's official teaching, namely, that sin is transmitted 'by propagation, not by imitation.' Sin is not a biological defect or merely culturally learned.[81] Historically, the RCC makes these claims to protect the goodness of the creation and reject Pelagianism. In other words, God does not create human beings as sinful and therefore defective; sin comes about due to human rebellion. And sin is not transmitted by imitation—they reject the heresy of Pelagianism.

Undaunted, Domning and Hellwig propose that the way to resolve the tensions between the RCC's doctrine and the claims of science is to pursue a theological and biological solution. Culture is the mechanism for the transmission of sin and biology explains the universality of sin.[82] Domning and Hellwig argue their case along the following lines. First, given the obscurity of ancient Hebrew, they claim that manuscripts may have been damaged in the Old Testament's long history of transmission. Ultimately, however, the creation account is ahistorical—it is myth. The account makes no effort to pinpoint the origin of evil, and even with Paul's Adam-Christ parallel, the apostle only juxtaposes two corporate personalities, not the actions of historical individuals. The Genesis account, therefore, only accounts for the existence of sin, not its origins.[83]

Second, contrary to common evangelical opinion, Darwinian evolution is a gift that explains the universality of sin.[84] All human life descended from a common bacteria-like life form, and the evolution of humanity has been marked by Darwin's process of

---

80. Domning and Hellwig, *Original Selfishness*, 5; cf. Piet Schoonenberg, *Man & Sin: A Theological View* (Notre Dame: University of Notre Dame Press, 1965).

81. Domning and Hellwig, *Original Selfishness*, 5.

82. Domning and Hellwig, *Original Selfishness*, 6.

83. Domning and Hellwig, *Original Selfishness*, 11-16.

84. Domning and Hellwig, *Original Selfishness*, 19.

natural selection—survival of the fittest. Domning and Hellwig, therefore explain:

> The innate, genetically-programmed drive to perpetuate oneself and one's posterity, and to sustain this effort by arrogating to oneself as much energy and resources as possible, is the most basic and necessary of all instincts. Because this drive is patently self-centered and ultimately (in a world of finite resources) succeeds only at the expense of others, there is no violence to language in calling it, in the simplest, most objective, non-psychological and non-pejorative sense, *selfish*.[85]

In other words, what theology calls original *sin*, Domning and Hellwig label original *selfishness*. Sin, therefore, is not a willful transgression of divine law but merely a biological necessity and consequence of the evolutionary process. God instigates the whole process and takes the risk of not controlling it; moreover, the process is ultimately neutral—natural selection is amoral. Attempts to deduce an ethical system from evolutionary principles is impossible.[86] Instead, Christians must seek their ethical norms that have been revealed through the incarnation of Christ.[87] Original selfishness is simply a consequence of our existence, and the task that lies before humanity is to evolve beyond our ingrained drive towards natural selection.[88] Humans must reject the inclination towards self-advancement and instead opt to advance the altruistic reign of God.[89] Jesus calls people to subvert, or convert, the evolutionary process and embrace His program of universal altruism.[90] Third, Domning and Hellwig exegetically support their arguments by excising a number of biblical claims. In their understanding, Adam was not responsible for introducing physical suffering or death into the creation. Science has decisively falsified the claims of Romans

---

85. Domning and Hellwig, *Original Selfishness*, 30.

86. Domning and Hellwig, *Original Selfishness*, 56, 110-11.

87. Domning and Hellwig, *Original Selfishness*, 56.

88. Domning and Hellwig, *Original Selfishness*, 108-09.

89. Domning and Hellwig, *Original Selfishness*, 125.

90. Domning and Hellwig, *Original Selfishness*, 127.

5:12-19. Like Enns, Domning and Hellwig claim that the Bible hardly mentions the fall and that it only incidentally appears in Romans 5, 1 Corinthians 15, and 1 Timothy.[91] In fact, *Adam* is not really a person at all but the common biological matter from which all living things originate.[92] *Adam* is simply a mythical designator for everyman.[93] But again, like Enns, Domning and Hellwig argue that denying a historical Adam does not therefore entail the denial of the historical Christ. The proper focus of Christian doctrine must be the historical second Adam, not on his allegorical twin, the first Adam.[94]

Fourth, and finally, Domning and Hellwig, acknowledge that God created the world good but nevertheless fallen.[95] Our proclivity is towards original selfishness, but we all have the choice to act differently: 'What God *has* done is put us in a position where we must and can choose: between the selfish way of natural selection, and the selfless way of Christ, which alone can liberate us from this world's futility.'[96]

In summary, Domning and Hellwig offer a Pelagian view of original sin and a moral influence theory of the work of Christ. Such convictions naturally sideline any concept of imputed guilt or righteousness. Domning and Hellwig accomplish their stated goal of arguing for the compatibility of evolutionary biology and the claims of the Bible by excising a number of problematic elements from the Scriptures—the Genesis narrative is mythical and allegorical, Paul's exegesis of the Genesis text has been falsified by science, and Jesus is a moral exemplar, not a vicarious redeemer.

Domning and Hellwig are not alone in their views. Daniel C. Harlow, religion professor at Calvin College, similarly argues that Adam and Eve are symbolic literary figures and Romans 5:12-21

---

91. Domning and Hellwig, *Original Selfishness*, 139.

92. Domning and Hellwig, *Original Selfishness*, 140.

93. Domning and Hellwig, *Original Selfishness*, 142.

94. Domning and Hellwig, *Original Selfishness*, 153.

95. Domning and Hellwig, *Original Selfishness*, 156.

96. Domning and Hellwig, *Original Selfishness*, 158.

is about humanity's plight, not Adam's imputed guilt. Harlow maintains a doctrine of original sin but along recalibrated scientific and biological lines suggested by Domning. Sin is a biologically inherited condition, and this means we must reconfigure the atonement along moral influence or *Christus Victor* models. Therefore, humanity has evolved and theology must follow suit. The church must shed the vestigial limbs of imputation and mistaken Pauline opinions, and walk upright on the feet of science and evolved theology.[97]

CONCLUSION

Despite the claims of fidelity to Christ and His word, it is difficult to square many contemporary engagements with an honest reading of Scripture. Schleiermacher and Bultmann completely sever Christian doctrine from its historical and scriptural roots. The lone individual stands in his own world divorced from any corporate connections, whether to Adam or Christ. Efforts to recover the doctrine of Scripture and wrestle with its claims in the formulations of Barth, Enns, and to a lesser extent Wright, nevertheless throw Adam overboard in an effort to calm the perceived storm of the claims of the ancient Near East or science—the Genesis narrative is myth or saga and therefore ahistorical and science supposedly rules out a historical Adam and Eve. Or, in the case of Domning, Hellwig, and Harlow, the doctrine of original sin has been entirely scuttled and has sunk to the bottom of a sea of irrelevance; original selfishness has taken its place. In a nutshell, Domning and Hellwig claim humanity is sinful because we were made this way.

Like Adam and Eve standing before God, present-day theologians have gathered whatever theological, philosophical, and scientific fig leaves they can find and verbally parry divine claims of sinfulness. By rejecting Adam's existence as myth, or setting him

---

97.   Daniel C. Harlow, 'After Adam: Reading Genesis in an Ages of Evolutionary Science,' *Perspectives on Science and Christian Faith* 62/3 (2010): 170-95, esp. 192.

forth as an illustration as everyman, sin is no longer a voluntary willful desertion of God and transgression of His covenant law. To God's, 'Where are you?' and His, 'Who told you that you were naked?' and, 'Have you eaten of the tree of which I commanded you not to eat?' Adam mythically responds, 'Come on, you know this isn't real. Sin just is. And besides, this is all your fault because you made me this way.' In rejecting claims of sinfulness and hence personal responsibility, there can be no imputed guilt, and if there is no imputed guilt then there can be no imputed righteousness. The details vary from theologian to theologian, but the twentieth century represents the resurrection of Pelagius. Despite suffering repeated blows in centuries past, 'Always after a defeat and a respite, the Shadow takes another shape and grows again.'[98]

---

98. J. R. R. Tolkien, *The Fellowship of the Ring: The Lord of the Rings*, Part I (1954; Boston: Mariner Books, 1994), 50.

Part I Summary

The survey of the history of the origins and development of the doctrine of imputation presents a number of issues for consideration in Parts II and III:

1. What is the nature of the connection between Adam and his offspring? Moral? Legal? Physical? Exemplary?

2. Are sin and guilt purely ontological and therefore require a physical means of transmission?

3. Is original sin merely the absence of righteousness or the active presence of sin?

4. Does Adam bear the Platonic ideal human nature?

5. Is imputed righteousness a theological novelty as the Council of Trent alleged?

6. Is a twofold covenantal structure warranted? Was God in covenant with Adam?

7. Should ontological or forensic categories take precedent in the question of determining the means by which God accounts people guilty or righteous?

8. Do believers receive Christ's essential righteousness through union with Him?

9. Does God impute both the active and passive righteousness of Christ to the believer?

10. Is mediate imputation truly a form of imputation?

11. Should we distinguish between guilt (*culpa*) and penalty (*reatus poenae*)? In other words, Does God merely impute the penalty for Adam's sin or also the guilt?

12. Must we affirm Adam's historical existence?

While different variations of these questions might arise, they summarize the various subjects that subsequent exegetical spadework and dogmatic formulation should address.

PART II:
EXEGESIS

1

Imputation in the Old Testament

Introduction

In the wake of the birth of higher critical studies and the advent of the modern theological curriculum, theologians no longer looked at the Bible as a unified whole but as a disparate collection of different theological reflections. Plenary inspiration, and thus an organically unified canon, ceased to exist for some portions of the church.[1] Theologians examined the various books of the Bible

---

1. See, e.g., Michael C. Legaspi, *The Death of Scripture and the Rise of Biblical Studies* (Oxford: Oxford University Press, 2010); Thomas Albert Howard, *Protestant Theology and the Making of the Modern German University* (Oxford: Oxford University Press, 2006).

in isolation and hence severed the testaments from one another. What theologians once joined together to produce a canonical portrait of doctrine was now splintered into a thousand different biblical shards. In contrast to higher-critical methods, early modern theologians employed the *locus* method of theology. Theologians gathered together in one place the exegetical occurrences of one doctrinal phenomenon because they assumed the organic unity and plenary inspiration of the whole Bible. Different biblical authors may have written the various texts to which they appealed, but the same Holy Spirit inspired the whole. Evidence of this conviction appears in the cited proof texts for the Westminster Confession of Faith (1647). Under its statements regarding imputed righteousness, the divines cite the following collection of texts: Romans 4:5-8; 2 Corinthians 5:19, 21; Romans 3:22, 24, 25, 27, 28; Titus 3:5, 7; Ephesians 1:7; Jeremiah 23:6; 1 Corinthians 1:30-31; and Romans 5:17-19.[2] The divines make no qualifications about the theology of Paul, Jeremiah, or so-called deutero-Pauline epistles. They simply appeal across the canon to support their claim regarding imputed righteousness.

Following this locus model, I offer a survey of four different Old Testament texts: Leviticus 16:21-22, Isaiah 53:11-12, Zechariah 3:1-5, and Isaiah 61:10. Each of these texts showcases different elements of the doctrine of imputation, and does so within the context of God's covenantal dealings with His people. These texts reveal the dynamic between the one and the many—how God imputes sin and righteousness. These texts are important because they form the foundational revelation upon which later New Testament authors, such as Paul, rest their own claims regarding imputation. These different texts form part of the bedrock for Paul's statements in Romans 4, 'Abraham believed God, and it was counted to him as righteousness' (Rom. 4:3). Paul's statement reaches back to Genesis 15:6, but many other Old Testament texts inform his subsequent exposition in 4:4-8. But before we proceed to

---

2. *The Humble Advice of the Assembly of Divines, Now by Authority of Parliament sitting at Westminster, Concerning a Confession of Faith* (London: 1647), XI.i.

these four texts, it is necessary to survey briefly the Old Testament's understanding of the relationship between the one and the many, a crucial element within the broader doctrine of imputation. Can one person's actions impact and affect the lives of others? More specifically, can one person legally assume responsibility for another? Can one person represent another, whether positively or negatively? The one and the many, or the individual's relationship to the corporate body, is an essential element of the doctrine of imputation that must be factored.

This chapter also considers an Old Testament text that some might consider an obstacle to the doctrine of imputation, namely, Jeremiah 31:29-30. This text states that individuals suffer for their own sins, which means they do not suffer for the sins of others. This chapter argues that this text does not overturn the doctrine of imputation but speaks to another issue, namely, generational retribution, which is a different phenomenon than imputed guilt. Imputation and generational retribution both coexist in the Old Testament and do not contradict one another.

THE ONE AND THE MANY

ACHAN'S SIN

When Israel entered the Promised Land the conquest was brought to a screeching halt due to the sin of one individual.[3] The individual-corporate dynamic appears in the opening verse of the narrative account: 'But the people of Israel broke faith in regard to the devoted things, for Achan the son of Carmi, the son of Zabdi, the son of Zerah, of the tribe of Judah, took some of the devoted things. And the anger of the LORD burned against the people of Israel' (Josh. 7:1). The text states that the people (lit. *sons*) of Israel committed a breach of that which was holy—they committed a מעל (*maal*; cf. Lev. 5:15) by taking what had been placed under the ban חרם (*herem*; cf. Josh. 6:17-19). The verse opens with the sons of

---

3. The following section on the one and the many is drawn from J. V. Fesko, *The Trinity and the Covenant of Redemption* (Fearn: Christian Focus, 2016).

Israel, focuses upon the act of one person, and then concludes with all of Israel suffering as a result of the actions of this one person. Moreover, the fact that the narrative provides Achan's genealogy also suggests corporate guilt despite the actions of a lone individual.[4] This text pulsates with the individual-corporate dynamic, evident in Israel's corporate solidarity, and hence its corporate guilt, as well as specifically naming Achan as the one who perpetrated the *maal*.[5] Achan as an individual was covenantally bound to Israel and, in this particular case, his breach of covenant fidelity became representative disobedience for all of Israel—all of Israel was covenantally, and hence legally, bound to Achan.[6]

DAVID'S CENSUS

Another occurrence of the individual-corporate dynamic occurs in David's sinful census of Israel (2 Sam. 24; cf. 1 Chron. 21). Against the advice of Joab, the commander of his armies, David proceeded with a census of Israel's armies in an effort to measure the nation's might (2 Sam. 24:3; cf. 1 Sam. 8:11-19; 14:6).[7] David was subsequently conscience-stricken, repented of his sin, and sought forgiveness from the Lord (2 Sam. 24:10). When David received a response to his entreaty, he discovered that God would give him one of three options: three months of famine, three months of fleeing from his enemies, or three days of plague in the land (2 Sam. 24:12). David chose the third option and seventy thousand Israelites perished. When David saw the messenger of the Lord striking down the people, he responded: 'I have sinned;

---

4. Richard S. Hess, *Joshua: An Introduction and Commentary*, TOTC (Downers Grove: InterVarsity Press, 1996), 143-44.

5. Marten H. Woudstra, *The Book of Joshua*, NICOT (Grand Rapids: Eerdmans, 1981), 120-21.

6. Important to note is that the individual-corporate dynamic at this point is earthly, typically illustrative, and not eternal. Only Adam and Christ are federal heads with eternal consequences (cf. Jer. 31:29-30; Ezek. 18:2-3, 20).

7. Cf. Kyle R. Greenwood, 'Labor Pains: The Relationship between David's Census and Corvée Labor,' *BBR* 20/4 (2010): 467-78; Shimon Bakon, 'David's Sin: Counting the People,' *Jewish Bible Quarterly* 41/1 (2013): 53-54.

I, the shepherd, have done wrong. These are but sheep. What have they done? Let your hand fall on me and my family' (2 Sam. 24:17). The text is clear—David the lone individual ordered the census and the nation as a whole suffered the consequences of his representative disobedience. In this particular case, David, unlike Achan, was the king, the earthly covenantal head of the nation. His individual actions had corporate implications. This is true not only in his disobedience but also in his quest for corporate forgiveness. David was told to build an altar to the Lord 'that the plague on the people may be stopped' (2 Sam. 24:21). After David paid fifty shekels for the oxen and altar site, he sacrificed burnt and fellowship offerings, at which point 'the LORD answered his prayer in behalf of the land, and the plague on Israel was stopped' (2 Sam. 24:25). We find, then, the corporate solidarity of Israel with her king—his sin brings their punishment and his repentance yields their healing.[8] A parting observation regarding David's census and sacrifice is in order—the location of his sacrifice became the future site of the Solomonic temple. In other words, David's action, seeking forgiveness, blankets David and the corporate body, and this all occurs at the site of the typical temple, which points forward to the antitypical reality of Christ.[9]

DANIEL'S SON OF MAN

Of the many titles that the Scriptures ascribe to Jesus, the most common is 'Son of Man,' an ascription that has roots in Daniel 7, among other texts (cf., e.g., Ps. 8; Gen. 1:26-28). Within the heart of Daniel's angst-inducing vision the prophet inquires about its meaning and is told: 'The saints of the Most High shall receive the kingdom and possess the kingdom forever, forever and ever' (Dan. 7:18). The immediate reference is clearly to multiple people,

---

8. Bruce Waltke, *An Old Testament Theology: An Exegetical, Canonical, and Thematic Approach* (Grand Rapids: Zondervan, 2007), 677-78; cf. Joshua J. Adler, 'David's Last Sin: Was it the Census?' *Jewish Bible Quarterly* 23/2 (1995): 91-95; Raymond Dillard, 'David's Census,' in *Through Christ's Word: A Festschrift for Dr. Philip E. Hughes* (Phillipsburg: P & R, 1985), 104-06.

9. Dillard, 'David's Census,' 106-07.

the 'saints' (cf. Dan. 7:22, 27). Some have therefore concluded that references to the Son of Man are corporate.[10] The individual beasts in Daniel's vision, for example, refer to nations, not individuals. Thus, they claim, the Son of Man title is a designation for Israel, for the people of God. But within the context of this vision, these beasts, first and foremost, represent kings, who in turn represent nations. In other words, efforts to swing the pendulum too hard in one direction or the other, individual versus corporate, fail to deal adequately with the particulars of the text. In Daniel's vision the references to the Son of Man have in view an individual who is the representative for the corporate group.[11]

In this case, that the Son of Man refers to one individual is evident in the fact that he enters the scene with the clouds of heaven. In the Old Testament the only one who rides on the clouds is Yahweh. Hence, the Son of Man cannot be a reference to a community of people but to a divine figure, who receives kingly authority to rule over the creation.[12] Jesus confirms this connection during His interrogation before the religious leaders—Jesus is the Son of Man that the prophet saw in his vision (cf. Matt. 24:30; 26:64; Mark 13:26; 14:62; Luke 21:27; Rev. 14:14). Hence, within the broader scope of Daniel 7, the Son of Man is the Messiah, the one to whom Yahweh gave a kingdom, authority, and power, and who reigns and represents the saints, those who 'receive the kingdom and possess the kingdom forever' (Dan. 7:18). The kingdom of God, of course, is a covenantal reality, evident in numerous places throughout the Old and New Testaments, and once again the covenant is the context that binds the king, the Son of Man, to His people, the saints.

---

10. See, e.g., C. H. Dodd, *According to the Scriptures: The Sub-Structure of New Testament Theology* (London: Nisbet & Co, Ltd., 1952), 117-19.

11. G. K. Beale, *A New Testament Biblical Theology: The Unfolding of the Old Testament in the New* (Grand Rapids: Baker, 2011), 394-95; R. T. France, *Jesus and the Old Testament: His Application of Old Testament Passages to Himself and His Mission* (Vancouver: Regent College Publishing, 1998), 169-71.

12. Beale, *Biblical Theology*, 396.

One element not disclosed in Daniel's vision, however, is the precise manner by which the Son of Man accomplishes His mission. In particular, Mark's gospel provides the link between the Son of Man's rule and the means by which He accomplishes His mission: 'For even the Son of Man came not to be served but to serve, and to give his life as a ransom for many' (10:45). This text links the Son of Man with elements that arise from Isaiah 53 and the suffering servant, the one who intervenes on behalf of the many.[13]

OLD TESTAMENT IMPUTATION TEXTS

The previous section surveyed three examples of how the Old Testament regularly binds together the one and the many. The lone individual acts and the corporate body either receives the blessings or suffers the consequences, which all hinges on whether the act was one of obedience or disobedience. Traffic on the imputation highway runs in both directions. As we drill down beneath the surface of the covenantal bonds between the one and the many, the Old Testament reveals two things: (1) that imputation lies at the heart of the connection between the individual and corporate body, and (2) that both righteousness and sin can be imputed.

LEVITICUS 16:21-22

Within the broader context of the book of Leviticus, chapter 16 and the famous Day of Atonement follow the ominous judgment that fell upon the sons of Aaron, Nadab and Abihu. The priestly brothers brought 'unauthorized fire before the Lord, which he had not commanded them' (Lev. 10:1). In judgment the Lord consumed the innovative brothers with fire; hence, the ensuing chapters (11-15) explain the differences between what is clean and unclean so Israel would explicitly know what was and was not acceptable in God's presence. The overall intent of these chapters is to show Israel that approaching God must be done according to

---

13. On the connections between Mark 10:45 and Isaiah 53, see France, *Jesus and the Old Testament*, 116-23; Seyoon Kim, *The Son of Man as the Son of God* (Grand Rapids: Eerdmans, 1983), 38-60.

His instruction and commands because they bear the uncleanness of sin.[14] A person's sin must be addressed before he can stand in God's presence without fear of immediate judgment. Moreover, another point these text highlight is that Israel's sinfulness, and hence uncleanness, defiles them and requires remedy before they can continue to dwell in God's presence.

Space prohibits an exhaustive exegesis of the text, but noting the broader structure proves beneficial for understanding the specific verses in question:

> vv. 1-2:   Introduction
> vv. 3-5:   Animals and priestly dress
> vv. 6-10: Outline of the ceremonies
> vv. 11-28: Description of the ceremonies
>
> > vv. 11-19: Blood-sprinkling rites
> > vv. 20-22: The Scapegoat
> > vv. 23-28: Cleansing of the participants
>
> vv. 29-34: Duty of the people

The instructions for the handling of the scapegoat present key elements of the doctrine of imputation. After it was chosen by lot (vv. 7-8), the high priest was supposed to take the scapegoat and confess the nation's sins over it:

> And Aaron shall lay both his hands on the head of the live goat, and confess over it all the iniquities of the people of Israel, and all their transgressions, all their sins. And he shall put them on the head of the goat and send it away into the wilderness by the hand of a man who is in readiness. The goat shall bear all their iniquities on itself to a remote area, and he shall let the goat go free in the wilderness (vv. 21-22).

In the broadest of terms, Aaron's actions transferred the nation's sins to the goat and the goat carried them away into the wilderness.

---

14. Gordon J. Wenham, *Leviticus*, NICOT (Grand Rapids: Eerdmans, 1979), 227.

But there are a number of elements within this text that require greater elaboration.

The first is the hand-laying ceremony—the high priest was supposed to lay both of his hands upon the head of the live goat. What does the imposition of the priest's hands signify? There are other similar actions in the Old Testament that indicate the transfer of something.[15] Moses, for example, laid his hands upon Joshua to signify the transfer of and investiture with authority (Num. 27:18, 20, 23; Deut. 34:9). Likewise, subsequent Old Testament priests were dedicated to temple service by the laying on of hands (Lev. 24:14). Other texts instruct the priests to lay their hands upon the heads of sacrificial animals (Exod. 29:10, 15, 19; Lev. 1:4, 10 (LXX); 3:2, 8, 13; 4:4, 15, 24, 29, 33; 8:14:18, 22; Num. 8:12; 2 Chron. 29:23). In these cases the laying on of hands indicates either the transfer of authority or sin. The priest's confession of sin over the scapegoat in conjunction with the laying-on of hands confirms the connection between the imposition of the hands and the transfer of sin: 'And Aaron shall lay both his hands on the head of the live goat, and confess over it all the iniquities of the people of Israel' (Lev. 16:21). Jacob Milgrom observes: 'A transfer thus takes place—not from the high priest, who is personally immune from the contamination produced by the sins he confesses—but from Israel itself; its sins, exorcised by the high priest's confession are transferred to the body of the goat, just as the sanctuary's impurities, absorbed by the purgation blood, are (originally) conveyed to the goat.'[16]

Other components confirm the transfer of sin to the goat is the fact that the passage specifically states: 'The goat shall bear all their iniquities on itself to a remote area' (Lev. 16:22). The goat *bears* (נָשָׂא) their sins (עָוֹן), what the Septuagint translates as *unrighteousness* (ἀδικίας). In the economy of Old Testament sin-bearing, ordinarily

---

15. René Péter, 'L'Imposition des Mains dans L'Ancien Testament,' *VT* 27/1 (1977): 48-55; cf. David P. Wright, 'The Gesture of Hand Placement in the Hebrew Bible and Hittite Literature,' *JAOS* (106/3 (1986): 433-46, esp. 434.

16. Jacob Milgrom, *Leviticus*, AB (New Haven: Yale University Press, 1991), 1043.

the one who transgresses God's law bears, holds, hauls, or carries about his sin. But when another party intervenes, which is usually God, he bears the sinner's burden. The weighty encumbrance no longer rests upon the shoulders of the sinner—God removes the load and its consequences (cf. Exod. 28:43; Lev. 5:1, 17; 7:18; 17:16; 19:8; 20:17, 19-20; 22:9, 16; 24:15; Num. 5:31; 9:13; 14:33-34; 15:30-31; 18:1, 22-23; 30:15).[17] To bear one's sin invites the consequential punishment, death (Num. 18:22), whereas in this case, to transfer the nation's sins to the goat by imposition of the hands and confession of sin over the goat's head brings continued life, though only for the next year.

There is great mystery surrounding the goat's ultimate destination, as the priest releases the goat into the wilderness never to return—the goat is ultimately for or destined to Azazel (Lev. 16:10, 26). Commentators disagree as to the precise meaning of this term and its significance—is Azazel a demonic name, a destination in the wilderness, or a state of destruction? Regardless of its significance, the intended meaning is clear—God removes and exterminates Israel's sin by having the goat carry it away into the wilderness.[18]

Another important element in this passage requires comment. We must not forget that the fiery judgment that fell upon Nadab and Abihu looms over the instructions for the Day of Atonement, indeed for all of the sacrifices. The priestly brothers fell under God's judgment because they brought unauthorized fire before the Lord—specifically, that which He had not commanded them. This means that there are two prerequisites for continued presence before God: (1) removal of the sin, evident by transferring the nation's sin to the goat; and (2) scrupulous attention to every detail of God's commands regarding offering the sacrifice. The smallest deviation from God's commands would result in disaster,

---

17. Baruch Schwartz, 'The Bearing of Sin the Priestly Literature,' in *Pomegranates & Golden Bells: Studies in Biblical, Jewish, and Near Eastern Ritual, Law, and Literature in Honor of Jacob Milgrom*, ed. David P. Wright, David Noel Freedman, and Avi Hurvitz (Winona: Eisenbrauns, 1995), 9.

18. Wenham, *Leviticus*, 235.

not just for the priest, as in the case of Nadab and Abihu, but for the nation. A failure on the Day of Atonement would have dire consequences and likely mean either God's departure from their midst or Israel's exile from His presence. In this text, therefore, the priest's adherence to the law undergirds and stabilizes the removal of the sin. Positive adherence to the law and the removal of sin is necessary for continued existence in the presence of God. The proper execution of the sacrifice, therefore, ensures the continued covenantal relationship between God and His people.

ISAIAH 53:11-12

A second critical text is Isaiah 53:11-12, which appears in what is perhaps the most famous of Isaiah's four servant songs. Within the broader context of his prophecy Isaiah tells of a future exile and explains how God Himself will deal with Israel's sin, the impelling cause of their banishment. God will send His servant who will offer a sacrifice, end the covenant curse, and repatriate Israel to the land of promise—God, not Israel, will personally end the exile. That this was God's plan is evident from Isaiah 53:10, 'It was the will of the LORD to crush him.' Within the recesses of the pre-temporal intra-trinitarian covenant it was the 'good plan' (NLT) to crush the suffering servant in order to end the curse of exile. The suffering servant would be righteous and submit to the will of Yahweh, and for this Yahweh would prolong his days, and the servant would divide the spoil with the strong (Isa. 53:12). This language evokes the blessings of the covenant, which were the effects of obedience to the terms of the covenant (cf. Deut. 6:25; 28:3-8).

In this midst of this passage, Isaiah states:

> Out of the anguish of his soul he shall see and be satisfied; by his knowledge shall the righteous one, my servant, make many to be accounted righteous, and he shall bear their iniquities. Therefore, I will divide him a portion with the many, and he shall divide the spoil with the strong, because he poured out his soul to death and was numbered with the transgressors; yet he bore the sin of many, and makes intercession for the transgressors (Isa. 53:11-12).

There are a number of contrasting terms and concepts in these two dense verses. Isaiah contrasts the righteous individual servant with the many, whom the prophet characterizes as transgressors, or sinners. The servant, therefore, keeps the terms of God's covenant whereas the sinners transgress and break it. But the antithetical contrast does not merely touch upon the moral character of the servant versus the many. Isaiah reports that there is an exchange between the servant and the many.

The servant makes 'many to be accounted righteous,' whereas conversely he bears 'their iniquities' (Isa. 53:11). The first important observation is Isaiah's statement regarding the servant's knowledge. The prophet does not refer merely to the acquisition of data. In the book of Isaiah lack of knowledge is the impelling cause of Israel's exile (Isa. 47:10). Idolaters lack knowledge (Isa. 44:19, 25). Yahweh possesses knowledge, whereas Israel does not (Isa. 40:14; 48:4). Yahweh anoints the servant with the Spirit of knowledge and the fear of the Lord, which is the proper disposition necessary to produce obedience (Isa. 11:2; 33:6; cf. Prov. 11:9).[19] If the prophet Hosea is any indication, to reject knowledge is to forget the law of God and thus to rush headlong into disobedience; conversely, to act with knowledge is to live in obedience to God's law (Hos. 4:6). Hence, the servant's obedience is the material source that makes 'many to be accounted righteous.' But what, precisely, does Isaiah mean when he states that the servant will make many to be accounted righteous? The overall thrust of Isaiah's prophecy is that the whole world, including Israel, is guilty of sin and unbelief. The servant changes the status quo, which Isaiah indicates by the verb צדק, which in this case appears in the hiphil imperfect. The hiphil (the causative) of צדק, 'to be righteous' should be translated as 'cause to be righteous,' and is usually followed by a direct object. For example, in Deuteronomy 25:1-2, the verb appears in the hiphil form followed by the direct objects of 'the innocent and … the

---

19. John Goldingay, *Message of Isaiah 40-55: A Literary-Theological Commentary* (London: T & T Clark, 2005), 514; cf. John Oswalt, *The Book of Isaiah: Chapters 40-66*, NICOT (Grand Rapids: Eerdmans, 1998), 403-04.

guilty,' indicated by the direct-object marker (אֵת). Here, however, Isaiah follows the verb with an indirect object governed by the preposition (לְ), which means, 'provide righteousness to.'[20] The latter half of Isaiah's statement, 'he shall bear their iniquities,' provides important interpretive data that helps us understand how, exactly, the servant provides righteousness, or makes the many righteous.

Isaiah's chosen terminology originates from the protocols of the Day of Atonement. On the Day of Atonement the high priest would lay his hands on the goat, confess Israel's sins over the goat, and then send the goat into the wilderness never to return. The goat would bear (נָשָׂא) or carry Israel's sins.[21] In this case, God does not place Israel's sins upon a goat but upon the shoulders of the suffering servant, and he carries or bears Israel's sins: 'He bore [נָשָׂא] the sin of many' (Isa. 53:12). The fact that the servant bears the sins of the many does not somehow compromise his status as righteous, which sheds light on the nature of how the many sinners receive the status of righteous. If an infused righteousness were in view, then in bearing the sins of the many the servant would be infused with their sins. Infused sin and righteousness are not in view. Rather, Isaiah's use of the hiphil of צָדַק with the indirect object and the governing preposition means that the righteous one will *justify* or *declare righteous* the many sinners, and will do so on the basis of his knowledge, his obedience. Hence, Yahweh imputes the obedience or righteousness of the servant to the many sinners and, conversely, He imputes the guilt of the many sinners to the righteous servant.[22]

Further confirmation of this exegesis appears in verse 12: 'Therefore, I will divide him a portion with the many, and he shall divide the spoil with the strong, because he poured out his soul to death and was numbered with the transgressors; yet he bore the

20. J. Alec Motyer, *The Prophecy of Isaiah: An Introduction & Commentary* (Downers Grove: InterVarsity Press, 1993), 441-42.

21. Goldingay, *Isaiah 40-55*, 510-11.

22. E. J. Young, *The Book of Isaiah*, 3 vols., NICOT (1965; Grand Rapids: Eerdmans, 1974), III:357-58.

sin of many, and makes intercession for the transgressors.' Isaiah's use of the term מָנָה ('numbered' or 'counted') indicates imputed rather than infused sin. In fact, the Septuagint translates this term with the verb λογίζομαι, which can be translated as *impute*. 'He was numbered with the transgressors' means, therefore, that God would look upon the servant as if he were sinful because he would bear the covenant curse on behalf of the many sinners. God would impute their sins to the servant.

Isaiah 53:11-12 adds important information that is lacking in Leviticus 16:21-22. The Leviticus text clearly portrays the imputation of sin to the scapegoat, which is but one element of the doctrine of double-imputation. Imputed righteousness is implicit in the text, as the priest had to follow perfectly the legal protocols; otherwise the sacrifice would be compromised, which would likely lead to the death of the priest and doom for the nation since they would still carry their own sins. The action of the one (the priest) would negatively impact the many (Israel). In this case his positive adherence to the sacrificial law and protocols undergirded the acceptability of the sacrifice. But the on-going increasing progressive nature of divine revelation sheds greater light upon imputation once Isaiah lays hold of these concepts and applies them to the work of the suffering servant. Like the scapegoat, the suffering servant clearly bears the sins of the many sinners, but under the light of progressive revelation we discover that God imputes the suffering servant's righteousness to the many sinners. At this stage in redemptive history, however, we still await the fullness of the revelation of God in Christ. In the light of Christ New Testament writers take up these very themes and concepts and explain the doctrine of imputation with greater precision and clarity. We will explore these numerous imputation texts in the following chapter. For now, we must first turn our attention to Zechariah 3:1-5.

ZECHARIAH 3:1-5

Isaiah's prophecy addressed Israel regarding an as-of-yet to occur exile, whereas Zechariah's prophecy occurs in the midst of Israel's return from their Babylonian exile. Israel was taken from the land, the temple was destroyed, the priesthood ceased to function, and hence the regular sacrificial cycle came to a screeching halt. When Cyrus issued the decree to return to the land, Israel's leaders began the rebuilding process, which, among other things, included rebuilding the temple and re-starting the sacrifices. But in order to regenerate the sacrificial system, Israel needed holy priests. Apart from a high priest, there was no one to conduct the sacrifices. At this point in redemptive history, however, the Levitical line was defiled and thus incapable and disqualified from making sin offerings on Israel's behalf. Zechariah offers his vision about Joshua, the high priest, which confirms the ineligible status of Israel's high priest, but he also receives a vision where God reconstitutes the Levitical priesthood and does so through the doctrine of imputation.

Zechariah's vision begins with Joshua the high priest standing in the presence of the Lord and the accuser, Satan (Zech. 3:1). Satan accused Joshua of being defiled by sin, which was evident by Joshua's 'filthy [צֹאִים] garments.' In this case, Joshua wears garments stained with excrement, which is one of the worst types of ceremonial defilement (cf. Deut. 23:14; Isa. 28:8; 36:12; Ezek. 4:12). But the term can also be used to depict sin (Isa. 4:4).[23] In stark contrast to Joshua's excrement-stained garments, the high priest was supposed to be clothed in the purest of dress (Lev. 16:4). The defiled high priest was supposed to be excommunicated from the covenant community, bathed and cleansed (Lev. 22:6-7), and given clean garments (cf. Ezek. 44:18-19).[24] Given this information, Satan's accusations are accurate and true—Joshua stands defiled before the presence of his holy covenant Lord.

Even though Joshua stands defiled before the divine bar, this is a courtroom like no other. Yahweh has a dual-function; He serves both as judge and advocate. The Lord declared to Satan: 'The Lord

---

23. Eugene H. Merrill, *Haggai, Zechariah, Malachi: An Exegetical Commentary* (Chicago: Moody Press, 1994), 134; Thomas McComisky, *Zechariah*, in *The Minor Prophets: An Exegetical & Expository Commentary*, 3 vols. (Grand Rapids: Baker, 1998), III:1070.

24. Baruch Halpern, 'The Ritual Background of Zechariah's Temple Song,' *Catholic Biblical Quarterly* 40 (1978): 167-90.

rebuke you, O Satan! The LORD who has chosen Jerusalem rebuke you! Is not this a brand plucked from the fire' (Zech. 3:2)?[25] Yahweh does not dispute Satan's characterization or description of Joshua but nevertheless rebukes him because Joshua has been designated as a recipient of God's mercy; he has been plucked from the fire of judgment (cf. Amos 4:11). He has been chosen by God's gracious election. That Yahweh speaks of Jerusalem rather than Joshua, indicates that as high priest, Joshua represents the nation, and hence mention of its capital city. Jerusalem serves as a metonymy for Joshua the high priest—the nation's representative before the divine bar.

The angel's actions that follow Yahweh's rebuke explain how Joshua remains in God's presence despite his defiled state. The angel said to the courtroom attendants: 'Remove the filthy garments from him.' Yahweh interprets this symbolic action as the removal of sin: 'Behold I have taken your iniquity away from you' (Zech. 3:4a).[26] But unlike the ritual cleansing of sin, Zechariah's use of the hiphil of עבר suggests that the removal of sin is an act of God's grace— God has completely removed it—nothing remains. But God's actions do not end here, as not only does the angel remove Joshua's filthy garments but Yahweh instructs him to clothe Joshua in 'pure vestments' (Zech. 3:5b). What do the pure vestments symbolize? If the defiled garments represent sin, then the pure vestments represent, not merely the absence of sin, but the positive presence of righteousness.[27] Such a conclusion is certainly logically reasonable, but is it exegetically warranted? There is exegetical evidence to sustain the conclusion that the pure priestly garments with which the angel clothed Joshua represent positive righteousness.

Within the conceptual framework of the temple and its accouterments, the priestly vestments were richly laden with symbolic meaning. Like the tabernacle, and later the temple, the priests were ritually purified by blood (Lev. 8) and ultimately given garments

---

25. Meredith G. Kline, *Glory in Our Midst: A Biblical-Theological Reading of Zechariah's Night Visions* (Overland Park, KS: Two Age Press, 2001), 98.

26. Merrill, *Zechariah*, 135.

27. Kline, *Glory in Our Midst*, 110.

woven of material similar to that of the tabernacle. The high priest also wore a turban with a gold plate that read, 'Holy to the LORD' (Exod. 28:36). The priest was essentially a miniature replica of the temple. The garments reminded the priest of his need for holiness and hence the need for righteousness.[28] Other portions of the Scriptures liken pure vestments to righteous works. One such text that we will explore below is Isaiah 61:10, 'My soul shall exult in my God, for he has clothed me with the garments of salvation; he has covered me with the robe of righteousness.' The apostle John employs this very imagery in his description of the Lamb's bride: "'And his Bride has made herself ready; it was granted her to clothe herself with fine linen, bright and pure"—for the fine linen is the righteous deeds of the saints' (Rev. 19:7c-8).[29] In fact, Revelation 19:8 has a unique parallel with the Targum (a fist-century Aramaic paraphrase of the Old Testament) of Zechariah 3:1-5.[30] The Targum renders Zechariah's, 'I will clothe you with pure vestments' with, 'I have removed your sins from you and have clothed you with *righteous deeds.*'[31] Hence, given this understanding of the pure vestments, instead of being found guilty for his sins, represented by the filthy garments, God forgives his sin and imputes righteousness to him, which the pure priestly vestments represent.[32]

ISAIAH 61:10

The last passage that deserves attention comes from Isaiah 61:10, and as noted above, contains themes similar to those found in Zechariah 3:1-5, 'I will greatly rejoice in the LORD; my soul shall exult in

---

28. Vern S. Poythress, *The Shadow of Christ in the Law of Moses* (Phillipsburg: P & R, 1991), 53-54.

29. G. K. Beale and D. A. Carson, eds., *Commentary on the New Testament Use of the Old Testament* (Grand Rapids: Baker, 2007), 1142; G. K. Beale, *The Book of Revelation*, NIGCT (Grand Rapids: Eerdmans, 1999), 934-44.

30. Beale, *Revelation*, 937.

31. Kevin J. Cathcart and Robert P. Gordon, *The Targum of the Minor Prophets: Translated, with a Critical Introduction, Apparatus, and Notes* (Wilmington, DE: Michael Glazier, Inc., 1989),

32. Beale, *Revelation*, 937; Kline, *Glory in Our Midst*, 110, 112.

my God, for he has clothed me with the garments of salvation; he has covered me with the robe of righteousness, as a bridegroom decks himself like a priest with beautiful headdress, and as a bride adorns herself with jewels.' Within its broader context, this verse falls under the prophet's reflections upon a broken but ultimately restored covenant relationship—a restoration that occurs through the work of the suffering servant (Isa. 53). With these words the prophet meditates upon the grandeur of the Lord's salvation. The speaker in this text is not God or the suffering servant, as neither He nor the servant require the garments of salvation.[33] The garments of salvation instead indicate the source of the vestments and that God's righteousness is a gift.[34] Moreover, note that Isaiah places *garments of salvation* in parallel with the *robe of righteousness*—these are synonymous expressions.[35]

In this case, once again, the conceptual framework that equates redemption with investiture has connections to other portions of the Bible, such as Psalm 45. The Psalmist describes the bride as one dressed in robes fragrant with myrrh, aloes, and cassia (Ps. 45:8). The bride's robe is interwoven with gold and made of multi-colored fabric (Ps. 45:13-14). In this context, only a righteous bride can wed the king, as Yahweh has 'loved righteousness and hated wickedness' (Ps. 45:7). Isaiah employs this conceptual metaphor in Isaiah 61:10 and so does John in the book of Revelation (19:7-8).[36] Important to note in these passages (Zech. 3:1-5; Isa. 61:10; Rev. 19:7-8) is that the recipient is passive—the person receives the pure garments, the robe of righteousness, as a divine gift. Yahweh specifically tells Joshua, 'I will clothe you with pure vestments' (Zech. 3:4). Isaiah says, 'He,' Yahweh, 'has covered me with the robe of righteousness' (Isa. 61:10), and John writes, 'It was granted [ἐδόθη] her to clothe herself with fine linen, bright

---

33. Young, *Isaiah*, III:465.

34. Oswalt, *Isaiah*, II:575.

35. Young, *Isaiah*, III:465.

36. Beale, *Revelation*, 938-41.

and pure' (Rev. 19:8).[37] The recipient passively receives the divinely given gift of the robe of righteousness.

GENERATIONAL RETRIBUTION

As some read the Old Testament they encounter a passage that appears to contradict the idea of imputed guilt, namely Jeremiah 31:29-30. The prophet Jeremiah states: 'In those days they shall no longer say: "The fathers have eaten sour grapes, and the children's teeth are set on edge." But everyone shall die for his own iniquity. Each man who eats sour grapes, his teeth shall be set on edge' (Jer. 31:29-30; cf. Ezek. 18:20; Deut. 24:16). The clear implication is that children will not suffer for the sins of their parents. How does this text fit with the four previously surveyed imputation passages?

Jeremiah 31:29-30 speaks to the issue of generational retribution, which is different than imputed guilt. Stated briefly, generational retribution is part of the Mosaic covenant and is the idea that future generations might suffer for the sins of their fathers. The most familiar occurrence of generational retribution occurs in the third commandment of the Decalogue. God visits the iniquity of the fathers on the children 'to the third and fourth generation of those who hate' Him (Exod. 20:5). Throughout the Old Testament God visits the sins of fathers upon their sons (1 Kings 14:10-18; 16:1-12; 17:18; Lev. 26:39-40; Isa. 14:21; Zech. 8:14; Ps. 109:14; Neh. 9:2). Yet, the Old Testament provides an important qualification when acknowledging the reality of generational retribution. God visits the sins of the fathers upon subsequent generations *if* they too hate God (Deut. 7:9-10). As Jacob Milgrom explains, 'God punishes individually, visiting punishment on the sinner; he in turn passes on the punishment to his progeny if they follow his evil ways.'[38] There are, however, two noteworthy observations concerning generational retribution.

---

37. Beale, *Revelation*, 939-40.

38. Jacob Milgrom, *Numbers*, JPS Torah Commentary (Philadelphia: Jewish Publication Society, 1990), 394.

First, in some cases God imposes a mitigated form of punishment upon future generations. The generation that entered the Promised Land had to suffer for the sins of their fathers by wandering in the wilderness: 'Your children … shall suffer for your faithlessness, until the last of your dead bodies lies in the wilderness' (Num. 14:33). The second generation did not suffer death but instead had to wander in the wilderness, which was due to their fathers' faithlessness.[39] Second, in other cases, the father might repent of his sin but his sons nevertheless suffer for his action. This pattern unfolds in the case of God's punishment for David's adultery with Bathsheba: 'Nathan said to David, "The LORD also has put away your sin; you shall not die. Nevertheless, because by this deed you have utterly scorned the LORD, the child who is born to you shall die"' (2 Sam. 12:13-14). The same pattern unfolds with Ahab's generationally postponed punishment: 'Because [Ahab] has humbled himself before me, I will not bring the disaster in his days; but in his son's days I will bring the disaster upon his house' (1 Kings 21:29; cf. 2 Kings 22:19-20).[40]

The point of Jeremiah's statement is that in the new covenant, generational retribution will cease to exist. This is evident when the prophet takes a prospective look forward to the days of the new covenant, evident by the words, 'In those days they shall no longer say …'[41] Immediately following these verses is the promise of the new covenant: 'Behold the days are coming, declares the LORD, when I will make a new covenant with the house of Israel and the house of Judah, not like the covenant that I made with their fathers on the day when I took them by the hand to bring them out of the land of Egypt, *my covenant that they broke*' (Jer. 31:31-32). Israel always lived under the looming shadow of the curse of the covenant and the specter of generational retribution, a point pressed upon Jeremiah's audience as they faced the

---

39. Milgrom, *Numbers*, 395.

40. Milgrom, *Numbers*, 394-95.

41. Bob Becking, 'Sour Fruit and Blunt Teeth: The Metaphorical Meaning of the māšāl in Jeremiah 31:29,' *SJOT* 17/1 (2003): 7-21, esp. 14-16.

covenant curse of exile. They dwelled under the dark clouds of Sinai and its threatened curses but under the new covenant God would send a redeemer, as Isaiah 53 makes clear, who would remove the threat of curse and generational retribution and bring the elect to Mt. Zion (Gal. 3:10-14; Heb. 12:18-29). The promise of the new covenant and the end of generational retribution does not mean that imputed guilt ceases to exist. In fact, generational retribution can only cease if the suffering servant bears the sins of the elect through imputation. Far from overturn the doctrine of imputation, generational retribution only highlights its absolute necessity. Apart from imputation, the Messiah cannot bear the sins of the many and thus free them from the curse of the covenant and generational retribution.

CONCLUSION

This brief survey reveals several important building blocks that comprise the Old Testament foundation for the doctrine of imputation. In contrast to post-Enlightenment views of radically individualized existence, the doctrine of the covenant binds the individual to the corporate body. No one is an island unto himself. People's actions impact the greater body. Achan's sin halted the conquest of the Promised Land. David's sinful census brought judgment upon the nation, and conversely his repentance brought healing. And Daniel's vision of the son of man points to the Messiah—the one person who serves as the kingly representative for His people, those whom He redeems. These same patterns continue in the four surveyed Old Testament texts: the protocols for the Day of Atonement have the high priest who scrupulously follows God's instructions, confessing Israel's sin and transferring them to the scapegoat. In Isaiah's famous fourth servant song, a lone righteous man makes many to be accounted righteous and alone bears their sins—God numbers him with the transgressors. The servant repairs the breach of the covenant but at the same time bears the covenant curse on behalf of the many. Isaiah's text presents what Martin Luther (1483–1546) called a glorious exchange—sinners receive righteousness and the servant receives their sin.

Other Old Testament texts such as Zechariah 3:1-5 and Isaiah 61:10 present the imputation in terms of removal of sin-stained garments and the investiture with garments of righteousness. All of these texts inform numerous New Testament passages that speak of imputation. The doctrine of imputation does not rest upon the meaning of one lone term, such as λογίζομαι ('impute'), nor upon a few isolated New Testament texts such as Romans 4:1-8. Rather, the Old Testament concepts of the one and the many and imputed sin and righteousness inform the New Testament's doctrine of imputation. We turn now to the New Testament to survey several key texts that rest upon this Old Testament foundation.

2

IMPUTATION IN THE NEW TESTAMENT

INTRODUCTION

In recent debates regarding the doctrine of imputation discussion has largely centered around several New Testament texts, chiefly Romans 4, Romans 5:12-21, and 2 Corinthians 5:17-21. Some New Testament scholars contend that Reformed appeal to these texts has either misunderstood Paul's arguments or has read medieval notions of merit into them. N. T. Wright's commentary on Romans, for example, maintains that Paul only uses his bookkeeping metaphor in Romans 4:4-5 this one time and that Reformed theologians have exaggerated its significance.[1] Michael Bird argues that notions of

---

1. N. T. Wright, *Romans*, in NIB, vol. 10 (Nashville: Abingdon, 2002), 491.

imputed righteousness have more to do with medieval views of merit, where God supposedly banks good deeds and dispenses them to believers to cover their account. He instead opts to maintain a view of incorporated rather than imputed righteousness: namely, those who are in union with Christ receive His righteous status.[2] Regardless of the criticisms, most of the debate largely focuses upon the meaning of λογίζομαι ('impute,' or 'account') in its isolated context. Few critics or defenders of imputation examine Paul's statements against their all-important Old Testament background.[3] In view of this methodological shortcoming, I present an examination of these three key texts in light of the exegetical spadework presented in the previous chapter. In other words, Paul's doctrine of imputation has a taproot that reaches back to the Old Testament, a doctrine informed by the ideas of the one and the many and especially key texts such as Leviticus 16 and Isaiah 53.

ROMANS 4

Romans 4 is one of the most important texts to the Reformation because it was frequently cited in disputes over the doctrine of justification. A number of Reformed confessions and catechisms, for example, appeal to this chapter in their explanations of justification.[4] This frequent citation was undoubtedly part of a greater renaissance

---

2. Michael F. Bird, 'Incorporated Righteousness: A Response to Recent Evangelical Discussion Concerning the Imputation of Christ's Righteousness in Justification,' *JETS* 47/2 (2004): 253-75; idem, 'Justification as Forensic Declaration and Covenant Membership: A *Via Media* Between Reformed and Revisionist Readings of Paul,' *TynB* 57/1 (2006): 109-30; idem, *The Saving Righteousness of God: Studies on Paul, Justification, and the New Perspective* (Milton Keynes: Paternoster, 2007), 60-87, 113-54; idem, 'Progressive Reformed View,' in *Justification: Five Views*, ed. James K. Beilby and Paul Rhodes Eddy (Downers Grove: InterVarsity Press, 2011), 145-52.

3. Ben C. Dunson, 'Do Bible Words Have Bible Meaning? Distinguishing Imputation as a Word and Doctrine,' *WTJ* 75 (2013): 239-60.

4. See, e.g., French Confession (1559), XX; Belgic Confession (1561), XXIII; Heidelberg Catechism, q. 60; and Second Helvetic Confession (1566), XV.iii-iv; cf. Charles Hodge, *Romans* (1835; Edinburgh: Banner of Truth, 1991), 108, 183.

of biblical exegesis and interest in Paul's epistle to the Romans.[5] Therefore, historically, Romans 4 merits our attention if only because it was frequently cited in discussions about justification. Exegetically and theologically, however, the passage warrants examination because Paul mentions the term λογίζομαι ('imputed,' 'accounted,' or 'accredited') eleven times (Rom. 4:3, 4, 5, 6, 8, 9, 10, 11, 22, 23, 24). If frequency statistics mean anything, Paul was eager to highlight the importance of this term and the concept behind it.

We should begin with Paul's first use of the term in Romans 4:3 and his famous quotation of Genesis 15:6, 'For what does the Scripture say? "Abraham believed God, and it was counted to him as righteousness."' Paul introduces this quote to explain why Abraham, the greatest patriarch of Israel, had no reason to boast before God (Rom. 4:1-2). Paul cites Genesis 15:6 for a number of reasons, one of which is because it is the first time the word *believe* (אמן) occurs in the Scriptures.[6] Here Paul repeatedly places believing in antithetical contrast to working or doing.[7] In fact, like the eleven times Paul mentions imputation, he mentions the word πιστεύω ('believe') six times (Rom. 4:3, 5, 11, 17, 18, 24) and the word πίστις ('faith') ten times (Rom. 4:5, 9, 11, 12, 13, 14, 16, 19, 20) for a total of sixteen occurrences of faith-related terms. In verse 3, Paul's point is that God reckons or imputes righteousness to Abraham because he believed God's promise. In short, the fact that God imputes righteousness to Abraham by faith means that this righteousness comes from God and does not inherently belong to Abraham.[8] This is a sound conclusion for three chief reasons.

First, Paul situates the relationship between faith and imputed righteousness within the broader context of his theology of the law.

---

5. See, e.g., T. H. L. Parker, *Commentaries on Romans: 1532-42* (Edinburgh: T & T Clark, 1986).

6. Douglas J. Moo, *The Epistle to the Romans*, NICNT (Grand Rapids: Eerdmans, 1996), 261.

7. Robertson, 'Genesis 15:6,' 270.

8. O. Palmer Robertson, 'Genesis 15:6: New Covenant Exposition of an Old Covenant Text,' *WTJ* 42 (1980): 265-66.

Paul writes: 'He [God] will render to each one according to his works: to those who by patience in well-doing seek for glory and honor and immortality, he will give eternal life; but for those who are self-seeking and do not obey the truth, but obey unrighteousness, there will be wrath and fury' (Rom. 2:6-8). The law functions in a *quid pro quo* manner—obey and you receive the blessing of eternal life, disobey and you receive condemnation and eternal death: 'For it is not the hearers of the law who are righteous before God, but the doers of the law who will be justified' (Rom. 2:13).[9] Paul does not quote the specific Old Testament text, but given his familiarity with the law in its Deuteronomic form he likely has the concept in view: 'And it will be righteousness for us, if we are careful to do all this commandment before the LORD our God, as he has commanded us' (Deut. 6:25). Obedience to the law is the means by which one receives the status of righteous. But Paul clearly states that God declared Abraham righteous, not because of his obedience to the law, but because of his faith in the promise. Paul repeatedly makes this point: 'For if Abraham was justified by works, he has something to boast about, but not before God' (Rom. 4:2). Abraham's justified status was not as a result of his works, or obedience.

Paul makes this point abundantly clear two more times: 'Now to the one who works, his wages are not counted [οὐ λογίζεται] as a gift but as his due. And to the one who does not work but believes in him who justifies the ungodly, his faith is counted [λογίζεται] as righteousness' (Rom. 4:4-5). Paul places works (obedience) in contrast to faith and imputed righteousness—he contrasts a merited accounting and an un-merited, or more properly a de-merited, accounting—one received as due wages (μισθὸς) and the other received as a gift, or grace (χάριν). An example of a merited accounting or imputation occurs with Phinehas's execution of the couple guilty of idolatrous adultery (Num. 25:6-13). The Psalmist describes God's response to Phinehas's action in the following manner: 'And that was counted to him as righteousness [καὶ ἐλογίσθη αὐτῷ εἰς δικαιοσύνην] from generation to generation

---

9. Hodge, *Romans*, 53-54.

forever' (Ps. 106:31 LXX). Phinehas's action qualifies as a case of merited accrediting—God rewarded Phinehas with a perpetual priestly covenant and accounted his action as a fulfillment of the law (Num. 25:13; cf. Deut. 6:25; 24:13; Num. 3–4).[10] Notably, here in Romans 4 Paul does not appeal to Phinehas as it would contradict his intended point regarding the gratuity of imputed righteousness received by faith apart from works. There is a difference between merited imputation (Phinehas) and demerited imputation (Paul)—the former is earned and the latter is given by free grace.

Another instance of 'impute' appears when Paul appeals to David's prayer of repentance: 'Just as David also speaks of the blessing of the one to whom God counts [λογίζεται] righteousness apart from works: "Blessed are those whose lawless deeds are forgiven, and whose sins are covered; blessed is the man against whom the Lord will not count [οὐ μὴ λογίσηται] his sin"' (Rom. 4:6-8). Through David's statement Paul makes the point that the forgiveness of sins is the non-imputation of sin. In other words, a person's good works do not erase the debt of sin but rather God's non-imputation constitutes forgiveness. This serves Paul's greater point that justification and the forgiveness of sins are free acts of God that have no legal basis in the person's good works. The imputation of righteousness and non-imputation of sin also further highlights that Paul has legal, not morally transformative, realities in view.[11]

Second, vital to recognizing that Paul has an alien righteousness in view, that is, a righteousness that is not inherent to Abraham, is the fact that he characterizes Abraham as *ungodly* (ἀσεβῆ) (Rom. 4:5). The term itself denotes a person who is irreverent, impious, or ungodly.[12] In other contexts, the ungodly ordinarily

---

10. Hodge, *Romans*, 110, 179; Gordon J. Wenham, *Numbers*, TOTC (Downers Grove: InterVarsity Press, 1981), 188-89; John Owen, *Justification*, in *The Works of John Owen*, 24 vols., ed. William H. Goold (Philadelphia: Leighton Publications, 1862), vol. 5; 168, 319.

11. Moo, *Romans*, 266.

12. BDAG, 141.

fall under God's judgment (Jude 15; cf. Deut. 33:2).[13] In fact, according to the apostle Peter, God is storing up fire 'until the day of judgment and destruction of the ungodly' (2 Pet. 3:7). Some have tried to defang Paul's statement by claiming that in this context ἀσεβής simply means *Gentile*.[14] Such an interpretation runs against the grain of Paul's argument as well as his broader understanding of salvation: 'For while we were still weak, at the right time Christ died for the ungodly [ἀσεβῶν]' (Rom. 5:6).[15] Moreover, both Jews and Gentiles are ungodly, a point Paul highlights in the opening of his epistle (Rom. 1:18; 3:9-19).

Paul's characterization of Abraham as ungodly, moreover, is glaringly different from typical first-century Jewish opinions. Philo (25 B.C. – A.D. 50), for example, described Abraham in the following manner: 'Now he [Abraham], being an admirer of piety, the highest and greatest of all virtues, labored earnestly to follow God, and to be obedient to the injunctions delivered by him.'[16] Statements about Abraham's virtuous character appear in other first-century Jewish literature. First Maccabees (ca. 104 B.C.) makes the opposite point as Paul: 'Was not Abraham found faithful when tested, and it was reckoned to him as righteousness?' (1 Macc. 2:52 NRSV). This statement falls under the category of wages counted as due, not as a gift (Rom. 4:4). Sirach describes Abraham as one who kept the law, entered into a covenant with God, certified the covenant in his flesh through circumcision, was tested and, 'Therefore the Lord assured him with an oath that the nations would be blessed through his offspring' (44:19-21 NRSV). Jubilees (ca. 160–40 B.C.) 23:10 states: 'For Abraham was perfect in all of his actions with the LORD and was pleasing through righteousness all of the days

---

13. G. K. Beale and D. A. Carson, eds., *Commentary on the New Testament Use of the Old Testament* (Grand Rapids: Baker, 2007), 1078.

14. So Joseph A. Fitzmeyer, *Romans*, AB (New York: Doubleday, 1992), 375.

15. Gerhard H. Visscher, *Romans 4 and the New Perspective on Paul: Faith Embraces the Promise* (New York: Peter Lang, 2009), 179.

16. Philo, *On Abraham*, in *Philo*, vol. 6, trans. F. H. Colson (Harvard: Harvard University Press, 1935), XIII (60).

of his life.'[17] These descriptions clash with Paul's characterization of Abraham as ungodly. In the mind of some Jews, Abraham's justified status was the result of his righteousness, whereas Paul indicates that Abraham was unrighteous.

Paul, in fact, specifically counters these common claims, namely, that Abraham's upright conduct (his circumcision or the sacrifice of Isaac) curried God's favor and thus earned him the status of righteous. Repeatedly invoking the term λογίζομαι, Paul demonstrates that Abraham's justified status preceded all of his upright conduct: 'For we say that faith was counted [ἐλογίσθη] as righteousness. How then was it counted [ἐλογίσθη] to him? Was it before or after he had been circumcised? It was not after, but before he was circumcised. He received the sign of circumcision as a seal of the righteousness that he had by faith while he was still uncircumcised' (Rom. 4:9-11). What was the point of this timing? 'The purpose,' writes Paul, 'was to make him the father of all who believe without being circumcised, so that righteousness would be counted [λογισθῆναι] to them as well' (Rom. 4:11). In other words, uncircumcised Gentiles could lay hold of the same gospel justification as Abraham so long as they did so by faith apart from works.

Third, Paul's stated doctrine stands in stark contrast to God's instructions to the Israelites that they should not justify the wicked. Paul's words in Romans 4:5 echo Exodus 23:7,* 'Keep far from a false charge, and do not kill the innocent and righteous, do not acquit the wicked [οὐ δικαιώσεις τὸν ἀσεβῆ]' (LXX). How can God justify ungodly Abraham? How can God declare Abraham righteous when he has no inherent righteousness of his own? Paul answers this question through the doctrine of imputed righteousness that is received by faith alone apart from works. These three points (faith and imputation, Abraham's ungodly status, and God's claim that He will not justify the ungodly) require us, therefore, to seek to understand better the nature of imputation and the specific term λογίζομαι.

---

17. James H. Charlesworth, ed., *The Old Testament Pseudepigrapha*, 2 vols. (New York: Doubleday, 1983), II:100.

The term λογίζομαι appears in a number of Old Testament texts in the Septuagint. Numbers 18:27 describes sacrifices that are reckoned to a person's advantage: 'And your contribution shall be counted [λογισθήσεται] to you as though it were the grain of the threshing floor, and as the fullness of the winepress.' In 2 Samuel 19:20 (MT) the underlying Hebrew term חשׁב appears; Shimei, who confessed his sin to David, asked him, 'Do not impute to me, my Lord, my guilt.' In this particular case, Shimei asks David to overlook his sinful conduct—to forgive him—and he does so in terms of the non-imputation of his sinful act.[18] Given this Old Testament lexical data, the upshot of Paul's quoted statement, 'Abraham believed God, and it was counted to him as righteousness' (Rom. 4:3), is that this legal declaration is not in accord with the facts if, and only if, the verdict rests solely upon Abraham's ungodly status.[19] But the fact that Paul highlights that God imputes righteousness as a gift apart from works points us in another direction for the source of righteousness (Rom. 4:4, 6).

So whence this righteousness? Paul provides an answer towards the end of Romans 4, an answer grounded in Isaiah 53 and Leviticus 16. Paul recounts the nature of Abraham's faith in God's promise and explains that the patriarch fully believed 'that God was able to do what he had promised. That is why his faith was "counted [ἐλογίσθη] to him as righteousness"' (Rom. 4:23). But Paul notes that Genesis 15:6 was not written for Abraham alone: 'It will be counted [λογίζεσθαι] to us who believe in him who raised from the dead Jesus our Lord, who was delivered up for our trespasses and raised for our justification' (Rom. 4:24-25). In these last two verses of the chapter, Paul employs language drawn from Isaiah 53.[20]

Several key features connect Romans 4:25 to Isaiah 53, such that we can say that this one verse concisely summarizes the fourth

---

18. Moo, *Romans*, 262 n. 35; Robertson, 'Genesis 15:6,' 265-66.

19. Hodge, *Romans*, 179.

20. What follows is drawn from J. V. Fesko, *The Trinity and the Covenant of Redemption* (Fearn: Mentor, 2016), 279-80.

servant song.[21] The first connection appears when we compare Romans 4:25 with the LXX text of Isaiah 53:

Romans 4:25a	Isaiah 53:12 LXX
παρεδόθη διὰ τὰ παραπτώματα ἡμῶν ('delivered up for our trespasses')	διὰ τὰς ἁμαρτίας αὐτῶν παρεδόθη ('delivered because of their iniquities')

In both cases, Paul, echoing the LXX, states that the Christ was παρεδόθη ('handed over,' or 'delivered up') for the sins of the many. The second line of Romans 4:25 continues to reflect the LXX text of Isaiah 53:11,

Romans 4:25b	Isaiah 53:11 LXX
ἠγέρθη διὰ τὴν δικαίωσιν ἡμῶν ('raised for our justification')	ἀπὸ τοῦ πόνου τῆς ψυχῆς αὐτοῦ, δεῖξαι αὐτῷ φῶς ('from the travail of his soul, to show him light')

The idea is that, after the servant's death, he will see light, or be raised from the dead, hence Paul's phrase, 'raised for our justification.'[22] The LXX's insertion of φῶς ('light') to the MT's phrase, 'Out of the anguish of his soul he shall see [מעמל נפשו יראה],' is an amplification of the idea of resurrection. In a number of Old Testament texts the expression 'to see light' is a metaphor for 'to live' (Ps. 36:9; 49:19; Job 3:16; 33:28-30; cf. Ps. 56:13).[23]

---

21. Otfried Hofius, 'The Fourth Servant Song in the New Testament Letters,' in *The Suffering Servant: Isaiah 53 in Jewish and Christian Sources*, ed. Bernd Janowski and Peter Stuhlmacher (Grand Rapids: Eerdmans, 2004), 180; Morna Hooker, 'Did the Use of Isaiah 53 to Interpret His Mission Begin with Jesus?' in *Jesus and the Suffering Servant: Isaiah 53 and Christian Origins*, ed. William Bellinger, Jr. and William R. Farmer (Eugene: Wipf & Stock, 1998), 101-02.

22. Hofius, 'Fourth Servant Song,' 180-81.

23. Hofius, 'Fourth Servant Song,' 181 n. 68; cf. Hans-Joachim Kraus, *Psalms 1-59* (Minneapolis: Fortress, 1993), 399-400, 483-84, 527; David J. A.

206 DEATH IN ADAM, LIFE IN CHRIST – PART II

Paul's use of these Isaianic phrases shows that Christ vicariously bore the sins of the many in His death—He is their vicarious representative. Taking the two texts combined (Rom. 4:25 and Isa. 53:11-12), the causative force of the prepositional διά indicates the cause of Christ being handed over, and in the second line the purpose and end goal in view: '[He was] delivered up for [*because of*] our trespasses, and raised for [*the purpose of*] our justification.'[24] Within the broader context of Romans 4, Paul echoes the themes of the fourth servant song, that Isaiah's 'transgressors' are 'accounted righteous' (Isa. 53:11) and the justification of the 'ungodly' (Rom. 4:5).[25] Noteworthy is the fact that both Paul and Isaiah employ λογίζομαι in their respective passages. Isaiah states that the suffering servant was τοῖς ἀνόμοις ἐλογίσθη ('numbered with the transgressors') and Paul explains in Romans 4:24b, ἀλλὰ καὶ δι' ἡμᾶς, οἷς μέλλει λογίζεσθαι ('it will be counted to us who believe'). Both employ imputation language.

But we must not forget that Isaiah 53 rests upon the foundation of Leviticus 16 and the procedures from the Day of Atonement. The suffering servant would bear the sin of many echoes the scapegoat, which bore Israel's sins and carried them away (Isa. 53:12; cf. Lev. 16:22). The high priest would lay his hands upon the goat, confess the nation's sins, and thus transfer or impute their guilt to the sacrificial animal. In this case, however, no mere animal bore Israel's sins but rather Jesus, the Son of God, bears the sins of the elect. Jesus was the source of Abraham's righteousness and forgiveness of sins that Abraham received by faith alone apart from works. Romans 4, therefore, is most certainly about justification by faith alone, but central to Paul's doctrine is the concept of imputation.

Important to note at this point are the two different phrases that Paul employs in Romans 4:5-6, namely: the believer's 'faith

---

Clines, *Job 1-20*, WBC, vol. 17 (Dallas: Word, 1989), 95; idem, *Job 21-37*, WBC 18a (Nashville: Thomas Nelson, 2006), 740.

24. Hofius, 'Fourth Servant Song,' 181; cf. Moo, *Romans*, 289.

25. Hofius, 'Fourth Servant Song,' 182.

is accounted for righteousness' and 'God imputes righteousness apart from works.' Some have claimed that Paul's phrase 'faith is accounted for righteousness' means that God looks upon Abraham's *faith* as righteousness, not that God imputes Christ's righteousness or obedience to Abraham. Michael Bird, for example, claims, 'There is no external source of righteousness identified. What is more, righteousness here is not a property to be transferred.'[26] Yet, we must read the statement 'faith is accounted for righteousness' in connection with Romans 4:6, namely: 'God imputes righteousness apart from works.' God does something here and it is not merely looking upon Abraham's faith favorably. Moreover, contra Bird, one cannot explain Roman 4:6 by arguing that it simply means 'God justifies.' In other words, Bird claims 'God counts righteousness apart from works' is the same as Romans 3:28, 'One is justified by faith apart from works of the law.'[27] If Isaiah 53 and Leviticus 16 comprise Paul's Old Testament subtext, then imputation is not the same thing as justification. Rather, imputation is a vital part of justification, but the latter requires both the imputation of righteousness and the forgiveness of sins to be complete. I argue that Romans 4:6, 'God counts righteousness apart from works' finds its parallel in Philippians 3:9 when Paul says that he does not have a righteousness of his own that comes from the law but rather one that 'comes through faith in Christ, the *righteousness from God* [ἐκ θεοῦ δικαιοσύνην]' (emphasis). Paul does not talk about his faith being treated as righteousness but that he receives an alien righteousness from God; the same holds true, therefore, for Abraham's faith in Romans 4:6. Paul's continued argument in Romans 5 confirms this conclusion.

---

26. Bird, 'Progressive Reformed View,' 147. Bird advocates what has been historically associated with an Arminian interpretation of Romans 4:6, an interpretation rejected in Reformed confessions (see J. V. Fesko, 'Arminius on Justification: Reformed or Protestant?' *Church History and Religious Culture* 94 [2014]: 1-21).

27. Bird, 'Progressive Reformed View,' 147.

Romans 5:12-21

Given that Paul invokes the term λογίζομαι eleven times in Romans 4, we might conclude that he has little else to say on the subject, but Paul nevertheless continues to expand upon the doctrine in Romans 5:12-21. This passage is one of the most significant for the doctrine of imputation since Paul places Adam and Christ in an antithetical parallelism to explain the relative effects of their respective acts of (dis)obedience. In Romans 4 Paul focuses upon imputation at a personal soteriological level, or as it relates to the *ordo salutis*. But here in Romans 5 Paul rises above the terrain and offers a bird's eye view of the *historia salutis*. Paul's interest lies in addressing the corporate significance of the work of the first and last Adams, which he accomplishes by oscillating back and forth between Adam and Christ with his 'just as … so also' comparisons. Adam's actions have detrimental universal consequences and Paul explains how God in Christ has counteracted those consequences. And though Paul's explanations follow his treatment of imputation in Romans 4, what he says here constitutes the theological foundation for all that has gone before since the opening of the epistle.[28] Paul discusses sin and righteousness, imputation, all within the context of the actions of the one and the implications for the many—a theme shot through the whole passage.[29]

Paul opens his fifth chapter reflecting upon the significance of Christ's death and our justification, namely, that Christ has died for the ungodly (Rom. 5:1-11). He then transitions to explain the reason behind this salvation (Διὰ τοῦτο) through the antithetical parallelism between Adam and Christ (Rom. 5:12).[30] Paul writes: 'Therefore, just as sin came into the world through one man, and death through sin, and so death spread to all men because all sinned' (Rom. 5:12). Paul explains that sin is a foreign

28. Moo, *Romans*, 314-15.

29. S. Lewis Johnson, Jr., 'Romans 5:12—An Exercise in Exegesis and Theology,' in *New Dimensions in New Testament Study*, eds. Richard N. Longenecker and Merrill C. Tenney (Grand Rapids: Zondervan, 1974), 301.

30. Johnson, Jr., 'Romans 5:12,' 301.

invader—it was not native to the original creation, which Genesis characterized as being 'very good' (Gen. 1:31). He lays the onus for this invasion upon Adam's shoulders, and does so with the phrase, δι' ἑνὸς ἀνθρώπου ('through one man').[31] The biblical narrative explicitly identifies Eve as the first one to sin, yet Paul lays the responsibility squarely upon Adam (Gen. 3:6; cf. 1 Tim. 2:13-14; 2 Cor. 11:3). Adam, not Eve, was the representative for humanity.[32] But in what way does Paul link the one man with οἱ πολλοί ('the many')?

The latter half of verse 12 involves the much-disputed meaning of ἐφ' ᾧ. Augustine (354–430) famously translated this phrase as, 'in whom.' That is, 'Just as sin came into the world through one man, and death through sin, and so death spread to all men; in whom [Adam] all sinned [*in quo omnes peccaverunt*].' Better grammatical analysis points us in a different direction. The disputed phrase most likely means *because*: 'Sin came into the world through one man, and death through sin, and so death spread to all men *because* all sinned' (emphasis; cf. 2 Cor. 5:4; Phil. 3:12). Moreover, the overall chiastic structure of this verse indicates that ἐφ' ᾧ has a causal meaning:[33]

A   sin (12a) produces

B   death (12b)
B[1] all die (12c)

A[1] because all sin (12d)

In other words, in some sense God views all of humanity as guilty of sin because of Adam's one transgression. And while arguing that all humanity participated in Adam's sin is an accurate conclusion, we must drill deeper into text to determine the precise nature of this participation.[34] In what way has all humanity sinned (ἥμαρτον)?

---

31. Johnson, Jr., 'Romans 5:12,' 302.

32. Moo, *Romans*, 319.

33. Moo, *Romans*, 321-22; Johnson, Jr., 'Romans 5:12,' 305.

34. Johnson, Jr., 'Romans 5:12,' 304.

Answering this question brings us to the shores of some heavily trafficked territory in the history of exegesis, which was evident in Part I of this study. There are largely four different views on the manner of humanity's participation in Adam's sin:[35]

1. Imitation – Pelagius (fl. ca. 390–418) famously argued that there is no legal or ontological connection between Adam and humanity. Rather, the connection is imitative.[36] Adam's progeny imitate his sin—Adam is a bad moral example. A predecessor to Pelagius appears in 2 Baruch 54:19, 'Adam therefore is not the cause, save only of his own soul, but each of us has been the Adam of his own soul.' Advocates of this view include Albert Barnes (1798–1870), C. K. Barrett (1917–2011), Emil Brunner (1889–1966), Rudolf Bultmann (1884–1976), as well as those who deny the historicity of Adam, such as Roman Catholics Daryl Domning and Monika Hellwig.[37] The problem with such exegesis is that it fails to engage the text responsibly. Paul makes the point six times that Adam's one sin caused the death of all people and that because of his sin ἁμαρτωλοὶ κατεστάθησαν οἱ πολλοί ('the many were constituted sinners'*) (Rom. 5:12, 15, 16, 17, 18, 19). Moreover, Paul contrasts Adam's one sin with the on-going sin of others: 'Yet death reigned from Adam to Moses, whose sinning was not like the transgression of Adam' (Rom. 5:14).

35. The following taxonomy of views is informed by Part I of this study in conjunction with Johnson, Jr., 'Romans 5:12,' 306-13.

36. Pelagius, *Pelagius's Commentary on St Paul's Epistle to the Romans*, trans. Theodore de Bruyn (Oxford: Clarendon Press, 1998), 92.

37. Albert Barnes, *Notes, Explanatory and Practical, On the Epistle of Romans* (New York: Leavitt, Lord, and Co., 1834), 127-29; C. K. Barrett, *Romans*, BNTC (Peabody: Hendrickson, 1991), 111; Emil Brunner, *The Christian Doctrine of Creation*, trans. Olive Wyon (London: 1952), 99; Rudolph Bultmann, 'New Testament and Mythology: The Mythological Element in the Message of the New Testament and the Problem of Its Re-interpretation,' in *Kerygma and Myth*, ed. Hans Werner Bartsch (New York: Harper & Row, 1961), 7; Daryl P. Domning and Monika K. Hellwig, *Original Selfishness: Original Sin and Evil in the Light of Evolution* (Aldershot: Ashgate, 2006).

2. Realism—this view was first made famous by Augustine who, based upon his mistranslation of Romans 5:12, believed that all humanity was seminally present in Adam. In some sense, then, humanity was really truly physically present. In addition to Augustine, similar views appear in John Calvin (1509–64), W. G. T. Shedd (1820–94) and James H. Thornwell (1812–62).[38] The pertinent question here is, does Adam pass sin onto his progeny by virtue of numerical or representative unity? The overall thrust of Romans 5:12-21 does not appear to be numerical unity, especially when Paul states that the many were 'constituted,' or 'appointed sinners' (κατεστάθησαν) by virtue of Adam's one sin (Rom. 5:19). There is also the fact that Paul repeatedly emphasizes the effects of Adam's one sin, but if humanity was seminally present in Adam why do they not bear the guilt of Adam's subsequent sins since they ostensibly would have been seminally present for those acts as well? Last, a realistic theory of participation muddies the waters of the Adam-Christ parallel. Paul places Adam and Christ and the effects of their respective acts in antithetical parallel: 'For as by the one man's disobedience the many were constituted sinners, so by the one man's obedience the many will be constituted righteous' (Rom. 5:19*). The means by which humanity participates in Adam's sin is the same manner in which believers participate in Christ's act of righteousness.

---

38. John Calvin, *The Epistles of Paul the Apostle to the Romans and to the Thessalonians*, CNTC (1961; Grand Rapids: Eerdmans, 1996), 112; idem, *Institutes of the Christian Religion*, trans. John Allen (Grand Rapids: Eerdmans, 1948), II.i.5-8; idem, John Calvin, *John 1-10*, CNTC (1960; Grand Rapids: Eerdmans, 1996), 66; W. G. T. Shedd, 'Original Sin,' in *Discourses and Essays* (Andover: W. F. Draper, 1856), 218-71; idem, *Dogmatic Theology*, 3 vols. (1888; Grand Rapids: Zondervan, 1969), II:168-260; James H. Thornwell, 'Nature of Our Interest in the Sin of Adam, Being a Review of Baird's Elohim Revealed,' in *Collected Writings*, vol. 1, ed. John B. Adger (Richmond: Presbyterian Committee of Publication, 1871), 515-68.

3. Mediate imputation – this view has been historically associated with Josua Placaeus (1596–1655).[39] Placaeus believed that humanity was guilty because they sinned; they did not sin because they were guilty. Is humanity's guilt antecedent or consequent? Do people sin because they are guilty, or are they guilty because they sin?[40] The main thrust of his argument is that humanity does not inherit Adam's guilt but a corrupt nature, and this corrupt nature leads them to sin. The so-called imputation occurs, therefore, through the means of an inherited corrupt nature. A noted advocate of this view is Henry Boynton Smith (1815–77).[41] Once again, this view does not pay close attention to the details of the text. Paul states that death spread to all men because all sinned (ἥμαρτον). The Greek term ἁμαρτάνω does not mean *to be* or *become corrupt* (cf. e.g., Matt. 18:15; 1 Cor. 15:34; Titus 3:11; John 5:14). The theory also rides roughshod over the Adam-Christ parallel (Rom. 5:19). Moreover, if the main concern was that guilt follow sin rather than precede it, the proposed solution of receiving a corrupt nature rather than the guilt of sin does not alleviate the perceived problem. To receive a corrupt nature presupposes some sort of guilt. In the end, though Placaeus called his view *mediate imputation*, in truth, he does away with the doctrine of imputation.[42]

4. Immediate imputation – this view appears in, among others, Francis Turretin (1623–87), the Westminster Confession of Faith (1647), the Savoy Declaration (1658), Second London

---

39. Josua Placaeus, *De Imputatione Primi Peccati Adami Josue Placaei in Academia Salmuriensi S. s. Theologiae Professoris Disputatio* (Saumur: Ioannem Lesnerium, 1661).

40. Hodge, *Romans*, 161, 164.

41. Henry Boynton Smith, *System of Christian Theology*, 2nd ed. (New York: A. C. Armstrong & Son, 1884), 306-17.

42. Turretin, *Institutes of Elenctic Theology* (Phillipsburg: P & R, 1992-97), IX.ix.5-6; cf. also Francis Turretin and Johannes Heidegger, *Formula Consensus Helvetica*, X-XII, in A. A. Hodge, *Outlines of Theology* (1860; Edinburgh: Banner of Truth, 1991), Appendix II (pp. 658-59).

Confession (1689), and Charles Hodge (1797–1878).[43] Advocates of this view maintain that God immediately (apart from any physical or real means) imputes both Adam's guilt and Christ's righteousness to those whom they represent. This view, in my judgment, best accounts for the exegetical data of Romans 5:12 and its immediate context.

Immediate imputation best explains a number of features in the text—there are five chief reasons.[44] First, Paul presents Adam and Christ as the respective representatives for humanity. Adam's dominion mandate (Gen 1:28) was not his alone but belonged to the human race. Hence, just as Christ's one act of obedience is representative and comprises the judicial ground for the justification of the elect, so Adam's one act of disobedience constitutes the judicial ground for the condemnation for those who are united to him.[45] Second, Paul implicitly relies upon the doctrine of immediate imputation when he describes humanity's legal state, a condition in which all people are born spiritually dead and under a curse—they are 'by nature children of wrath' (Eph. 2:3). Third, the concept of the one representing the many is not new or foreign to the Scriptures, as was evident in the previous chapter—Achan's sin, David's sinful census, Daniel's vision of the Son of Man, Leviticus 16 and the Day of Atonement, and Isaiah's suffering servant all feature the concept of immediate imputation. One acts and the many bear the positive or negative consequences. Fourth, immediate imputation better accounts for the Adam-Christ parallels. Paul repeatedly states that the respective actions of *one* impact the many, either for life or death. Most pointedly, *all* die because *one* sinned. Fifth, immediate imputation best explains why Adam's progeny only bear the guilt and consequences of his first and not his subsequent sins.

43. Turretin, *Institutes*, IX.ix.11, 16; WCF VI.i; Savoy Declaration VI.i; Second London Confession, VI.iii; Charles Hodge, *Systematic Theology*, 3 vols. (rep.; Grand Rapids: Eerdmans, 1993), II:196-203.

44. For what follows, see Johnson, Jr., 'Romans 5:12,' 312-13.

45. Hodge, *Romans*, 170.

Immediate imputation, therefore, best explains Romans 5:12-21, though there are several other elements in this passage that merit examination, namely, the historicity of Adam, the Old Testament background, and the implicit covenantal context. One of the more important points in Romans 5:12-21 is that Paul compares two historical people, Adam and Christ, and two historical actions. Despite the efforts of some exegetes and theologians to categorize Adam as a mythic icon that explains the human fallen condition, such efforts must ignore the plain meaning of the text.[46] When Paul identifies Adam as a 'type [τύπος] of the one to come' (Rom. 5:14), he has in mind a comparison between historical, not mythical, realities. Such is the nature of biblical typology—it places Old Testament historical events, places, and people in an analogous relationship to New Testament historical events, places, and people.[47] To argue that Adam is a mythic figure or did not truly exist means Paul's argument ultimately crumbles.[48] How can God impute the non-existent mythical act of one non-historical mythical figure to the rest of humanity? If Adam did not exist, then there is no act of disobedience to impute, which means either there is no corporate solidarity with him and hence no corporate guilt, or that God created human beings defective with a predisposition towards sin. Such a conclusion not only strikes at the goodness of the creation but at the very heart of the doctrine of God. How can a holy and upright God create humanity with a proclivity towards sin and then hold them accountable if they were unable to act otherwise?

Another important feature is the Old Testament background to Paul's argument. As already noted, the concept of immediate imputation is not foreign to the Scriptures—it appears throughout

---

46. E.g., Peter Enns, *The Evolution of Adam: What the Bible Does and Doesn't Say about Human Origins* (Grand Rapids: Brazos, 2012), 79-87.

47. Leonhard Goppelt, *Typos: The Typological Interpretation of the Old Testament* (Grand Rapids: Eerdmans, 1982), 17-20; Richard M. Davidson, *Typology in Scripture: A Study of Hermeneutical τύπος Structures* (Berrien Springs, MI: Andrews University Press, 1981), 313-16.

48. D. A. Carson, 'Adam in the Epistles of Paul,' in *In the Beginning*, ed. Nigel M. de Cameron (Glasgow: Biblical Creation Society, 1980), 28-44.

the Old Testament. Beyond the broader connections to the Old Testament, there are a number of elements within Romans 5:12-21 that connect this passage to Isaiah 53. Through one (ἑνὸς) man, Adam, sin entered the world and 'death spread to all men because all sinned' (Rom. 5:12). Paul labels those affected by Adam's sin as τοὺς πολλοὺς ('the many'). Conversely, echoing Isaianic themes, Paul explains: 'For the judgment following one trespass brought condemnation, but the free gift following many trespasses brought justification' (Rom. 5:16). In contrast to Adam's disobedience, Christ, the last Adam, offers His representative righteousness, or obedience, which brings justification. Paul oscillates back and forth between the actions of one and the effect upon the many, whether unto condemnation or justification. The fact that Paul mentions that the οἱ πολλοί 'will be constituted righteous' (δίκαιοι κατασταθήσονται οἱ πολλοί, Rom. 5:19*) likely arises directly from Isaiah 53:11b (LXX).[49]

The last key observation is the implicit covenantal context for Paul's argument. Paul never invokes the term, but the concept of the one and the many as well as his allusion to Isaiah 53 grow out of the rich covenantal soil of the Old Testament. The covenant binds the one and the many together, and in other places in his epistles Paul references the concept (Rom. 9:4; 11:27; 1 Cor. 11:25; 2 Cor. 3:6, 14; Gal. 3:17; 4:24; Eph. 2:12). Moreover, Paul understood that Christ's intercessory work was connected to the fulfillment of Jeremiah's prophesied new covenant given that Christ identified His shed blood as that which ratified the new covenant (cf. Jer. 31:31-34; Matt. 26:28; Mark 14:24; Luke 22:20; 1 Cor. 11:25; cf. Heb. 9:15).

49. Hofius, 'Fourth Servant Song,' 182; cf. Brian Vickers, *Jesus' Blood and Righteousness: Paul's Theology of Imputation* (Wheaton: Crossway, 2006), 122; Moo, *Romans*, 345-46; Albrecht Oepke, καθίστημι, in *Theological Dictionary of the New Testament*, vol. 3, ed. Gerhard Kittel (Grand Rapids: Eerdmans, 1965), 445; Charles Hodge, *Romans* (1835; Edinburgh: Banner of Truth, 1989), 173-74; Ben C. Dunson, *Individual and Community in Paul's Letter to the Romans* (Tübingen: Mohr Siebeck, 2012), 148-54; Sang-Won (Aaron) Son, *Corporate Elements in Pauline Anthropology: A Study of Selected Terms, Idioms, and Concepts in the Light of Paul's Usage and Background* (Rome: Pontifico Instituto Biblico, 2001), 61, 77.

All of these different elements, therefore, confirm that Paul's doctrine of imputation was informed by the Old Testament. Imputation was no novelty but rather went back into the earliest days of Israel's existence. Given the Adam-Christ parallel, it also stands to reason that Adam and humanity exist in covenantal relationship.[50] More will be said about this in Part III, the dogmatic formulation of the doctrine of imputation.

2 Corinthians 5:17-21

A third and final text for consideration is 2 Corinthians 5:21, which has Paul's famous statement: 'For our sake he made him to be sin who knew no sin, that in him we might become the righteousness of God.'[51] One of the most recent challenges to citing this text in support of the doctrine of imputation comes from N. T. Wright.[52] Wright contends that Paul's statement should not be treated as an isolated bit of soteriology that purports to disclose the imputation of sin to Christ and the imputation of Christ's righteousness to sinners. Instead, Paul's statement comes within the context of a defense of his ministry, and that Paul does not have in view soteriology but God's covenant faithfulness, His righteousness. Wright argues that, when Paul says that Christ became sin so that 'we might become the righteousness of God,' it should be understood that he and the other apostles have become a manifestation of God's covenantal faithfulness, which they carry out in their apostolic ministry. Another recent challenge to employing this verse in the service of imputation comes from Michael Bird, who claims that if forensic realities are in view, such as imputation, then Paul's word-choice is odd, since he states that in Christ 'we become' (γενώμεθα) the righteousness of God.[53] This, in Bird's assessment, is not legal-forensic nomenclature (e.g.,

---

50. Hodge, *Romans*, 156; Robert Haldane, *Romans* (1874; Edinburgh: Banner of Truth, 1996), 213, 232-33.

51. The following section is drawn from Fesko, *Covenant of Redemption*, 287-95.

52. Wright, 'On Becoming the Righteousness of God,' 68-76; idem, *Paul and the Faithfulness of God*, 2 vols. (Minneapolis: Fortress, 2013), 881-85.

53. Bird, 'Progressive Reformed View,' 149.

λογίζομαι).[54] Rather than treating the subject of imputation, Bird believes the statement addresses the fact that believers 'experience the status of "righteousness."'[55] In dogmatic terms, the contested verse is not about imputation but a broader statement about soteriology. Once again, the Old Testament background to this text is vital to determining Paul's meaning. As with the aforementioned Pauline passages, this text also has the literary complex of Isaiah 40-66 as its subtext.[56] That Paul operates within the orbit of Isaiah 40-66 is evident from 2 Corinthians 5:17*, with his invocation of the concept of new creation: 'Therefore, if anyone is in Christ, he is new creation. The old has passed away; behold, the new has come.' Paul not only talks of the new creation, but he uses a phrase evocative of two different passages in Isaiah, evident by the following terminological parallels (indicated by bold print):[57]

Isaiah 43:18-19	
μὴ μνημονεύετε τὰ πρῶτα καὶ **τὰ ἀρχαῖα** μὴ συλλογίζεσθε. **ἰδοὺ** ποιῶ **καινὰ** ('Remember not the former things, and do not consider the ancient things. Behold, I do new things'*)	**2 Corinthians 5:17** εἴ τις ἐν Χριστῷ, **καινὴ** κτίσις· τὰ **ἀρχαῖα** παρῆλθεν, **ἰδοὺ** γέγονεν **καινά**
Isaiah 65:17 ἔσται γὰρ ὁ οὐρανὸς **καινὸς** καὶ ἡ γῆ **καινή**, καὶ οὐ μὴ μνησθῶσιν τῶν προτέρων ('For there will be a new heaven and a new earth, and they will not remember the former'*)	('If anyone is in Christ, he is new creation. The old has passed away, behold, the new has come')

54. Cf. Harris, *Second Corinthians*, 451, 454-55.

55. Bird, 'Progressive Reformed View,' 149.

56. Mark Gignilliat, *Paul and Isaiah's Servants: Paul's Theological Reading of Isaiah 40-66 in 2 Corinthians 5:14-6:10* (London: T & T Clark, 2007), 45-50, 57.

57. G. K. Beale, 'The Old Testament Background of Reconciliation in 2 Corinthians 5-7 and Its Bearing on the Literary problem of 2 Corinthians 6:14-7:1,' in *The Right Doctrine from the Wrong Texts: Essays on the Use of the Old Testament in the New*, ed. G. K. Beale (Grand Rapids: Baker, 1994), 219-20.

Paul echoes the Isaianic ideas of new creation contrasted with the old, evident in the repetition of the terms τὰ ἀρχαῖα ('the old') and καινὰ ('new') and even does so with the same emphatic ἰδοὺ ('behold') as Isaiah. Yet, how does this statement fit within Paul's overall argument? Wright is correct to claim that the chief function of 2 Corinthians is Paul's apology for his ministry.[58] But contra Wright, Paul does not merely state that God's covenant faithfulness is manifest in Paul's ministry (note Wright's much controverted definition of δικαιοσύνη θεοῦ).[59] There is another covenantal concept to describe God's fidelity, namely His *hesed*. God keeps His covenant promises, and in this vein He is covenantally faithful (e.g., Deut. 7:9; cf. 1 Cor. 1:9, 10:13; 2 Cor. 1:18-20).

As much as God's covenant faithfulness undergirds Paul's ministry, this is not the specific subject under consideration. Rather, Paul invokes the concept of God's righteousness. In this particular case, Paul urges the Corinthians to be reconciled to him, and not to evaluate his ministry κατὰ σάρκα ('according to the flesh') (2 Cor. 5:16), that is, the standards of this present evil age. They must instead evaluate Paul and the other apostles according to the standards of the new creation—'the old has passed away; behold the new has come' (2 Cor. 5:17). If they understand this tectonic shift in redemptive history, the in-breaking of the eschaton and new creation, then they will evaluate Paul's ministry in the proper light.[60] Paul appeals and alludes to the literary complex of Isaiah 40-66 not only to announce that the new creation has burst onto the scene of history with the ministry of Christ, but also because the

---

58. Wright, 'On Becoming the Righteousness of God,' 72.

59. For a critique of Wright's definition of God's righteousness as covenant faithfulness, see C. Lee Irons, 'Dikaiosyne Theou: A Lexical Examination of the Covenant-Faithfulness Interpretation' (Ph.D. Diss., Fuller Theological Seminary, 2011). One thing to note is that the LXX employs the term δικαιοσύνη to translate the Hebrew term *hesed* (חסד) in nine different places, which some might believe mitigates my argument. On these nine texts, see Irons, *Dikaiosyne Theou*, 208-23.

60. Beale, 'Background of 2 Corinthians 5-7,' 219; Scott J. Hafemann, *2 Corinthians*, NIVAC (Grand Rapids: Zondervan, 2000), 243.

Isaianic text originally dealt with the reconciliation and restoration of Israel.[61] Paul desires that the Corinthians would be reconciled to him. Reconciliation in the church is not simply a matter of conflict resolution but is based upon the reconciliation wrought by God in Christ. Hence Paul appeals to this Isaianic passage that deals with reconciliation.

How precisely did God accomplish this reconciliation? He accomplished it through the obedience and intercession of His servant. His servant ushered in the new creation by breaking the grip of sin and death through His vicarious representative obedience and suffering. Hence Paul states: 'For our sake he made him to be sin who knew no sin, so that in him we might become the righteousness of God' (2 Cor. 5:21). Paul appealed to the Corinthians to embrace this reconciliation, which meant embracing Paul and his ministry because he was God's ambassador—to reject Paul and his message was to reject God's reconciliation (2 Cor. 5:20).[62] In this instance, Paul's description of the exchange, Christ becoming sin and those who are united to Him becoming righteousness, reflects the categories that lie at the heart of Isaiah 53—the one and the many and the vicarious and representative work of the servant. Isaiah 53 stands in the background not only because of these elements but also because of Paul's phrase, 'he made him to be sin' (ἁμαρτίαν ἐποίησεν) which echoes Isaiah 53:9*, 'although he had committed no sin [ἀνομίαν οὐκ ἐποίησεν]' (LXX).[63]

Due to the absence of legal-forensic language in 2 Corinthians 5:20-21 question undoubtedly arises whether Paul had in mind representative obedience and suffering, let alone the doctrine of imputation. As noted above, Bird objects to appealing to this text as a basis for the doctrine of imputation because Paul uses the verb γίνομαι, 'so that we might *become* the righteousness of God'

---

61. Beale, 'Background of 2 Corinthians 5-7,' 222; Gignilliat, *Paul and Isaiah*, 54, 60.

62. Beale, 'Background of 2 Corinthians 5-7,' 223-25.

63. Victor Paul Furnish, *II Corinthians*, AB, vol. 32a (New York: Doubleday, 1984), 340; Hafeman, *2 Corinthians*, 247.

(2 Cor. 5:21; emphasis).[64] Hence, Paul has something other than forensic categories in mind. But as others have observed, Paul's allusion to Isaiah 53 is general and free, and at verse 21 he adheres neither to the language of the MT or LXX.[65] The general nature of Paul's statement applies in the terminology he uses to discuss not only Isaiah's justification of the many ('so that in him we might become the righteousness of God'), but also the manner by which Christ bore the sins of the many ('he made him to be sin') (cf. Rom. 8:3).[66]

Bird offers an unsatisfactory explanation: 'So Paul does not say that "God imputed our sin to the sinless one, and imputed God's righteousness to us." We can say what the text says, no more and no less: Christ was made sin probably in the sense of carrying, bearing and taking sins upon himself, and those who are in Christ share in the "righteousness of God."'[67] Ironically, Bird does not follow his own rule, namely, saying only what the text states. Paul says God *made* Christ to be sin. On the ground of Bird's objections, Paul's use of the verb ποιέω becomes equally problematic. The verb, like γίνομαι, is not strict legal nomenclature. In fact, the LXX employs the term ποιέω to translate the Hebrew ברא, to create or make. On Bird's analysis, we would have to conclude that God actually made Christ to be sin—it was not a legal imputation but an ontological transformation. Yet Bird invokes imputation categories, 'carrying, bearing and taking sins,' (terms used in Leviticus 16 and Isaiah 53 associated with imputation) which are not reflected by the word ποιέω. But as others have noted, exegesis does not merely involve

---

64. Bird, 'Progressive Reformed View,' 149.
65. John Hoad, 'Some New Testament References to Isaiah 53,' *ExpT* 67 (1957): 254-55.
66. Murray Harris suggests the possibility that when Paul invokes the term *sin* (ἁμαρτία), that he does not intend the category, but the LXX rendering of sin- and guilt-offering, hence Paul has Isaiah's חטאת in view (Murray J. Harris, *The Second Epistle to the Corinthians*, NIGTC [Grand Rapids: Eerdmans, 2005], 452).
67. Bird, 'Progressive Reformed View,' 149.

repeating the language of the biblical text but interpreting what it means.[68]

How to interpret Paul's statement, consequently, should not be decided merely by a lexical appeal and definition of individual words or one lone statement. Rather, how does Paul's statement in 2 Corinthians 5:21 fit within the broader context of his argument, and how does it sit within the bigger canonical context? In this case, the immediate surrounding context presents strong evidence to suggest that Isaiah 40-66 is the subtext of Paul's argument, and that he focuses on Isaiah 53 in 2 Corinthians 5:21. We can safely conclude these connections not only because of the similarities between the two passages mentioned above (Christ's impeccability, the one and the many) but also because of the exchange of sin and righteousness, key subjects in the fourth servant song. Regarding the issue of Paul's terminology (ποιέω and γίνομαι), the answer appears in the nature of his appeal to Isaiah 53.[69] Paul clearly does not quote Isaiah 53; he alludes to it. An allusion is when an author offers a brief expression and is consciously dependent upon an Old Testament passage without reproducing its exact wording of the text. The text need only present parallel wording, syntax, or concepts to qualify as an allusion.[70] In this instance, therefore, Paul's terminology is inconsequential against the broader Isaianic backdrop. He alludes to the fourth servant song and the reader should understand that they receive Christ's righteousness in the same manner as Christ receives their sin, namely, through imputation.[71]

There is one further possible objection to consider: Paul specifically states that we become the δικαιοσύνη θεοῦ ('righteousness of God'), thus how can we speak of *Christ's* imputed righteousness if Paul states that it is *God's*?[72] Two simple points

68. Dunson, 'Imputation as Word and Doctrine,' 256.

69. Oepke, καθίστημι, 445

70. G. K. Beale, *Handbook on the New Testament Use of the Old Testament: Exegesis and Interpretation* (Grand Rapids: Baker, 2012), 31.

71. Gignilliat, *Paul and Isaiah*, 104-05; Harris, *Second Corinthians*, 455.

72. Bird, 'Progressive Reformed View,' 149; also, Gundry, 'Nonimputation of Christ's Righteousness,' 41-42.

sufficiently answer this query. First, within the Isaianic subtext, the suffering figure is Yahweh's chosen servant (Isa. 43:10; 44:1-2; 44:21; 45:4; 49:3, 6). This point especially comes to the forefront at the beginning of the fourth servant song: 'Behold, my servant shall act wisely' (Isa. 52:13).[73] Second, Paul states that we become the righteousness of God ἐν αὐτῷ ('in him'), in Christ, the servant. Paul repeats this: 'God, who through Christ reconciled us to himself …' and, 'In Christ God was reconciling the world to himself …' (2 Cor. 5:18-19). God's righteousness does not come immediately to sinners apart from Christ. In this sense, sinners receive the imputed righteousness of Christ, which ultimately comes from God because God was in Christ reconciling the world to Himself.

What, however, does Paul specifically mean when he writes that ἐν αὐτῷ ('in him') we become the righteousness of God? Paul's use of the preposition with the dative has three different possible readings.[74] It could refer to realm transfer, as it does in 2 Corinthians 5:17, anyone who is 'in Christ' is part of the new creation. But Paul's use of the verb γίνομαι mitigates this possibility because Paul does not describe believers as entering into a realm of righteousness but becoming the righteousness of God. The 'in him' could be instead instrumental, which means that Paul intends to convey the idea that God accomplishes redemption by the agency of Christ. This idea is certainly in view in verses 18-19, as Paul states that God reconciled διὰ Χριστοῦ ('through Christ').

The third and most likely reading, however, is that the 'in him' refers to union with Christ. Believers are justified by the representative obedience and vicarious suffering of Christ, benefits they enjoy through union with Christ. This is the most likely reading given the symmetry between Christ being made sin and sinners becoming the righteousness of God. This symmetry weakens the instrumental reading because if believers became righteous instrumentally through Christ, it is not clear how this

---

73. Harris, *Second Corinthians*, 455 n. 207.

74. For what follows, see Constantine R. Campbell, *Paul and Union with Christ: An Exegetical and Theological Study* (Grand Rapids: Zondervan, 2012), 185-88.

parallel would work with Christ being made sin. Christ's sharing in the condemnation of sinners means that sinners are made righteous by sharing in His right standing—this occurs through imputation. On this point, note Paul's similar use of the ἐν αὐτῷ construction: 'I have suffered the loss of all things and count them as rubbish, in order that I may gain Christ and be found in him [ἐν αὐτῷ], not having a righteousness of my own that comes from the law, but that which comes through faith in Christ, the righteousness from God that depends on faith' (Phil. 3:8-9).[75] Once again, Paul does not rest in his own law-keeping, but in the representative law-keeping of Christ, the servant of Yahweh.

CONCLUSION

The three surveyed texts, Romans 4, Romans 5:12-21, and 2 Corinthians 5:17-21, therefore, rest upon the Old Testament's understanding of the relationship between the one and the many and pulses with the doctrine of imputation. Those who are united to Christ receive His imputed righteousness and conversely Christ bears their imputed sin. This is Paul's major emphasis in Romans 4, evident by the fact that he invokes the term λογίζομαι eleven times and astonishingly explains that ungodly Abraham was declared righteous before the divine bar, not for what he had done, but because he believed in the promise. In Romans 5:12-21 Paul further elaborated by what means Abraham and anyone else who believes in Christ can be righteous before the throne of God. But Paul also explains that the road runs both ways—by Adam's one act of disobedience the many were constituted sinners and by the last Adam's one act of obedience the many were constituted righteous. But God did not merely write off the sin or forget it. Rather, in imagery drawn from Isaiah and grounded in Israel's Day of Atonement, Christ shouldered the burden of sin and paid the debt. Far from a cold and calculated balancing of the ledger, Paul characterizes this double imputation as grace and gift (Rom. 5:15).

---

75. Silva, *Philippians*, 159-63; cf. O'Brien, *Philippians*, 391-400.

PART II SUMMARY

The survey of key Old and New Testament texts provides answers to questions generated by the historical survey of the origins, development, and reception of the doctrine of imputation:

1. What is the nature of the connection between Adam and his offspring? Moral? Legal? Physical? Exemplary?

In one sense, the exegetical data reveals that Scripture presents all of these connections. All people are in natural union with Adam, to borrow the language of classic Reformed theology. Similarly, Scripture upholds Adam as a negative moral example—believers should not follow his path of apostasy. But the question deals with the specific manner by which God holds all humanity accountable for Adam's one sin. The survey of Romans 5 reveals that God does not base humanity's unity upon biological, moral, physical, or exemplary but a federal-legal connection. One man sinned therefore all sinned. The one man's act of disobedience constituted many sinners—they were appointed to this status.

2. Are sin and guilt purely ontological and therefore require a physical means of transmission?

Paul does not posit a physical means of transmission in his Adam-Christ parallel. Against the backdrop of the Old Testament, there is no physical connection between Achan and Israel or David and Israel, for example, when God holds the nation accountable for their individual actions. The bond is legal, or more specifically, covenantal. The covenant binds the individual and the corporate body.

3. Is original sin merely the absence of righteousness or the active presence of sin?

Paul does not characterize original sin, or in exegetical terms the effects of Adam's first sin, merely as a privation of righteousness as medieval theologians believed. Rather, the Day of Atonement conveys the idea that sin is not merely the absence of righteousness but a real negative presence that the sacrificial goat must bear or carry. Likewise, Isaiah presents the same picture in the Messiah's work when He carried the grief, sorrows, and the iniquity of the elect (Isa. 53:6). God does not merely impute a privation of righteousness to Christ but rather the legal responsibility for the transgressions of God's law, which originate from a heart twisted by the active presence of sin.

4. Does Adam bear the Platonic ideal human nature?

According to Anselm and Aquinas, individuals are members of human nature, a view that Calvin also shares and weds to his concept of the divine ordination of humanity's culpability. Adam corrupts the ideal nature that all human beings share, and thus all human beings receive Adam's guilt. Adam corrupts the form and thus all subsequent people bear the imprint of his defect. Divorced from the Platonic concept of ideal forms, there is a certain truth to these observations. Like produces like, sinful Adam produces sinful offspring. But Paul does not characterize Adam's sin in terms of the corruption of an ideal nature but in federal or representative terms. Part III reflects upon this question in greater detail.

5. Is imputed righteousness a novelty as the Council of Trent alleged?

No. The Old Testament and Paul's Adam-Christ parallels prove the validity of imputed guilt and righteousness.

6. Is a twofold covenantal structure warranted? Was God in covenant with Adam?

Initial evidence points in this direction on two counts: (a) God deals with His people on the basis of covenant. God held Israel accountable for Achan's and David's sins because of their shared covenantal bond. (b) The Adam-Christ parallel supports the idea of a twofold covenantal structure. There is no doubt about Christ's covenantal representative role as the surety of the new covenant. It stands to reason that Adam has a similar covenantal representative role. Part III presents more evidence to validate historic Reformed claims regarding the covenants of works and grace.

7. Should ontological or forensic categories take precedent in the question of determining the means by which God accounts people guilty or righteous?

Initial evidence points in the direction of granting priority to forensic categories. God does not communicate Adam's sin ontologically but federally; the same is true of Christ's imputed righteousness. Part III elaborates upon the priority of legal-forensic categories to ontological ones.

8. Do believers receive Christ's essential righteousness through union with Him?

The exegetical evidence does not support the notion that believers receive Christ's essential righteousness. When Paul, for example, explains the legal basis for constituting the many as righteous, he does not appeal to Christ's essential righteousness but to His 'one act of righteousness' (Rom. 5:18) or His 'one act of obedience' (Rom. 5:19). Imputed righteousness rests upon the historical blood, sweat, and tears of the God-man—His act of obedience—not Christ's essential righteousness.

9. Does God impute both the active and passive righteousness of Christ to the believer?

The exegetical evidence supports the historic Reformed claim that believers receive the imputed active and passive obedience of Christ. Paul does not distinguish or separate, for example, Christ's active and passive righteousness. Those who say believers only receive the passive obedience of Christ rend Christ's seamless garment of His perfect obedience asunder. To *distinguish* (not separate) Christ's active and passive obedience merely acknowledges that His unified law-keeping has two sides—fulfilling the law and paying the penalty for its violation. The surveyed Old Testament texts showcase the active and passive obedience quite clearly. While most focus their attention upon the typified passive obedience of Christ with the goat's role on the Day of Atonement, we must not forget that all the protocols of that special day typify the person and work of Christ. Both the goat and the high priest's scrupulous obedience to the legal instructions for conducting the sacrifice typify Christ. Similarly, when the prophet Zechariah sees the vision of Joshua's justification, God does not merely purify his soiled garments, or remove them. He removes the fouled priestly robe and replaces it with a completely new vestment. Ancient Jewish Targums of Zechariah interpret this given garment as one comprised of righteous deeds, or perfect law-keeping. There is sufficient warrant, therefore, to affirm the necessity of Christ's imputed active and passive obedience. Part III elaborates upon the necessity of Christ's inseparable twofold obedience and the priority of the active to the passive.

10. Is mediate imputation truly a form of imputation?

No. Mediate imputation relies upon an ontological basis for the transmission of guilt. Again, Achan's and David's imputed sins required no means of communication—the legal bonds of Israel's covenant were sufficient to communicate immediately the consequences of their sins to the nation. Paul employs the same covenantal-representative relationship in his Adam-Christ parallel. Moreover, if ontology was the basis of shared guilt, then we must ask why God does not hold humanity accountable for all of Adam's sins. Paul clearly states, 'Just as sin came into the world through one man, and death through sin, and so death spread to all men because all sinned.' God constitutes the many as sinners (Rom 5:19) prior to their existence and prior to any guilt or corruption they might receive through biological means.

11. Should we distinguish between guilt (*culpa*) and penalty (*reatus poenae*)? In other words, Does God merely impute the penalty for Adam's sin or also the guilt?

While we may distinguish guilt and penalty, there does not appear to be sufficient exegetical warrant to separate them. As venerable as the Old Princetonians are, Paul does not separate guilt from penalty. All humanity shares in Adam's penalty, namely, death (Rom. 5:12). But Paul also states that God constitutes all humanity as *sinners* (Rom. 5:19). The wages of sin is death (Rom. 6:23), hence only those guilty of sin merit the penalty of death. God imputes, therefore, Adam's guilt and penalty to all humanity.

12. Must we affirm Adam's historical existence?

Yes. The Scriptures do not give the least hint that Adam is anything less than a real flesh and blood historical person. Part III will briefly reflect upon the necessity of affirming the historicity of Adam.

PART III:

DOGMATIC FORMULATION

1

THE DOCTRINE OF IMPUTATION

INTRODUCTION

The doctrine of imputation has historically rested upon the exegesis of a few key Pauline texts, whether in the hands of its critics or proponents. But as the previous chapters have argued, the doctrine of imputation appears in numerous places across the canon of Scripture. Recognizing this fact inexorably draws us into the warp and woof of the historical details of these various texts. All too often, it seems, theologians wrestle with the question of imputation from one side of the issue—they address the universality of sin or Christ's imputed righteousness. Seldom do they realize that they behold a coin that has two sides: Adam's imputed guilt and Christ's imputed righteousness. Yet Paul saw no such dichotomies—he presented both sides of the coin in the fifth chapter of Romans. Despite the protestations of some who believe Paul is not interested in how sin spread to all humanity but in how Christ delivers us from it, the apostle presents the doctrine of imputation as the explanation for the universality of sin and death and the particularity of salvation.

But Paul's explanation rests upon the two epochs of world history—the aeons of the two Adams. This means that we have to explore Adam's pre-fall estate in terms of his work and its goals, the consequences of failure, and how these things relate to the doctrine of imputation. Conversely, we must explore Christ's work and its goals, the consequences of success, and how these things relate to the doctrine of imputation. As we explore these things, we must pay careful attention to Adam's context in the Garden of Eden. All too often exegetes and theologians myopically examine Genesis 1-3 and put blinders on where the rest of the canon is concerned. Yet, Genesis 1–3 is not an island but is just the tip of a continent that provides the interpretive context and lexicon for the events that transpire in Eden. In simpler terms, we must explore Genesis 1–3 in the light of the rest of the Old Testament, especially the book of Deuteronomy, Israel's national covenantal charter. How would an Israelite steeped in the Mosaic covenant look at Adam's state in the garden? Such a contextually sensitive question provides the necessary data to understand how the doctrine of imputation functions as it relates to the respective works of Adam and Christ.

In brief, this chapter sets forth an exposition and defense of the doctrine of threefold imputation whereby God immediately imputes the guilt of Adam's sin to all people, the sins of the elect to Christ, and Christ's alien righteousness to the elect. The chapter begins with a brief statement about two key presuppositions for the doctrine of imputation: the historicity of Adam and the doctrine of the covenant. The doctrine of imputation stands or falls with Adam's real life flesh and blood existence. If there was no Adam who committed sin, then there is nothing to impute. The doctrine of the covenant is also a necessary presupposition because it provides the means by which God binds the actions of the one to the lives of many. The chapter then proceeds with examinations of how imputation relates to the respective works of Adam and Christ. The chapter explores a few objections to the doctrine of immediate imputation and then concludes with summary observations. In short, this chapter explains how we find death in Adam and life in Christ.

Necessary Presuppositions

Historicity of Adam

There are certain elements within Christian doctrine that rest upon other key pillars—move them and the doctrinal edifice comes crashing down. One such pillar for the doctrine of imputation is the historicity of Adam. In instances where people deny the historicity of Adam, they inevitably have to reconfigure entirely not merely the doctrine of imputation but also the nature of sin and the gospel. Karl Barth (1886–1968) was one of the most prominent twentieth-century theologians to deny Adam's historicity—Adam was a mythic archetypal figure that symbolically represented every person.[1] Apart from a historical adamic anchor, Barth focuses upon redemption, and in a sense renders history superfluous. What Reformed Orthodox theologians once accomplished through the doctrine of imputation, Barth carried out with his doctrine of election.[2] Barth attempts to build a doctrinal cathedral of redemption in Christ suspended in mid-air apart from a concrete historical foundation.[3] Such edifices might appear in science fiction and fantasy but ultimately have no real existence.

---

1. Karl Barth, *Church Dogmatics*, 14 vols. (Edinburgh: T & T Clark, 1936–68), IV/1:508.

2. Bruce L. McCormack, '*Justitia Aliena*: Karl Barth in Conversation with the Evangelical Doctrine of Imputed Righteousness,' in *Justification in Perspective: Historical Developments and Contemporary Challenges*, ed. Bruce L. McCormack (Grand Rapids: Baker, 2006), 190-93.

3. Cf. John Murray, *Romans*, NICNT, 2 vols. (Grand Rapids: Eerdmans, 1959, 1965), I:384-90; Cornelius Van Til, *An Introduction to Systematic Theology* (Phillipsburg: P & R, 1974), 29.

Others have followed Barth's lead. Peter Enns, for example, claims that one can embrace Paul's theological claim about the origin of sin but nevertheless reject the apostle's belief in a historical Adam.[4] Enns uses the Neo-Orthodox distinction between the infallibility and inerrancy of Scripture. Scripture is not inerrant, as it contains errors of fact, science, and history, but it is infallible, in that it accurately speaks to theological matters and infallibly accomplishes its divinely intended end. Yet, how can one claim theological accuracy built upon factual or historical error? If Luke, for example, places Adam in Christ's genealogy, then who else does Luke erroneously place in the Messiah's line that never really existed? If Adam did not truly exist, then he did not actually sin, so what accounts for the presence of sin in the world? To say as N. T. Wright does that the Bible is not concerned with how sin became a reality but rather how God will set things right ignores the express statements of Scripture.[5]

Things only devolve in other denials of Adam's existence, whether with Roman Catholics, Daryl Domning and Monika Hellwig, or Reformed theologian Daniel Harlow. All three authors reject the historicity of Adam and consequently the doctrine of original sin. Domning and Hellwig contend that humanity's problem is an inherent proclivity towards selfishness, which is a biologically inherited condition—Christ redeems 'fallen' humanity by being a moral exemplar.[6] Their denial of Adam's historicity sends a tsunami throughout the rest of their theological system—God creates the world good but fallen and Christ is not actually a vicarious mediator.[7] They advocate a Pelagian understanding of redemption. Building

---

4. Peter Enns, *The Evolution of Adam: What the Bible Does and Doesn't Say about Human Origins* (Grand Rapids: Brazos, 2012), 123, 135.

5. N. T. Wright, 'Paul's Use of Adam,' in John H. Walton, *The Lost World of Adam and Eve: Genesis 2–3 and the Human Origins Debate* (Downers Grove: InterVarsity Press, 2015), 169-80.

6. Daryl P. Domning and Monika K. Hellwig, *Original Selfishness: Original Sin and Evil in the Light of Evolution* (Aldershot: Ashgate, 2006), 158.

7. Domning and Hellwig, *Original Selfishness*, 156.

off the work of Domning and others, Harlow also jettisons the traditional doctrine of original sin and recognizes that the doctrine of the atonement must be reconfigured—he advocates a *Christus Victor* or moral influence theory of the atonement. What was once considered heresy is now commonplace and is supposedly the only remedy to keep Christianity intellectually credible and culturally relevant.[8]

Space prohibits a full-blown defense of the historicity of Adam, as others have ably done this elsewhere.[9] Suffice it to say that few who deny the historicity of Adam claim that the Bible teaches something other than Adam's real, historical, flesh and blood existence. In other words, those who deny Adam's historicity claim that the Bible erroneously reports Adam's existence. The biblical evidence is clear that, whether in the genealogies (Gen. 5:1ff; 1 Chron. 1:1; Luke 3:38; Jude 14), the prophetic interaction with the creation narratives (Hosea 6:7), or Paul's later engagement with the same (Rom. 5:12-21; 1 Cor. 15:22-28, 45; 1 Tim. 2:13), the Bible uniformly takes Adam's historical existence as an unquestioned fact. Hence, a responsible handling of the biblical text does not worry about potential cultural irrelevance or intellectual impropriety but rather represents accurately what the text states. In this case, a biblical doctrine of imputation rests upon the affirmation of a

---

8. Daniel C. Harlow, 'After Adam: Reading Genesis in an Age of Evolutionary Science,' *Perspectives on Science and Christian Faith* 62/3 (2010): 192.

9. The following works vary in the type of case they make for Adam's historicity, but readers should nevertheless consult the following: J. P. Versteeg, *Adam in the New Testament: Mere Teaching Model or First Historical Man?*, 2nd ed., trans. Richard B. Gaffin, Jr. (1977; Phillipsburg: P & R, 2012); Matthew Barrett, Ardel B. Caneday, eds., *Four Views on the Historical Adam* (Grand Rapids: Zondervan, 2013), 89-254, 267-79; C. John Collins, *Did Adam and Eve Really Exist? Who They Were and Why You Should Care* (Wheaton: Crossway, 2011); idem, 'Adam and Eve in the Old Testament,' in *Adam, the Fall, and Original Sin: Theological, Biblical, and Scientific Perspectives*, eds. Hans Madueme and Michael Reeves (Grand Rapids: Baker, 2014), 3-32; William VanDoodewaard, *The Quest for the Historical Adam: Genesis, Hermeneutics, and Human Origins* (Grand Rapids: Reformation Heritage Books, 2015); John H. Walton, *The Lost World of Adam and Eve: Genesis 2–3 and the Human Origins Debate* (Downers Grove: InterVarsity Press, 2015).

historical Adam as fixed pillar without which both the doctrine and the gospel itself disintegrate.

COVENANT

A second key presupposition is the doctrine of the covenant. Historically, the doctrine of the covenant of works has been a common staple within classic Reformed theology, though in recent years it has come under significant criticism and outright rejection.[10] Again, space prohibits a full-blown defense and explanation of the covenant of works, as others have ably done this.[11] Nevertheless, there are several important factors to keep in mind. First, there is no debate—the term *covenant* berit (בְּרִית) does not appear in the creation narrative (Gen. 1–3). But we should not commit the word-concept fallacy, namely, the term's absence means the concept's absence. Do other indicators point to the concept's presence? In this particular case numerous elements within Genesis 1–3 point to the presence of covenantal activity.

If the Mosaic covenant provides a benchmark for covenantal activity, then all signs point to the presence of covenant in Genesis 1–3: issuing the command not to eat from the tree of knowledge (cf. Gen. 2:17; Exod. 20:13-15), the presence of the sacramental trees of life and knowledge as signs of the covenant (cf. Gen. 9:13-16; 17:9-14; Exod. 31:13), the invocation of the covenant-name of

---

10. See, e.g., Barth, *Church Dogmatics*, IV/1: 55-66; John Murray, 'The Adamic Administration,' *Collected Writings*, vol. 2 (1977; Edinburgh: Banner of Truth, 1996), 47-59; G. C. Berkouwer, *Sin*, Studies in Dogmatics (Grand Rapids: Eerdmans, 1977), 207; Anthony A. Hoekema, *Created In God's Image* (Grand Rapids: Eerdmans, 1986), 119-21; Herman Hoeksema, *Reformed Dogmatics* (Grand Rapids: Reformed Free Publishing Association, 1966), 214-26.

11. For historical and exegetical arguments see, e.g., Richard A. Muller, 'The Covenant of Works and the Stability of Divine Law in Seventeenth-Century Reformed Orthodoxy: A Study in the Theology of Herman Witsius and Wilhelmus à Brakel,' *CTJ* 29 (1994): 75-101; Cornelis P. Venema, 'Recent Criticisms of the Covenant of Works in the Westminster Confession of Faith,' *MAJT* 9/3 (1993): 165-98; Bryan D. Estelle, 'The Covenant of Works in Moses and Paul,' in *Covenant, Justification, and Pastoral Ministry*, ed. R. Scott Clark (Phillipsburg: P & R, 2007), 89-132.

God, Yahweh (cf. Gen. 2:4; Exod. 3:14ff), as well as the blessing-curse formula—obedience and life vs. disobedience and death (cf. Gen. 2:9, 16-17; Deut. 27:1–28:68). To recognize that Adam and Eve were in a covenant with God is not the lone opinion of Reformed theologians but has precedent in ancient Jewish tradition: 'The Lord created human beings out of earth ... He bestowed knowledge upon them, and allotted to them the law of life. He established with them an eternal covenant, and revealed to them his decrees' (Sirach 17:1, 11-12).

Another example of Jewish claims of a covenant in Eden appears in *Genesis Rabbah*, a rabbinic commentary. The commentary argues that Adam's failure to keep God's commandment and his subsequent exile foreshadow Israel's similar failures. *Genesis Rabbah* 19.9 explains:

> It is written, 'But they are like a man [Adam], they have transgressed the covenant' (Hosea 6:7) 'They are like a man,' specifically, like the first man. [We shall now compare the story of the first man in Eden with the story of Israel in its land.] 'In the case of the first man, I brought him into the garden of Eden, I commanded him, he violated my commandment, I judged him to be sent away and driven out ... So too in the case of his descendants, I brought them into the Land of Israel, I commanded them, they violated my commandment, I judged them to be sent out and driven away.'[12]

Such post-biblical comparisons between Israel and Adam originate from the prophetic intra-canonical exegesis of the creation narrative: 'But like Adam they [Israel] transgressed the covenant' (Hosea 6:7a).[13]

---

12. *Genesis Rabbah: The Judaic Commentary to the Book of Genesis*, trans. Jacob Neusner, 3 vols. (Atlanta: Scholars Press, 1985), 19.9 (vol. I, 208-09); also Seth D. Postell, *Adam as Israel: Genesis 1–3 as the Introduction to the Torah and Tanakh* (Cambridge: James Clarke and Co., 2012), 6-7; Carlos Bovell, 'Genesis 3:21: The History of Israel in a Nutshell,' *ExpT* 115 (2004): 361-66.

13. Byron G. Curtis, 'Hosea 6:7 and Covenant-Breaking like/at Adam,' in *The Law Is Not of Faith: Essays on Works and Grace in the Mosaic Covenant*, eds. Bryan D. Estelle, J. V. Fesko, and David VanDrunen (Phillipsburg: P & R, 2009), 170-209.

Hermeneutically, one must therefore avoid reading Genesis 1–3 in isolation from the rest of the Old Testament, but especially Deuteronomy, as some have done. John Murray (1898–1975) isolates Genesis 1–3 from the rest of the Pentateuch and concludes by the absence of the term that there is no covenant.[14] Israelite readers knowledgeable of the Pentateuch, evident by the Jewish sources cited above, read the creation narrative within the context of Israel's covenantal charter, Deuteronomy, and observed many parallels between Eden, Sinai, and Gerazim and Ebal.[15] In addition to foreshadowing the last Adam, God's faithful son (Rom. 5:14), Genesis 1–3 anticipates Israel's failure to keep the Mosaic covenant and their future exile from the Promised Land. Both Adam and Israel point to Jesus, the last Adam—the only one in a post-fall world who completed Adam's failed work. Adam's failure to subdue the seditious serpent, his temptation, covenant apostasy, and subsequent exile is Israel's story in miniature.[16] Adam's apostasy and exile in Genesis 1–3 forms an inclusio with Israel's foretold apostasy and exile in Deuteronomy 32:1-43. This sets up God's work in the 'last days' where he will rectify Adam's and Israel's failures (Deut. 30:6).

The doctrine of the covenant is a key element of the doctrine of imputation because it provides the ligatures that connect the one

---

14. Murray, 'Adamic Administration,' 47-60.

15. On the inter-textual symbiotic relationship between Genesis 1–3 and Deuteronomy see, e.g., Mary Douglas, *Purity and Danger: An Analysis of the Concepts of Pollution and Taboo* (London: Routledge & Kegan Paul, 1966), 41-57, esp. 55ff; T. Stordalen, *Echoes of Eden: Genesis 2–3 and Symbolism of the Eden Garden in Biblical Hebrew Literature* (Leuven: Peeters, 2000), 33; Tryggve N. D. Mettinger, *The Eden Narrative: A Literary and Religio-Historical Study of Genesis 2–3* (Winona Lake: Eisenbrauns, 2007), xii, 49-50, 57; John Van Seters, *Prologue to History: The Yahwehist as Historian in Genesis* (Louisville: Westminster John Knox, 1992), 127-29; Norbert Lohfink, *The Christian Meaning of the Old Testament* (Milwaukee: Bruce Publishing Co., 1968), 58-62. Note, one need not adopt the text-critical stance of commentators who posit a late-date for the Genesis material in order to accept the interpretive relationship between Genesis 1–3 and the rest of the Pentateuch, especially Deuteronomy.

16. Postell, *Adam as Israel*, 3-4, 108-19, 130, 134-48.

and the many. In other words, how do you account for the actions of one person impacting the lives of the many? If you eliminate the doctrine of the covenant, there are only three other options to explain the universality of sin: social, biological, or decretal bonds. In other words, theologians have tried to account for the universality of sin and death. Why do all human beings die? Pelagius (fl. ca. 390–418), for example, argued that original sin is exemplary—the bond between Adam and his offspring is social. In the simplest terms, Pelagius affirms a monkey-see, monkey-do, doctrine of original sin. People sin because they follow the bad example of others within their social context. Yet, common sense and experience tells us that there are always holdouts and exceptions in society. How could everyone imitate the same pattern of sinful behavior with no exceptions? The wages of sin is death, right (Rom. 6:23)? And everyone dies, right? Pelagius avoided this conflict with the biblical text by asserting that humanity was created mortal—human mortality is a correlate of creation, not the fall, never mind the fact that this runs against the grain of the biblical text at several points (e.g., Gen. 2:16-17; Rom. 5:12-14; 6:23). A social-imitative bond does not adequately account for the universality of death.

Apart from the covenant, theologians have sought to account for the transmission of sin and guilt through biological means (e.g., Augustine, Shedd). With no other viable means available, sin must be passed through procreation. Yet Paul places Adam and Christ in parallel in Romans 5 and contrasts their respective roles in constituting (κατεστάθησαν) many as sinners or righteous (Rom. 5:19). Moreover, Paul specifically states that when Adam sinned, 'all sinned' (Rom. 5:12), which rules out a biological means for accounting for the universality of sin and guilt. A third option is a decretal means of accounting people sinners in Adam. In other words, God decrees that because of Adam's sin, all of his offspring are thus guilty. This is one of the chief elements in John Calvin's (1509–64) doctrine of original sin. While God does decree the guilt of all humanity based upon Adam's personal sin, at the same time to recourse to the decree takes us back into the eternal counsel of God rather than explain Adam's sin and its consequences as a historical phenomenon. In other words, what historical mechanisms account for humanity's universal guilt and subjection to death? In what way does Adam's violation of God's command bring guilt and death upon humanity? How does God bind the one (Adam) and the many (humanity)?

The biblical answer to these questions comes with the doctrine of the covenant, the means by which God binds the one and the many in numerous other places in Scripture. When Achan alone sinned, the rest of the nation suffered (Josh. 7:1-26). When David took a forbidden census, the rest of the nation suffered (2 Sam. 24; 1 Chron. 21). Conversely, when Christ suffered and lived in obedience to the law, those who are united to Him benefited (Rom. 5:12-21). Society, biology, and God's decree do bind people to one another in some sense but they do not sufficiently explain the precise relationship between the one and the many—how one person's actions can impact and affect others. As we look at the various aspects of the doctrine of imputation, whether with Adam's imputed guilt or Christ's imputed righteousness, we must take into account the doctrine of the covenant as a necessary element.

DEATH IN ADAM

The doctrine of imputation has an exegetical and historical context, which for original sin comes in the opening chapters of the Bible and pre-redemptive history. In this respect we need to understand the nature of Adam's work and goals and the consequences for failure. By setting the overall context of imputation, we will be equipped to understand the doctrine and how it functions with respect to Adam and imputed guilt.

ADAM'S WORK AND GOALS

If we are to understand Adam's work, we should begin with his identity as an image-bearer of God. God created man (male and female) in His image and they were given a task: 'And God blessed them. And God said to them, "Be fruitful and multiply and fill earth and subdue it, and have dominion over the fish of the sea and over the birds of the heavens and over every living thing that moves on the earth"' (Gen. 1:28). We should not separate humanity's identity as God's image-bearers from the command to exercise dominion over the earth. God's command functions as an organic explanation of the chief elements of what it means to be an image-bearer.[17] The chief element of bearing God's image is ruling over the creation, but humanity's rule was not for an indefinite period of time—it had a terminus, a goal. They were supposed to subdue the earth and fill it, which means at some point they were supposed to complete their labors. In theological terms, there was an eschatological goal to their labors, which means there is an eschatological goal that is inherent to humanity's identity as an image-bearer. This eschatological aspect finds its origins in God's Sabbath-rest at the conclusion of His own creation work (Gen. 2:1-4). As God works and rests, so creatures made in His image work and rest.

Important are the parallels between God's creative activity and Adam's exercise of dominion over the creation. Adam initially exercised dominion over the creation when he named all of the animals (Gen. 2:18-19). In the ancient Near Eastern context in which Genesis originated, to name something is to have authority over it. Adam's kingly activity points back to God's own authoritative naming-activity.[18] God spoke the cosmos into existence. He said, 'Let there be light,' and there was light. He called the light *day* and the darkness *night* (Gen. 1:3-4). God exercised dominion over the creation by virtue of His kingly fiats, but these were not bare utterances of raw creative power but were ultimately *covenantal* declarations. God speaks through the prophet Jeremiah and states: 'Thus says the LORD: If you can break my covenant with the day and my covenant with the night, so that day and night will not come at their appointed time, then I will reject the offspring of Jacob and David my servant and will not choose one of his offspring to rule

---

17. David VanDrunen, *Divine Covenants and Moral Order: A Biblical Theology of Natural Law* (Grand Rapids: Eerdmans, 2014), 48-50; also J. Richard Middleton, *The Liberating Image: The Imago Dei in Genesis 1* (Grand Rapids: Brazos, 2005), 50-55.

18. Graeme Auld, '*Imago Dei* in Genesis: Speaking in the Image of God,' *ExpT* 116 (2005): 259-62; VanDrunen, *Divine Covenants*, 51.

over the offspring of Abraham, Isaac, and Jacob' (Jer. 33:25-26). God announces through the prophet that His covenant fidelity to Israel and David, especially in the covenant promise to give David an heir to sit upon his throne and rule over Israel (2 Sam. 7:14ff), is as strong as His covenant with the day and the night—covenantal events that first unfolded in the opening verses of the Bible.

Other instances of the convergence of creation and covenant occur in Psalm 148:5-6, 'For he commanded [צוה] and they were created. And he established them forever and ever; he gave a decree [חק], and it shall not pass away.' The parallel between *command* and *decree* points to the fact that God's verbal creative acts parallel the covenantal administration of His laws. Similar parallels occur in Psalm 147:18-19 with a seamless transition from creation to covenant: 'He sends out his word [דברו], and melts them; he makes his wind blow and the waters flow. He declares his word to Jacob, his statues and rules [חקיו ומשפטיו] to Israel.'[19] When God issues commands, He does so as a king, as Lord of His covenantally binding word. In every command there is a tacit covenantal obligation, whether in the case of God's fiat to create light and darkness or in His commands to Adam and Eve to be fruitful and subdue the earth.[20]

CONSEQUENCES OF FAILURE

The covenantally binding nature of God's word becomes especially relevant when we examine His second command to Adam: 'And the Lord God commanded the man, saying, "You may surely eat of every tree of the garden, but of the tree of the knowledge of good and evil you shall not eat, for in the day that you eat of it you shall surely die"' (Gen. 2:16-17). Once again, an important note is that the text employs the covenantal name of God, *Yahweh Elohim*. Moreover, the curse itself is constitutive of a covenantal agreement. Note this connection between covenant and curse in Deuteronomy 29:12* (MT 11), which states:

---

19. Middleton, *Liberating Image*, 67.

20. Kevin Vanhoozer, *First Theology: God, Scripture, and Hermeneutics* (Downers Grove: InterVarsity Press, 2002), 200-01.

לעברך בברית יהוה אלהיך ובאלתו אשר יהוה אלהיך כרת עמך היום

So that you may enter the covenant of the LORD your God and into
his oath-curse which the LORD your God has made with you this day
(cf. 1 Sam. 14:24; 1 Kings 8:31; 2 Chron. 6:22).

In this one statement we find the covenant name of God, the
terms for covenant (ברית), making a covenant (כרת), and oath-
curse (אלה).[21] An Israelite would not hesitate to think that Adam
was in anything but a covenantal relationship with God given the
presence of God's covenantal name along with a threatened curse
of death for violating His command. This would especially be the
case in light of the parallels between God's command not to eat
of the tree of knowledge and the similarly worded commands of
the Decalogue, which when combined with the covenant name,
point in the direction of a covenantal relationship (Exod. 20:1-17,
esp. cf. Exod. 20:2; Gen. 2:16). Recognizing the covenant context
is not merely window-dressing—there are significant implications
for Adam's context that immediately bear upon the doctrine of
imputation. There are three things we should investigate: (1)
Adam as a representative figure, (2) the covenantal nature of
God's command, and (3) the significance of Adam's post-fall exilic
existence.

First, Genesis 1–2 presses the point that Adam is a representative figure. God creates man (male and female), gives them the
dominion mandate, but the text specifically states that God gave
the command not to eat from the tree of knowledge to the man:
'And the LORD God commanded the man ... [אלהים על האדם
ויצו יהוה]' (Gen. 2:16a). At this point in the Genesis 2 recapitulation of the Genesis 1 creation narrative, the woman has yet to be
created. This means that, as an imager-bearer, as a kingly figure,
Adam has the responsibility to communicate the covenantal law to

---

21. Anne Marie Kitz, *Cursed Are You! The Phenomenology of Cursing in Cuneiform
and Hebrew Texts* (Winona Lake: Eisenbrauns, 2014), 13, 26-27; cf. Ludwig
Koehler and Walter Baumgartner, *The Hebrew and Aramaic Lexicon of the Old
Testament*, 2 vols. (Brill: Leiden, 2001), I:51.

his fellow image-bearer upon her creation and to any subsequent offspring. Even if Adam did not communicate the threatened covenantal curse, his offspring were still liable to it. Note, for example, when Saul imposed a covenantal curse upon his army. The whole army was covenantally bound to the king's command even if not present to hear it; Jonathan did not hear his father's covenantal curse but was nevertheless bound to it. Jonathan's subsequent fracture of the covenant required his death, which caused the army to ransom him from the curse (1 Sam. 14:24, 26-28).[22]

Further evidence of Adam's representative role surfaces in subsequent intra-canonical exegesis of the creation narratives. The Genesis narrative clearly indicates that the woman sinned first before Adam, yet the prophet Hosea and Paul repeatedly lay the onus squarely upon Adam's shoulders:

- But like Adam they transgressed the covenant (Hosea 6:7a).

- Death reigned from Adam to Moses, even over those whose sinning was not like the transgression of Adam (Rom. 5:14).

- For as in Adam all die ... (1 Cor. 15:22).

- The first man was from the earth, a man of dust ... As was the man of dust, so also are those who are of the dust ... (1 Cor. 15:47-48).

Paul even recognizes that Eve, not Adam, was first deceived, but this does not detract from Adam's representative function (1 Tim. 2:13-14).

Second, God issues a command, which is like that of a ruler (or father) to a subordinate (cf. Gen. 12:20; 44:1; 2 Sam. 14:8; 1 Kings 2:43; Jer. 39:11; Esther 2:10, 20). Notable is that this command form occurs 85 times in the Pentateuch (e.g., Exod. 35:1; 38:22; 39:1; 40:21), which supports the claim that this edenic command is like God's subsequent covenantal commands in the

---

22. Kitz, *Cursed Are You*, 113-14.

Pentateuch.[23] The Old Testament often juxtaposes the term 'command' (צוה) with the phrase 'obey,' or literally, 'listen to the voice of' (בקל שמע). In fact, Adam's chief failure is that he 'listened to the voice of' his wife rather than God (Gen. 3:17).[24] Adam's obedience, therefore, was essential and foundational to carrying out his dominion labors. Failure to obey the command would constitute a breach of the covenant. Once again, any Israelite listening to or reading these statements would naturally draw these conclusions given the same architecture present in the Mosaic covenant. God tells the Israelites, 'Now therefore, if you will indeed obey my voice [בקלי ושמרתם] and keep my covenant, you shall be my treasured possession' (Exod. 19:5). In this Mosaic covenantal context, God then issued a series of Eden-like commands in the Decalogue.

The same pattern appears in the covenantal renewal ceremony at the bases of Mts. Ebal and Gerazim:

> You shall therefore obey the voice of the LORD your God, being careful to do all his commandments that I command you today, the LORD your God will set you high above all the nations of the earth. And all these blessings shall come upon you and overtake you, if you obey the voice of the LORD your God (Deut. 28:1-2).
>
> But if you will not obey the voice of the LORD your God or be careful to do all his commandments and his statutes that I command you today, then all these curses shall come upon you and overtake you (Deut. 28:15, cf. v. 45).

An Old Testament Israelite familiar with the Pentateuch would not only recognize the connections between obeying the voice of the Lord and blessing or curse, but he would also connect these outcomes to life and death: 'I call heaven and earth to witness against you today, that I have set before you life and death, blessing and curse. Therefore choose life, that you and your offspring may live' (Deut. 30:19; cf. Gen. 2:17; Gen 26:11; Exod. 19:12; 21:15-17; Lev. 20:9-16; 26:1ff).[25] The fact that Deuteronomy places blessing

---

23. Stordalen, *Echoes of Eden*, 226; Estelle, 'Covenant of Works,' 111.

24. Estelle, 'Covenant of Works,' 111-12.

25. Stordalen, *Echoes of Eden*, 447-48; Mettinger, *Eden Narrative*, 57; R. W. L.

and curse in parallel with life and death confirms that the stated penalty for violating God's Eden-command constitutes the curse of this Adamic covenant.

The stated covenantal curse is death: 'For in the day that you eat of it you shall surely die' (Gen. 2:17). Understanding the nature of the covenantal curse is vital for a robust doctrine of imputation. Many assume or argue that the threatened curse is immediate physical death but that God relented and offered a stay of execution given that Adam physically died 930 years after his fall in the garden (Gen. 5:5).[26] While physical death was undoubtedly a consequence of his covenantal apostasy, we should not too quickly assume that it exhausts the nature of the curse. In order to understand the threatened curse, we must explain it in the light of the rest of the Old Testament's understanding of death. Additionally, we must correlate the concept of death with physical location of where God formally issues the covenant and its attending sanction.

Vital to understanding the nature of the threatened death is recognizing Eden's status as the first earthly temple.[27] If Adam and Eve were blessed by being given life in the presence of God, then geography (sacred space) and movement (exile) play a key function in understanding the text's threatened sanction of death. The original Israelite audience would not have read this text in isolation from the rest of the Old Testament but with a keen awareness of the geography, architecture, and boundaries of the Promised Land.

Moberly, 'Did the Serpent Get It Right?' *JTS* 39/1 (1988): 4.

26. E.g., Hermann Gunkel, *Genesis* (Macon, GA: Mercer University Press, 1997), 10.

27. On the garden's status as the first earthly temple, see G. K. Beale, *The Temple and the Church's Mission: A Biblical Theology of the Dwelling Place of God* (Downers Grove: InterVarsity Press, 2004), 66-80; J. V. Fesko, *Last Things First: Unlocking Genesis 1–3 with the Christ of Eschatology* (Fearn: Mentor, 2007), 57-76; L. Michael Morales, *The Tabernacle Pre-Figured: Cosmic Mountain Ideology in Genesis and Exodus* (Leuven: Peeters, 2012), 51-120; cf. similar conclusions by Stordalen, *Echoes of Eden*, 307-10; Jon D. Levenson, *Sinai and Zion: An Entry Into the Jewish Bible* (San Francisco: Harper San Francisco, 1985), 128-33; Michael Fishbane, *Biblical Interpretation in Ancient Israel* (Oxford: Clarendon, 1988), 368-72.

Deuteronomy equates dwelling in God's presence in the land with life itself: 'The LORD your God ... is your life and length of days' (Deut. 30:20). In fact, the Psalmist longs to dwell, not merely in the land, but especially in the house of the Lord: 'One thing I have asked of the LORD, that I may dwell in the house of the LORD all the days of my life, to gaze upon the beauty of the LORD and to inquire in his temple' (Ps. 27:4; cf. Ps. 23:6). If the Old Testament idealizes life as dwelling in God's presence in the temple, then conversely how does it characterize death? The Old Testament answers this question in very large print with its characterization of Israel's banishment from the land and God's presence. Ezekiel portrays Israel as lying in an exilic graveyard—away from the presence of God they have no life—Israel lies in a barren valley as a pile of dry bones (Ezek. 37).[28]

Stated simply, presence is life and exile is death.[29] These connections appear a number of times in Deuteronomy. Exile is a consequence of covenantal infidelity (Deut. 4:25-28; 28:58-68). Exile is the final consequence of Israel's utter abandonment of the covenant (Deut. 29:24) and a rejection of God's commands (Deut. 28:15, 58). In fact, exile is ultimately the result of idolatry (Deut. 4:25; cf. Prov. 5:5, 20-23; 7:21-27) and the violation of the first two commandments of the Decalogue (Deut. 28:20).[30] These violations cause Israel's destruction: 'I call heaven and earth to witness against you today, that you will soon utterly perish from the land that you are going over the Jordan to possess. You will not live long in it, but will be utterly destroyed' (Deut. 4:26; cf. 28:63). In this vein Israel suffers the consequences of the *lex talionis*, an eye for an eye (Deut. 19:21). If the individual suffers death for idolatry, then corporate death is the fitting punishment for national idolatry (Deut. 4:3; 13:2-5, 6-11, 13-16; 17:2-7).[31]

28. Stephen G. Dempster, *Dominion and Dynasty: A Theology of the Hebrew Bible* (Downers Grove: InterVarsity Press, 2003), 126, 153.

29. Moberly, 'Did the Serpent Get it Right?' 18.

30. Moberly, 'Did the Serpent Get it Right?' 16-17.

31. Kenneth J. Turner, *The Death of Deaths in the Death of Israel: Deuteronomy's*

This contextual exegetical data informs us that an Israelite would not have seen Adam's 930-year life as a stay of execution or that God somehow relented. Rather, they would have seen Adam's fate in a far worse light. From within their own context they would have realized that, first and foremost, the threatened curse was exile from the garden—Adam would be cast out of paradise and forced to live east of Eden in a state of exilic death (cf. Num. 5:1-4; 12:1-15; 2 Kings 7:3-8).[32] He would be ejected from his dwelling in God's temple-presence. To be sure, Adam's death also entailed his spiritual and physical death. The noetic effects of sin disrupted all his faculties and he eventually returned to the dust.

Third, there are important corollaries in the recognition that the chief penalty for violating the covenant was exile from God's presence in the temple-garden. In previous discussions about original sin and imputed guilt, one element that I seldom, if ever, find is relating imputation to the doctrine of the Holy Spirit. The Spirit, I believe, is a crucial missing piece of the imputation puzzle. The creation narrative announces the Spirit's presence in the opening words of the Bible: 'And the Spirit of God was hovering over the face of the waters' (Gen. 1:2). But we should not think that the Spirit only participated in the opening moments of the creation. If the rest of the Bible gives us any clue, recognizing the garden as the first temple means that the Garden of Eden was also the realm of the Spirit. God's Spirit typically dwells in the various temples scattered throughout Scripture.

The Spirit was present over the desert tabernacle in the form of a cloud by day and pillar of fire by night (e.g., Exod. 13:21; Num. 9:15-16; 11:25). In the context of constructing the post-exilic temple, the prophet Haggai connects God's temple with the presence of the Spirit: 'I am with you, declares the LORD of

---

Theology of Exile (Eugene: Wipf & Stock, 2010), 225-26.

32. Cf. Moberly, 'Did the Serpent Get It Right?' 13-17; Mettinger, *Eden Narrative*, 58-59; Kitz, *Cursed Are You*, 138, 238-39; J. Pedersen, *Israel, Its Life and Culture*, vol. 1/1-2 (Oxford: Oxford University Press, 1926), 451-52.

hosts, according to the covenant that I made with you when you came out of Egypt. My Spirit remains in your midst' (Hag. 2:4-5; cf. Neh. 9:19-20; Isa. 63:11-14).[33] In Ezekiel's prophecy, God promises to place His Spirit within His people and return them to the Promised Land (Ezek. 36:27). These types give way to the antitypical reality when tongues of fire rested upon the heads of the disciples at Pentecost (Acts 2:3-4), a fact confirmed by Paul's repeated statements about the people of God comprising His final dwelling place—the eschatological Spirit-filled temple (1 Cor. 3:16; 6:19; Eph. 2:22).[34]

If the temple is the location of the Spirit's presence, then this means that the Spirit imparts life to anyone within the confines of Eden's sacred space. Several places in Scripture confirm this Spirit-life connection. In the book of Job, for example, Elihu states: 'The Spirit of God has made me, and the breath of the Almighty gives me life' (Job 33:4). This text echoes themes present in the creation narrative, both in terms of the Spirit's participation in the creation of the cosmos (Gen. 1:2) as well as God breathing life into Adam's nostrils (Gen. 2:7). Conversely, the absence of God's Spirit means death: 'If he should set his heart to it and gather to himself his Spirit and his breath, all flesh would perish together, and man would return to dust' (Job. 34:14-15*).[35] Elihu's comments present a reversal of the Spirit's participation in the creation and breathing life into Adam's nostrils. All of this means that if he disobeyed the covenantal command not to eat from the tree of knowledge, Adam would be sent into exile away from the presence of God and His

---

33. Meredith G. Kline, *Images of the Spirit* (1980; Eugene: Wipf & Stock, 1998), 15; J. Luzaraga, *Las Tradiciones de La Nube en la Biblia y en el Judaismo Primitivo* (Rome: Biblical Institute Press, 1973), 234-45.

34. G. K. Beale, 'The Descent of the Eschatological Temple in the Form of the Spirit at Pentecost: Part I,' *TynB* 56/1 (2005): 73-102; idem, 'The Descent of the Eschatological Temple in the Form of the Spirit at Pentecost: Part II,' *TynB* 56/2 (2005): 63-90.

35. Tremper Longman, III, *Job*, BCOTWP (Grand Rapids: Baker, 2012), 393-94; David J. A. Clines, *Job 21-37*, WBC, vol. 18a (Nashville: Thomas Nelson, 2006), 774.

life-giving Holy Spirit. This is why exilic death inexorably leads to physical death.

ADAM AND IMPUTATION

These three factors (Adam's status as a representative, the covenantal nature of God's command, and the significance of Adam's post-fall exilic existence) are profoundly relevant for the doctrine of imputation. All too often some theologians remove the doctrine of imputation from its exegetical and pre-redemptive historical context and discuss it purely in terms of an abstract mechanism by which God holds all people accountable for Adam's sin (e.g., Murray). As true as it is, for example, that immediate imputation accounts for Adam's imputed guilt and Christ's imputed righteousness, the contextual exegetical data give opportunity for a fuller account of the doctrine. This brings us, then, to the specific nature of how imputation functions with regard to Adam's disobedience.

When God placed Adam in the garden-temple and gave him the two commands (the dominion mandate and the prohibition about eating from the tree of knowledge), God revealed an explicit relationship between obedience and eschatological life. The creation narrative attests to the fact that God created Adam good, indeed 'very good' (Gen. 1:31), which other portions of Scripture describe as a state of righteousness (Eccles. 7:29).[36] But given the two commands, we must recognize that Adam's righteousness was untested and unconfirmed. Any Israelite reading the creation narrative and God's commands would likely connect it with similar commands in the Pentateuch, such as Leviticus 18:5, 'You shall therefore keep my statues and my rules; if a person does them, he shall live by them: I am the LORD.' The life promised here is not merely longevity in the land, although that is certainly in view (cf. Lev. 18:26, 28; 20:22; 26:3-5), but ultimately eschatological life. Simply stated, obedience to God's law yields eschatological life (cf. Gal. 3:12; Rom. 10:5).[37]

---

36. Tremper Longman, III, *The Book of Ecclesiastes*, NICOT (Grand Rapids: Eerdmans, 1998), 207.

37. Preston M. Sprinkle, *Law and Life: The Interpretation of Leviticus 18:5 in Early*

Another relevant consideration is how Deuteronomy links obedience with righteousness: 'And it will be righteousness for us, if we are careful to do all this commandment before the LORD our God, as he has commanded us' (6:25; cf. 2 Kings 23:3).[38]

God created Adam in a state of unconfirmed righteousness and he was supposed to obey God's command, which would have secured eschatological life. Adam would have confirmed his righteous status and thereby earned the ability to dwell eternally in the presence of his covenant Lord. He would have secured this indefectible blessing for both himself and his offspring. God would have credited Adam's obedience to those whom he represented. Important to note is the priority that the Scriptures assign to Adam's active obedience. In other words, prior to the entrance of sin into the world, which necessitated humanity's redemption and suffering the penalty for violating God's law, the eschatological goal of the creation stood before Adam. In simpler terms, eschatology precedes soteriology. Eschatology is the exponent of protology (creation) not soteriology (redemption).[39] This means that Adam was supposed to confirm his righteous status and consequently usher in the eschaton—he would have effected the eschatological outpouring of the Spirit. God would have justified Adam—declared him righteous on the basis of his obedience, which would have unleashed the power of the age to come, the Holy Spirit. Adam's obedience would have guaranteed eschatological life for all of Adam's offspring whom he represented.

Judaism and in Paul (Tübingen: Mohr Siebeck, 2008), 31-33, 177-78; Bryan Estelle, 'Leviticus 18:5 and Deuteronomy 30:1-14 in Biblical Theological Development: Entitlement to Heaven Foreclosed and Proffered,' in *The Law Is Not of Faith: Essays on Works and Grace in the Mosaic Covenant*, ed. Bryan Estelle, J. V. Fesko, and David VanDrunen (Phillipsburg: P & R, 2009), 109-46.

38. Georg Braulik, 'The Development of the Doctrine of Justification in the Redactional Strata of the Book of Deuteronomy,' in *The Theology of Deuteronomy: The Collected Essays of Georg Braulik, O. S. B.*, trans. Ulrika Linblad (North Richland Hills, TX: Bibal Press, 1994), 151-64.

39. Geerhardus Vos, *The Pauline Eschatology* (1930; Phillipsburg: P & R, 1996), 325n. 1.

Rather than obey God's commands, Adam committed covenantal apostasy. He violated the prohibition and ate from the tree of knowledge, which implicitly entailed the abandonment of his divine vocation, the dominion mandate and his kingly role. Although Samuel's words were directed to Saul, they also accurately describe the consequences of Adam's covenantal apostasy: 'Because you have rejected the word of the LORD, he has also rejected you from being king' (1 Sam. 15:22–23). Adam's disobedience cost him his kingly office and also brought upon him the promised covenantal curse, death. But the precise nature of how this curse functions and affects Adam and his offspring hinges upon its covenantal, judicial, and geographic contexts.

Adam violated God's covenantal law, and as the representative for his offspring, this meant that his action was the action of all of his offspring. The covenant binds the actions of the one to the lives of the many. The apostle Paul makes this point explicitly: 'By the one man's disobedience the many were constituted sinners' (Rom. 5:19a). As Charles Hodge (1797–1878) and others rightly point out, immediate imputation best explains Paul's statement. Paul mentions nothing of biological descent or sociological imitation. People are sinners because they are guilty of Adam's sin; they are not guilty because they are sinners (contra mediate imputation). In a post-fall world, people are guilty because they are sinners, but in this case their guilt arises from their actual sins, which are distinct from Adamic imputed guilt. The means by which God conveys Adam's guilt to his offspring is purely forensic. Those who are federally, or covenantally, united to Adam receive his guilt by virtue of God's judicial declaration, both in terms of the threatened sanction, 'In the day you eat of it you shall surely die' (Gen. 2:16b), and also in terms of the judicial curses God pronounces upon Adam and woman.

Immediately on the heels of Adam's sin the narrative records Yahweh's arrival in the garden-temple. Most English translations render God's arrival in the following manner: 'And they heard the sound of the LORD God walking in the garden in the cool of the day' (Gen. 3:8; cf. Deut. 4:12). A better translation of this phrase reveals a slightly different picture: 'And they heard the sound of the Lord God walking in the garden in the Spirit of the day.' The language of the 'Spirit of the day,' refers not to the cool breezes that undoubtedly marked the garden-temple of Eden but rather the Spirit of judgment that attends the divine throne—God the Spirit came to justify or condemn His covenant servant (cf. Judg. 3:10; Isa. 28:5-6; 42:1; Zeph. 1:14; Num. 12:1-15, esp. 4-5).[40] God would either justify Adam in the Spirit or condemn him. When God called 'the man,' not Eve, it was a summons to appear before the throne of judgment (Gen. 3:9). The man's physical and verbal fig leaves proved woefully insufficient to cover his covenant apostasy and God therefore issued His forensic declaration of condemnation—He enacted the covenant sanctions. God not only cursed the serpent and the woman for their roles in Adam's apostasy, but He cursed the creation thus making man's existence one of a continual state of turmoil. God introduced vanity into the creation as an aspect of the covenantal curse (cf. Eccles. 1:2ff LXX; Rom. 8:20).[41] Old Testament readers would undoubtedly associate this curse with their own covenant sanctions for covenant apostasy. The animals would no longer live in submissive fear to man's rule but would instead rule over man (cf. Lev. 26:6, 22; Deut. 28:26; 32:24).

But key in God's declarative judgment is the curse that He pronounced over Adam as a consequence of his rebellion. God cursed Adam's labors, 'by the sweat of your face you shall eat bread,' and He also declared Adam's death: 'Till you return to the ground, for out of it you were taken; for you are dust, and to dust you shall return' (Gen. 3:19). Death does not come about simply by virtue of Adam's disobedience, as it if it were an inanimate natural mechanism that triggered Adam's mortality. The tree of knowledge, for example, did not have poisonous properties that spread a viral contagion to all humanity. The tree of knowledge was

40. Kline, *Images of the Spirit*, 97-106; Jeffrey Niehaus, 'In the Wind of the Storm: Another Look at Genesis 3:8,' *VT* 44/2 (1994): 263-67; VanDrunen, *Divine Covenants*, 54; cf. Christopher L. K. Grundke, 'A Tempest in a Teapot? Genesis III 8 Again,' *VT* 51/4 (2001): 548-51.

41. Kitz, *Cursed Are You*, 202.

a visual representation, even a sacrament, of God's law.[42] Adam's violation of God's law merited the covenantal sanction of death, which comes about by God's verbal curse. Apart from God's curse Adam would not suffer death.

But equally important as the verbal nature of the covenantal curse is the geographic context in which all of these events transpired. Adam's apostasy occurred within the sacred space of the garden-temple, the dwelling of the life-giving Spirit of God. When Adam violated the covenant, he in effect abandoned the life-giving power of the Spirit who would have assisted him in obeying the divine commands. As the first prophet, priest, and king, Adam possessed the anointing of the Spirit. But when God enacted the covenant curse upon Adam, the verbal curse was the impelling cause for Adam's loss of office and ejection from the garden-temple, the realm of the life-giving Spirit. Robert Rollock (ca. 1555–99) most clearly captures the nexus between covenantal curse and death:

> This efficacy of that sin is by reason of that word and covenant which God made with Adam in his creation, as it were in these words; 'If man will stand and persist in that his innocency which he had by creation, he shall stand for his own good and for his progeny; but if he do not stand, but fall away, his fall shall turn to his own damage, so to the hurt of his posterity; and whatsoever evil shall betide him, the same shall ensue to all his offspring.'[43]

The penalty of death finds its material cause in Adam's sin and its formal cause in 'that word and covenant which God made with Adam.'[44]

Geerhardus Vos (1862–1949), offers a similar explanation when he writes:

---

42. David J. A. Clines, 'The Tree of Knowledge and the Law of Yahweh,' *VT* (1974): 8-14.

43. Robert Rollock, *A Treatise on God's Effectual Calling*, in *The Select Works of Robert Rollock*, ed. William Gunn, 2 vols. (Edinburgh: The Woodrow Society, 1849), XXV (vol. I, p. 175).

44. Cf. A. C. Thiselton, 'The Supposed Power of Words in the Biblical Writings,' *JTS* 25 (1974): 283-99.

If Adam had remained unfallen and kept the probation command, then God would have justified him—that is, God would have taken into account Adam's holy and steadfast condition and would have had a state of immutable righteousness follow. Conversely, when Adam sinned, it was the condemnation of God that followed on the heels of this sin that transferred him from a state of rectitude into a state of damnation.[45]

Just as Israel's later covenant curse would mean the undoing of their redemption, so Adam's curse meant the undoing of his very creation (Deut. 28; cf. Gen. 1:2; Deut. 32:10-11; Jer. 4:23-26).[46] When God said, 'Let there be light,' light ensued in accord with God's word. If Adam had obeyed, God's, 'Well done, good and faithful servant,' would have yielded the fruit of eschatological life (cf. Deut. 28:1-14). But on the heels of Adam's apostasy, God uttered the words of covenantal curse, 'To dust you shall return' (Gen. 3:19; cf. Deut. 28:15-68, esp. 68).[47]

In technical terms, God's covenantal curses are performative utterances—the means by which He exercises His authority and brings about a state of affairs.[48] God's words are neither magical incantations nor utterances that bring about natural and physical effects.[49] Rather, they have effect given the established covenant ('In the day you eat of it you shall surely die') and by virtue of God's authority as covenant lord.[50] For example, if I say, 'I do,' when a minister asks me, 'Do you take this woman to be your wife,' my words have no intrinsic power in and of themselves. My words only bring about a state of affairs (my marriage) given the established convention of marriage and the laws of the state to unite a man and

---

45. Geerhardus Vos, *Reformed Dogmatics*, 5 vols., ed. Richard B. Gaffin, Jr. (Bellingham, WA: Lexham Press, 2012–), IV:138.

46. Turner, *Death of Deaths*, 133-37; Postell, *Adam as Israel*, 97.

47. Turner, *Death of Deaths*, 134.

48. Thiselton, 'Power of Words,' 296; cf. J. L. Austin, *How To Do Things With Words* (Oxford: Oxford University Press, 1965), 154-58.

49. Thiselton, 'Power of Words,' 293.

50. Thiselton, 'Power of Words,' 293; Austin, *How To Do Things With Words*, 159.

woman by virtue of their verbal declarations. When God, therefore, utters the sanction, 'To dust shall you return,' these words effect a state of affairs given God's authority as covenant lord and the established convention of the covenant, 'In the day you eat of it you shall surely die.'

Adam would dwell in a state of exile from the garden-temple and thus his physical death ensued. But Adam's exile was not an isolated individual punishment. Once again, the covenant binds the actions of the one to the lives of the many, and hence Adam's ejection meant that all of his offspring would dwell in a state of exilic death. All humanity suffers death because of Adam's one transgression by which they were constituted sinners, and as such, they all are born east of Eden, in a state of exile and hence they suffer death. They only know of the temporary life-preserving role of the Spirit, what is common to all fallen humanity and inevitably ends in the first and second deaths (Rev. 2:11; 20:6, 14; 21:8). Given their state of exile, humanity suffers other consequences, such as the noetic effects of sin. Because of humanity's exile from the life-giving presence of the Spirit, they suffer corruption of the faculties, degeneration of their bodies, and ultimately death.

LIFE IN CHRIST

Blessedly, God declared more than a judicial sentence against Adam— He embedded a promise of hope in the midst of the curses—the *protoevangelium*. Adam's cursed state is markedly different from that of the serpent or Cain (Gen. 4:16). Cain was driven into permanent exile with no hope of reconciliation whereas God promised that the seed of the woman would crush the head of the serpent and deliver Adam and Eve from covenant curse (Gen. 3:15).[51] Adam publicly professed his faith in this promise by renaming his wife—he called her Eve, 'Because she was the mother of all living' (Gen. 3:20). Eve would give birth to the promised redeemer. God then sent Adam and Eve into exile but they wore garments of hope. No longer did they hold up their fig leaves to cover their nakedness but God

---

51. Kitz, *Cursed Are You*, 237-38.

clothed them in animal skins (Gen. 3:21), which was a foreshadow of a greater covering yet to come. God would send another, like the son of man, Adam, to execute faithfully the divine vocation that God had originally given to Adam and Eve. God did not rewrite Adam's vocation but instead sent one who would faithfully carry it out.[52] In systematic theological terms, God would send His Son to fulfill the broken covenant of works. As with the work of Adam, we should examine Christ's work and goals, the consequences of success, and Christ and imputation.

CHRIST'S WORK AND GOALS

One of the clearest pictures of Christ's recapitulation of Adam's probation appears in His own wilderness wanderings on the heels of His baptism. Like Adam, God anointed His Son with the Holy Spirit, which occurred through the heavenly descent of the dove as Christ emerged from the waters of His baptism (Matt. 3:16 // Mark 1:9-11 // Luke 3:22 // John 1:32). The Spirit then led Christ into the wilderness where He was, like Adam, tempted by the serpent. There are, of course, significant dissimilarities between Adam and Christ. Unlike Adam, Christ was tempted in the wilderness, a haunt of wild animals, a sign that the world was upside down, under a covenantal curse (cf. e.g., Jer. 17:5-6 LXX; Mark 1:12-13).[53] By contrast, Adam was tempted in the plush confines of the garden-temple. Adam was presumably tempted on a full belly given that every fruit of the garden, save one, was available for his consumption, whereas Christ fasted for forty days.

Unlike Adam, who was only tempted once, Satan tempted Christ three times. In fact, in His response to Satan's three temptations, Christ responds with three texts from Deuteronomy 6 and 8, which is the same complex in which Deuteronomy 6:25 appears, 'And it will be righteousness for us, if we are careful to do all this commandment before the LORD our God, as he has commanded

---

52. N. T. Wright, *The New Testament and the People of God* (Philadelphia: Fortress, 1992), 262-64.

53. Kitz, *Cursed Are You*, 250-52.

us' (cf. Matt. 4:1-11; Deut. 8:3; 6:16; 6:13).[54] We ought not to think that when Christ quoted these three verses that He narrowly only had the specific words in view. Rather, we should think of them in terms of the entire contextual complex in which the verses appear.[55] These three verses are the anchor points from which Christ lifts the entire Deuteronomic complex of laws and commands to prove that He, unlike the first Adam, was faithful and would love the Lord His God with all His heart, soul, mind, and strength (Deut. 6:4ff). Christ, unlike Adam, came to fulfill every jot and tittle of the law (Matt. 5:17). In line with Deuteronomy 6:25, Christ tells John the Baptist that He must be baptized by him, 'to fulfill all righteousness' (Matt. 3:15). The overarching theme of large portions of the New Testament is that Jesus is the faithful last Adam in contrast to the unfaithful first Adam.

One of the big differences between Adam and Christ's work is that Adam only had to offer his active obedience to the law—to fulfill the requirements of God's commandments in order to secure eschatological life. In addition to the requisite active obedience, Christ had to offer His passive obedience—He had to suffer the penalty of the law for the sake of Adam's original transgression as well as all of the other sins of the elect.[56] Christ had to offer, therefore, both His active and passive obedience to God to secure the redemption of the elect. There are two important observations regarding those who would deny the necessity of the imputation of Christ's active and passive obedience.

First, to say that believers only require the passive obedience of Christ rends the seamless garment of Christ's obedience asunder (contra Piscator, e.g.). His active fulfillment of the law is equally as necessary as His suffering the penalty of the law—to say that

---

54. G. K. Beale and D. A. Carson, eds., *The New Testament Commentary on the Use of the Old Testament* (Grand Rapids: Baker, 2007), 14-17.

55. G. K. Beale, *Handbook on the New Testament Use of the Old Testament: Exegesis and Interpretation* (Grand Rapids: Baker, 2012), 44-46.

56. In this respect, we need to distinguish between original and actual sin— Adam's first sin imputed to his offspring and all of the subsequent personal sins which people individually commit.

believers only receive one aspect of Christ's obedience is an attempt to separate the inseparable. Second, to assume that Christ's active obedience only qualified Him to serve as the sinless sacrifice and is consequently not imputed to the believer confuses the relationship between eschatology and soteriology. Christ's role as covenant surety requires His impeccability to legitimize His intercessory work—Christ must be the spotless lamb in order to take away the sins of the world. But we must remember that eschatology is the exponent of protology, not soteriology. In other words, Christ comes not merely as Messiah but also as the last *Adam*—Adam's state in the garden and the necessity for confirmed righteousness logically and temporally precedes the need for redemption (1 Cor. 15:45). Therefore, believers require Christ's active and passive obedience in order to free them from the curse of the law and to secure their indefectible state in the eschaton. If Christ only presents His passive obedience, then there is no anchor of confirmed righteousness by which believers can secure eschatological life. If all Christ does is serve as an enabler, a Messiah who returns believers to Adam's state in the garden for one more shot at eschatological life, then He is not truly a redeemer.

THE CONSEQUENCES OF SUCCESS

As with Adam, the same original eschatological goals stand before the last Adam—obedience secures eschatological life. The Spirit-anointed Adam was supposed to unleash the Spirit from the garden-temple so that he would re-create the good but nevertheless un-subdued world. In like manner the Father anointed the last Adam with His Spirit to empower His work as mediator and upon the completion of His successful work unleash the outpouring of the Spirit upon the creation (Isa. 42:1; 61:1; Luke 4:18-21; Heb. 9:14; Acts 2:32-35).[57] As Paul succinctly writes: 'Thus it is written, "The first man Adam became a living being; the last Adam became a

---

57. Geerhardus Vos, 'Paul's Eschatological Concept of the Spirit,' in *Redemptive History and Biblical Interpretation: The Shorter Writings of Geerhardus Vos*, ed. Richard B. Gaffin, Jr. (Phillipsburg: P & R, 1980), 96.

life-giving Spirit"' (1 Cor. 15:45*).[58] God approached apostate Adam in the Spirit of the day to bring a reckoning, a judgment that left curse and death in its wake due to Adam's disobedience. By contrast, God the Father justified, or declared righteous, His Son in the power of the Spirit: 'He,' Christ, 'was manifested in the flesh, *justified in the Spirit*, seen by angels, proclaimed among the nations, believed on in the world, taken up in glory' (1 Tim. 3:16,* emphasis added).[59] Once again, we must factor the Spirit's role in doctrine of imputation. Paul clearly states that God justified Christ in the Spirit. But what does it mean that Christ was justified in the Spirit?

Simply stated, the Son came to the judgment throne of God convicted of gross sin and blasphemy by the religious leaders of Israel and God overturned the verdict by raising Jesus from the dead. Death is the consequence of sin (Rom. 3:23), hence given Christ's impeccability, death had no hold upon Him. But far more than being sinless, Christ was also righteous, which meant that He was able to secure eschatological life for those who were united to Him. God came in the Spirit of the day to judge Adam and found him wanting; God subsequently judged Christ, the last Adam, in the 'Spirit of the day' and justified Him. There are several key passages that testify to this cause-and-effect relationship between righteousness and eschatological life. The first passage is Galatians 3:10-14 where Paul places faith and works in stark antithesis. Sin-fallen humanity lies under a curse, hence no person is justified before God by the law, 'For the righteous shall live by faith' (Gal. 3:10-12; cf. Hab. 2:4). The law, Paul writes, 'is not of faith.' Rather, 'The one who does them shall live by them' (Gal. 3:12; cf. Lev. 18:5). Christ does not save by His faith but by His obedience to the law. Christ was obedient to the law (Lev. 18:5) and suffered its curse for those who are united to Him (Gal. 3:13; cf. Deut. 27:26), hence anyone united to Him receives the promised Spirit by faith (Gal. 3:14). The Spirit is the life-giving agent of the eschaton, not merely the

---

58. Vos, 'Eschatological Concept,' 107-14.

59. I. Howard Marshall, *The Pastoral Epistles*, ICC (Edinburgh: T & T Clark, 1999), 525-26.

life-preserving agent of this sin-fallen world. The Spirit is the 'power of the age to come' (Heb. 6:4).

The second passage appears in Paul's letter to Rome: 'But if Christ is in you, although the body is dead because of sin, the Spirit is life because of righteousness' (Rom. 8:10). The eschatological outpouring of the life-giving Spirit is the exponent and consequential fruit of the imputed active obedience of Christ (Rom. 5:21).[60] Christ secures the outpouring of the Spirit through His life-long perfect obedience to the law and because He suffers the consequences and penalties of the law on behalf of those who are in union with Him. Adam forfeited life in the sacred space of the garden-temple of Eden, but the last Adam brings the life-giving Spirit and sacred space of the eschatological temple to sin-fallen man. Christ ends the state of exilic death for the elect through the outpouring of the Spirit, and though the Spirit imparts life in stages, first raising sinners according to their inner man, and then at the last day raising redeemed sinners according to their outer man, He brings an end to life east of Eden (2 Cor. 4:16-18). The last Adam causes the fearsome cherubim to abandon their posts at the gates of Eden and return to their station before the throne of God (cf. Gen. 3:24; Exod. 25:18; Rev. 4:6-8). The last Adam re-opens the gates of paradise so that His bride may once again dwell in God's presence, but in a state far greater than Adam's edenic existence. Our state in God's presence is permanent and secure because the last Adam has ushered in the eschaton. Humanity finally enters the eschatological Sabbath-rest of Yahweh, as the last Adam delivers the elect and the creation from its covenantally-cursed estate of vanity (cf. Rom. 8:20; Eccles. 1:2ff LXX).

CHRIST AND IMPUTATION

As with Adam's imputed guilt, God employs the same mechanism to give believers the last Adam's righteousness. By Adam's one act of disobedience many were constituted sinners, and conversely by Christ's one act of righteousness many were constituted righteous—

---

60. Douglas J. Moo, *The Epistle to the Romans*, NICNT (Grand Rapids: Eerdmans, 1996), 491-92.

His obedience 'leads to justification and life for all men' (Rom. 5:18). Just as with Adam, there is no intermediate biological means by which God communicates the righteousness of Christ (contra realistic and mediate views of imputation). Moreover, Paul does not state that Christ serves as a moral exemplar so that believers can follow His footprints in the ethical sand (contra imitation theories). Rather, God 'constitutes' or 'appoints' people as righteous due to the obedience of the one man. The covenant, once again, accounts for the actions of the one and how it affects the lives of the many. The covenant binds the actions of the one individual, Jesus Christ, to the many for their salvation. While Adam's covenantal role implicitly appears in the Genesis narrative, Christ's covenantal role is quite explicit. He is the mediator and surety of the new and better covenant (Heb. 7:28; 9:15; 12:24; cf. Jer. 31:31). Christ's role as surety means that He legally fulfills the covenantal obligations on behalf of another. In Pauline terms, He secures these benefits on behalf of all those who are 'in Christ.' In systematic theological terms, Christ secures these benefits for all who are federally united to Him. In typological terms, Adam's garments of skin and Joshua's pure white robe give way to the antitypical reality of Christ's robe of righteousness (Gen. 3:21; Zech. 3:1-4).

God imparts this robe of righteousness by means of His forensic declaration and sentence of justification first over His Son and then over anyone united to His Son. In the first forensic declaration the Father declared His Son righteous, a sentence revealed in His resurrection from the dead, a sentence that gave His Son right and title as Lord of the eschatological Sabbath. Christ secured eschatological life because of His loving obedience to His Father's commands and He earned the right to pour out the life-giving Spirit upon the entire creation, which is for the gathering of His elect bride and for the judgment of the unbelieving world. In the second forensic declaration the Father constitutes as righteous anyone united to His Son by a Spirit-wrought faith. United to Christ they thus have right and title to eschatological life because in the moment of their justification by faith alone, God immediately imputes to them the perfect obedience and satisfaction (active and passive obedience) of Christ and constitutes them righteous in His sight.

As we hold the two Adams side by side we finally see the broader context of the threefold imputation that rests upon the pillars of the covenantal, geographic, historical contexts (pre- and post-fall). God first imputes Adam's sin to those whom he covenantally represents. Hence, they are guilty of sin and suffer the curse of the covenant—exilic death, a life subject to vanity, their return to dust, and the second death. Christ, the last Adam, steps onto the stage of redemptive history to take up Adam's failed work. But Christ must yield His obedience to the law to secure eschatological life and He must suffer the curse for those who are covenantally united to Him. God, therefore, makes Christ sin—this is the second imputation. God imputes Adam's first sin and the guilt of all the actual sins of each and every one of the elect to Jesus—in this way Christ suffers the curse. Christ does not actually commit sin, nor does He become sin incarnate. Rather, like the goat on the Day of Atonement, He bears or carries the sins (original and actual) of the elect. God imputes their guilt and sin to Christ. The third and final imputation occurs when God imputes the righteousness of Christ to the elect. God declares the elect righteous when they receive Christ's imputed righteousness by faith alone by God's grace alone—it is the free gift of God. We receive the alien righteousness of Christ, which means that it is outside of us. Christ's work for us is the basis of His work in us.[61] That it is alien and imputed means that our salvation rests entirely in Christ's work for us—the sole legal and covenantal basis for the salvation of God's people.

This threefold imputation (Adam to all people, the sins of the elect to Christ, and Christ's righteousness to the elect) comprises the covenantal basis for the universality of death and the particularly of eschatological life. In Adam all die, but all in Christ shall be made alive (1 Cor. 15:22). 'As was the man of dust, so also are those who are of the dust, and as is the man of heaven, so also are those who are of heaven. Just as we have borne the image of

---

61. Vos, *Reformed Dogmatics*, IV:164.

the man of dust, we shall bear the image of the man of heaven' (1 Cor. 15:48-49).

OBJECTIONS

As Part I demonstrates, there have always been a number of different views regarding imputed guilt and righteousness. The nineteenth century witnessed significant discussion and debate, especially concerning imputed guilt. One of the most recent objections to the immediate imputation of Adam's guilt comes from Oliver Crisp. He presents three objections to the doctrine of immediate federal imputation. First, Adam's appointment as federal head 'as our legal representative is dependent on the divine will alone.'[62] Crisp objects to this idea because, in his view, 'God alone is responsible for bringing about what appears to be a deeply immoral and unjust arrangement whereby all those who come after Adam are culpable and punishable for his primal sin—a sin they did not commit and did not authorize a representative to commit either.' He labels this, the *arbitrary divine will objection*.[63]

Crisp labels the second problem as, the *authorization objection*. He explains, 'I have not authorized Adam to act on my behalf as Jones authorizes Smith.' In other words, if a person authorizes another to act on his behalf, then there are legal grounds to hold accountable the one who authorized the action. Moreover, no one human being has the authority to authorize Adam to serve as the sole legal representative for the entire human race. Crisp adds additional objections under this category, namely, why is Adam's first sin the only action imputed to his offspring, why not subsequent sins? Conversely, why does God not impute his first virtuous act to his offspring in a similar manner? In Crisp's judgment, covenantal imputation faces the obstacle of God acting unjustly under such an arrangement.[64]

---

62. Oliver Crisp, 'Original Sin,' in *Christian Dogmatics: Reformed Theology for the Church Catholic*, ed. Michael Allen and Scott R. Swain (Grand Rapids: Baker, 2016), 202.

63. Crisp, 'Original Sin,' 203.

64. Crisp, 'Original Sin,' 203.

Crisp calls the third difficulty the *fiction objection*. God holds humanity guilty for Adam's first sin (original sin) apart from the commission of any actual sins of their own. How can God hold people accountable for something they have not actually personally done? Crisp believes that adherents to the view of immediate imputation deflect this objection by appealing to the inscrutability of the divine will. God has the right to bring about whatever state of affairs He so chooses. However true this might be, argues Crisp, such an answer does not provide any moral or legal justification for God imputing Adam's sin to his offspring.[65]

Crisp recognizes that by rejecting the imputation of Adam's sin, that some might claim that he proves too much, in that he also undercuts the basis for the imputation of Christ's righteousness. Crisp, however, appeals to the dissimilarity between the Adam-Christ parallel of Romans 5:12-19. The relationship between Adam and his offspring is natural, whereas the link between Christ and the redeemed is supernatural. Arguing for a legal imputation in the former is problematic (because of the three aforementioned objections) whereas the latter does not suffer from the same obstacles.[66] Crisp therefore argues that the bond between Adam and his offspring involves a real rather than a legal union, whereas there is a legal union between Christ and the redeemed. Humanity, consequently, is not in covenant with Adam, but the redeemed are presumably in covenant with Christ and hence share a legal union with Him.[67]

In response to these objections, I offer three counter-observations. First, when he raises the *arbitrary divine will objection*, he states that, according to advocates for immediate imputation, Adam's appointment as our legal representative rests upon the divine will alone. On the one hand, this is true. The apostle Paul admits this very fact: 'And he made from one man every nation of mankind to live on all the face of the earth, having determined allotted

---

65. Crisp, 'Original Sin,' 205.

66. Crisp, 'Original Sin,' 205 n. 18.

67. Crisp, 'Original Sin,' 206.

periods and the boundaries of their dwelling place' (Acts 17:26). Not only has God appointed Adam, but even many other things within human history and existence. This statement certainly fits the *divine will* portion of Crisp's objection, but I contend that it is anything but *arbitrary*. God has His reasons for ordaining things as He does, and they are not arbitrary. In fact, Paul states that God has ordained this state of affairs so 'that they,' fallen human beings, 'should seek God, and perhaps feel their way toward him and find him' (Acts 17:27). On this count, Paul clearly elsewhere states that God chose us in Christ, 'according to the purpose of his will' (Eph. 1:5). God does sovereignly establish Adam as our federal representative, but this is anything but arbitrary—it is in accordance with the mysterious and inscrutable yet holy and righteous will (Rom. 11:33-36).

Second, the *authorization objection* falters at numerous levels, but most notably at the exegetical level. Scripture provides numerous examples where God holds the many accountable for the actions of the one lone individual (e.g., Adam, Achan, David). To this we can also add examples of generational guilt (such as the wilderness generation suffering for the sins of their fathers, Num. 14:33; David's son suffering for his sin with Bathsheba, 2 Sam. 12:13-14; or Ahab's sons bearing his punishment, 1 Kings 21:29). Moreover, Paul clearly states: 'Sin came into the world through *one man*, and death through sin, and so death spread to all men because *all sinned*' (Rom. 5:12; emphasis added). Paul does not say that one man sinned, and thus all became corrupt or infected, although human corruption is certainly a consequence of Adam's sin. Rather, when Adam sinned, 'all sinned.' Crisp's objection seems to rest upon a modern individualist assumption of the inviolability of the sovereignty of the individual. No one individual has the right to authorize Adam's role as representative for the human race sounds like a principle of Lockean political philosophy, namely that political rule derives from the consent of the governed, rather than what the Scriptures state about God's appointment of Adam or other instances of collective guilt due to the actions of one person.

Third, the *fiction objection* fails because Crisp assumes that the only legitimate type of guilt is that based upon personal action. Once again, this assumes the supremacy of the individual—one shorn from any kind of corporate, or more properly, covenantal bond. The covenant is the basis for binding Achan and Israel—Achan's sin halted the conquest of the Promised Land. The same holds for David's sinful census. Individual Israelites did not personally ratify David's appointment as their king—God directly appointed him. No individual Israelite personally authorized David to take the sinful census—in fact, the opposite was true—Joab advised against it (2 Sam. 24:3). Nevertheless, God held David *and* Israel collectively responsible. David was Israel's king and functioned in a representative capacity (cf. Deut. 17:14-20). There are, therefore, several types of guilt in Scripture: personal and collective (familial, generational, national). The collective categories typically rest on a legal-covenantal basis.

Pace Crisp, his objections to immediate imputation are unconvincing because he merely proposes objections without offering substantial exegetical argumentation. On face value, his objections run against the grain of numerous examples. He raises his objections on very narrow footing, namely, the ontological connection between Adam and humanity. There is undoubtedly a connection, but apart from other factors, such as Adam's covenantal role as federal head, the garden-temple context, and other categories of guilt beyond the personal, Crisp's objections amount to a decontextualized analysis of Adam's place and function regarding original sin.

CONCLUSION

Imputation has been a contested doctrine because previous examinations and formulations have looked at the question from a very narrow point of view, chiefly through the doctrine of anthropology. Even among those theologians who rightly recognized that Adam was in covenant with God, this acknowledgement typically serves as window-dressing—a beautiful frame for a magnificent portrait, but attention often falls only upon the portrait. When we consider that God the divine artisan not only painted the portrait but also carefully and expertly constructed the beautiful frame, admirers learn a great deal more about the portrait's intended message. We must acknowledge the covenantal frame so that we rightly understand the interaction between Adam and God in the brushstrokes of the portrait, particularly the blessings and curses. Upon closer examination we also discover that the Adamic portrait has details in the background that reveal that Adam was created to dwell in God's temple-presence. When God, therefore, casts Adam and Eve out of the garden, we learn other important facts about the nature of Adam's death. God paints this portrait and constructs this frame with the brush of His voice—His spoken word. By His word He brought worlds into existence, made man, and gave to him a covenantal task, which promised unimagined blessings but also threatened nightmarish curses. Accounting for all of these factors provides us with the proper context in which we can rightly understand the doctrine of immediate imputation.

Part III Summary

At the end of Part II, I provided answers to a number of questions that arose in the survey of the historical origins, development, and reception of the doctrine of imputation. Part II answered many of those questions but there were some things that required greater reflection. The remaining issues include the following:

1. Is a twofold covenantal structure warranted? Was God in covenant with Adam?

The initial exegetical survey provided sufficient data to answer *yes* to this question. But in the dogmatic formulation, we read the Genesis 1-3 account within the context of the canon, and especially the Pentateuch. Read in context, all signs point to the existence of a covenant between God and Adam—even early Jewish interpretation of the creation account arrives at this conclusion. In this respect, the book of Deuteronomy plays a crucial role as Israel's covenantal charter. We cannot merely look for the term *covenant*, acknowledge its absence from Genesis 1-3, and hastily conclude that Adam is not in covenant with God. We must instead look at all of the exegetical evidence and recognize that Genesis 1-3 stands at the beginning of the Pentateuch's narrative and functions as an inclusio meant to be read against its Deuteronomic counterpart.

2. Should ontological or forensic categories take precedent in the question of determining the means by which God accounts people guilty or righteous?

Rollock and Vos offer important observations about the root cause of Adam's judicial state—namely, the word of the covenant or God's covenantal curse upon Adam. When God formally established the covenant with Adam by issuing commands, fill the earth and subdue it, and do not eat from the tree, these covenantal utterances created the federal context for the consequences of obedience or disobedience. In Adam's case his disobedience brings death—God's curse is the formal cause of his expulsion from Eden, which ultimately results in his death and the exilic state of death for his offspring. To acknowledge the priority of the forensic does not eliminate or sideline ontology. We must not pit forensic versus ontological categories. Instead, we must account for a covenantal ontology. In other words, God's covenantal dealings define the nature of man's being. All humanity suffers the effects of Adam's first sin by virtue of the consequences of his covenantal failure. Non-covenantal attempts to account for the Adam-humanity connections (e.g., realistic theories of imputation) must rely upon biological connections but ultimately inadequately consider the nature of God's words to Adam. When God tells Adam not to eat from the tree, He formalizes Adam's covenantal existence. And when God tells Adam that he will return to dust should he violate the covenant, the curse is the impelling cause of his ejection and consequential condemned deathly existence. The converse holds true for Christ's imputed righteousness. God constitutes the many as righteous by virtue of Christ's appointment at covenant surety and His completed work—His life, death, and resurrection. Believers do not receive Christ's essential righteousness but the consequences of His obedience. Christ's alien righteousness is the judicial ground of their redemption, not Christ's indwelling or the supposed communication of His essential righteousness.

3. Does God impute both the active and passive righteousness of Christ to the believer?

Sinners require both the active and passive obedience of Christ, as Part II demonstrated. But the active takes priority to the passive obedience. Why? God required Adam's active obedience prior to the entrance of sin into the world. In technical terms, eschatology precedes soteriology—eschatology is of greater antiquity—it is part of pre-redemptive history, whereas soteriology is part of redemptive history. I believe some theologians have rejected the necessity of the active obedience because they have not satisfactorily wrestled with the Adamic origins of eschatology. Viewed within the architecture of the covenants of works and grace, we can clearly see the necessity of both the active and passive obedience of Christ.

4. Must we affirm Adam's historical existence?

Absolutely, yes. We cannot establish the historical work of the last Adam upon a mythical foundation.

CONCLUSION

The doctrine of imputation is of vital importance for a right and robust understanding of the doctrine of justification and ultimately the gospel. Some might characterize this doctrine and the surrounding debate as technical hairsplitting. Why do we have to be specific about the nature of our redemption? Can we not simply acknowledge that Adam somehow brought sin into the world and that Christ delivers us from this stricken state? From one vantage point this is certainly a legitimate question. But if the Bible specifies and explains the nature of the connection between Adam and humanity and Christ and the elect, then it behooves the church to study and embrace its teaching. While Romans 5:12-21 is not the only passage that speaks to the issue, the church must explain how one man sins and God therefore constitutes all people as sinners. Conversely, we must also ask how one act of righteousness or obedience leads to justification for all who place their faith in Christ. Why do we receive death in Adam and life in Christ? The simple answer is, the imputed sin and righteousness of the first and last Adams. The Scriptures clearly teach the threefold immediate imputation of Adam's guilt and Christ's righteousness within the context of the covenants of works and grace. God imputes the guilt of Adam's sin, which renders all human beings subject to death since they dwell in covenantal exile, east of Eden, away from the eschatological life-giving power of the Holy Spirit. Only the imputed obedience and satisfaction of Christ received by faith alone by God's grace alone grant right and title to eternal life and restore fallen sinners into a new covenantal relationship with the triune God.

Such truths are sublime and, while they do not present the entirety of the gospel, they certainly represent its chief elements. The pastoral and practical implications of the doctrine of imputation are significant. One of the most telling statements from the history of the doctrine comes from Jesuit theologian Diego Laynez and his three-hour speech against imputation. He rejected the doctrine for many reasons, but the most prominent was the fact that imputed righteousness left no room for personal merit. The opening analogy for his speech reveals the starkly different understandings of imputation and consequently salvation. In his parable Laynez spoke of the king's son who had inherited all of his father's wealth and the son who wanted his servants to win the possession of a precious gem. To one servant the son said: 'Only believe, and I, to whom all of the king's wealth has been promised, will obtain the gem and freely give it to you.' The son told another servant that he would free him from servitude, ensure his well being, and give him weapons so that he could fight for and earn the gem. These two different servants represented the Protestant doctrine of imputed righteousness and the Roman Catholic doctrine of infused righteousness. The differences are clear and, quite frankly, stunning.

For those who carry the burden of a doubt-stricken conscience, questions undoubtedly arise about personal fidelity, unworthiness, or eternal security. While it is a blessing to have Christ release you from the bondage of sin and equip you for good works, if you must secure the gem of your salvation by your own efforts, who is sufficient for such a task? At what point are my works sufficient? Will my own personal unworthiness weigh me down into the depths of hell? How do I know whether I will persevere to the end? Such questions are not uncommon and have answers within the Roman Catholic understanding of salvation. Your works may not be sufficient and thus you must suffer in purgatory. You may be saved now but should you commit grievous sin you will lose your salvation unless you make use of penance, the second plank of justification. You very well may not persevere to the end, but if a priest offers you last rites, you can receive an extra measure of grace to fend off the temptation to apostatize in the waning moments of your life. Security is always fleeting and imperiled at every turn.

Aside from these issues, the more fundamental question presses upon us, namely, to what degree does Layñez's parable reflect the teaching of Scripture? Do God's people place their good works alongside of Christ's in the hopes that they sufficiently tip the scale towards a favorable verdict at the divine bar? Or was Layñez blind to many key passages of Scripture, such as Ephesians 2:8-9, 'For by grace you have been saved through faith. And this is not your own doing; it is the gift of God, not the result of works, so that no one many boast.' The first servant in Layñez's parable who received the gem as a freely given gift best reflects this famous Pauline text. Moreover, Paul repeatedly invokes this term to characterize justification and especially imputation. According to Paul we 'are justified by [God's] grace as a gift, through the redemption that is in Christ Jesus' (Rom. 3:24). In his discussion of imputed righteousness, Paul writes: 'Now to the one who works, his wages are not counted as a gift but as his due' (Rom. 4:4). The converse is true, namely, that justification and hence imputation is a free gift.

Paul invokes the term *gift* (χάρισμα or δωρεά) in Romans 5:15-17, which lies in the heart of his explanation of the Adam-Christ imputation parallel:

> But the *free gift* is not like the trespass. For if many died through one man's trespass, much more have the grace of God and the *free gift* by the grace of that one man Jesus Christ abounded for many.

And the *free gift* is not like the result of that one man's sin. For the judgment following one trespass brought condemnation, but the *free gift* following many trespasses brought justification. For if, because of one man's trespass, death reigned through that one man, much more will those who receive the abundance of grace and the *free gift* of righteousness reign in life through the one man Jesus Christ (Rom. 5:15-17, emphasis added).

In the short span of three verses Paul characterizes Christ's imputed righteousness as a free gift five times. Layñez ultimately believed that Christ was an enabler, but it is difficult to characterize Him as a redeemer. In stark contradistinction, Paul presents Christ as a redeemer and believers receive His imputed righteousness as a free gift, a gift that irrevocably, immutably, and indefectibly secures the blessing of eternal life (Rom. 5:19-21; 6:23).

The free gift of imputation should fill our hearts with praise and gratitude for the generosity of our triune Lord—for the Father's gift, the Son's willingness to fulfill the law on our behalf and suffer the consequences for its violation, and the Spirit's application of Christ's work to us through His effectual calling and the gift of faith, the alone instrument by which believers lay hold of Christ's imputed righteousness. We stand with Joshua the high priest and do not have to fear the accuser's charges. Apart from Christ we are unworthy of salvation and justly deserve God's wrath and condemnation. But Christ has said to Satan, 'The LORD rebuke you, O Satan! The LORD who has chosen Jerusalem rebuke you! Is this not a brand plucked from the fire?' (Zech. 3:2). The Father cries out, 'Remove the filthy garments,' and clothe him with pure vestments (Zech. 3:4). The Father clothes us in the seamless robe of Christ's righteousness. Unlike Jacob, who had to wear his brother's coat to deceive his father Isaac to receive the blessing of the covenant, our heavenly Father has freely given us the coat of our elder brother, Jesus, so that we may boldly stand in His presence and receive His blessings. Our lives are 'hidden with Christ in God' (Col. 3:3) with the full knowledge and consent of the triune God. The doctrine of imputation is, therefore, of the greatest pastoral and practical relevance.

On the last day we cannot claim to stand alone—no man is an island. We cannot say, 'I am the master of my fate, I am the captain of my soul,' and reject the representative actions of Adam and Christ. We must stand with one of these two epoch-shaping representatives—we either stand with Adam or Christ. The fact that Adam repented of his sin informs us where we should all stand. When Laýnez rejected the doctrine of imputation because it left no room for personal merit, he was exactly right. The Protestant reformers knew that salvation cannot depend upon us but must rest solely upon Christ. The words of Horatius Bonar's (1808–89) well-known hymn, 'Thy Works, Not Mine, O Christ,' beautifully capture the essence and nature of the doctrine of imputation:

> Thy works, not mine, O Christ,
> Speak gladness to this heart;
> They tell me all is done,
> They bid my fear depart.
> To whom save Thee, who canst alone
> For sin atone, Lord, shall I flee?
> ...
>
> Thy cross, not mine, O Christ,
> Has borne the awe-full load
> Of sins that none could bear
> But the incarnate God.
> To whom save Thee, who canst alone
> For sin atone, Lord, shall I flee?
> ...
>
> Thy righteousness, O Christ,
> Alone can cover me;
> No righteousness avails
> Save that which is of Thee.
> To whom save Thee, who canst alone
> For sin atone, Lord, shall I flee?

Adam's imputed guilt brings death, but Christ's imputed righteousness brings life. His imputed righteousness imparts assurance of salvation and the hope of eternal life. There is no other foundation for salvation save but in Christ's imputed righteousness.

BIBLIOGRAPHY

Á Brakel, Wilhelmus. *The Christian's Reasonable Service.*
    Translated by Bartel Elshout. 4 vols. Morgan: Soli Deo
    Gloria, 1992.

Adler, Joshua J. 'David's Last Sin: Was it the Census?' *Jewish Bible
    Quarterly* 23:2 (1995): 91-95.

Andrada, Diego. *Orthodoxarum Explicationum Libri Decem.*
    Coloniae: Maternum Cholinum, 1564.

Annesley, Samuel. *The Morning Exercises at Cripplegate.* Vol. 6.
    1675; London: Thomas Tegg, 1844.

Anselm of Canterbury. *Anselm of Canterbury: The Major Works.*
    Edited by Brian Davies and G. R. Evans. Oxford: Oxford
    University Press, 1998.

Arand, Charles P. 'Two Kinds of Righteousness as a Framework
    for Law and Gospel in the Apology.' *Lutheran Quarterly* 15
    (2001): 417-39.

Arand, Charles P., Robert Kolb, and James A. Nestingen, editors. *The Lutheran Confessions: History and Theology of the Book of Concord.* Minneapolis: Fortress, 2012.

Aristotle. *Nicomachean Ethics.* 2nd edition. Translated by Terence Irwin. Indianapolis: Hacket Publishing Co., 1999.

Auld, Graeme. 'Imago Dei in Genesis: Speaking in the Image of God.' *Expository Times* 116/8 (2005): 259-62.

Austin, J. L. *How To Do Things With Words.* Oxford: Oxford University Press, 1965.

Aquinas, Thomas. *Commentary on the Letter of St. Paul to the Romans.* Translated by Fabian R. Larcher. Vol. 37. *Latin/English Edition of the Works of St. Thomas Aquinas.* Edited by John Mortensen and Enrique Alarcón. Lander, WY: Aquinas Institute for the Study of Sacred Doctrine, 2012.

_____. *Commentary on St. Paul's Letters to the Galatians and Ephesians.* Translated by Fabian R. Larcher and Matthew L. Lamb. Vol. 39. *Latin/English Edition of the Works of St. Thomas Aquinas.* Edited by John Mortensen and Enrique Alarcón. Lander, WY: Aquinas Institute for the Study of Sacred Doctrine, 2012.

_____. *Summa Theologica.* 5 vols. Allen: Christian Classics, 1948.

Augustine. 'City of God.' Translated by Marcus Dods. In *A Select Library of the Nicene and Post-Nicene Fathers*, edited by Philip Schaff, Series 1. Vol. 2, 1-511. 1887; Peabody, MA: Hendrickson Publishers, 1994.

_____. *The Literal Meaning of Genesis.* Translated by John Hammond Taylor. Ancient Christian Writers. Vol. 41. New York: Paulist Press, 1982.

_____. 'On the Merits and Remission of Sins, and on the Baptism of Infants.' Translated by Peter Holmes and Robert Ernest Wallis, and revised by Benjamin B. Warfield. In *A Select Library of the Nicene and Post-Nicene Fathers*, edited by Philip Schaff, Series 1, vol. 5, 12-78. 1887; Peabody, MA: Hendrickson Publishers, 1994.

_____. 'On the Predestination of the Saints.' In *Four Anti-Pelagian Writings*, translated by John A. Mourant and William J. Collinge, 218-270. Vol. 86, *Fathers of the Church*. Edited by Thomas P. Halton. Washington: Catholic University of America Press, 1992.

_____. 'To Simplician - On Various Questions.' In *Augustine: Earlier Writings*, edited and translated by John H. S. Burleigh, 370-406. Library of Christian Classics. Edited by John Baillie. Vol. 6. Philadelphia: Westminster, 1953.

_____. 'A Treatise on Grace and Free Will.' Translated by Peter Holmes and Robert Ernest Wallis, and revised by Benjamin B. Warfield. In *A Select Library of the Nicene and Post-Nicene Fathers*. Edited by Philip Schaff, Series 1, vol. 5, 436-465. 1887; Peabody, MA: Hendrickson Publishers, 1994.

_____. 'A Treatise on the Origin of the Human Soul, Addressed to Jerome.' Translated by J.G. Cunningham. In *A Select Library of the Nicene and Post-Nicene Fathers*. Edited by Philip Schaff, Series 1, vol. 1, 523-32. 1886; Peabody, MA: Hendrickson Publishers, 1994.

Baird, Samuel. *The First Adam and the Second: The Elohim Revealed in the Creation and Redemption of Man*. Philadelphia: Lindsay & Blakiston, 1860.

Ballor, Jordan J. *Covenant, Causality, and Law: A Study in the Theology of Wolfgang Musculus*. Göttingen: Vandenhoeck & Ruprecht, 2012.

Bakon, Shimon. 'David's Sin: Counting the People.' *Jewish Bible Quarterly* 41/1 (2013): 53-54.

Barnes, Albert. *Notes, Explanatory and Practical, On the Epistle of Romans.* New York: Leavitt, Lord, and Co., 1834.

Barrett, Matthew and Ardel B. Caneday, editors. *Four Views on the Historical Adam.* Grand Rapids: Zondervan, 2013.

Barth, Karl. *Christ and Adam: Man and Humanity in Romans 5.* 1956; Eugene: Wipf & Stock, 2004.

_____. *Church Dogmatics.* 14 vols. Edited by G. W. Bromiley and T. F. Torrance. Edinburgh: T & T Clark, 1936-68.

Bastingius, Jeremias. *An Exposition or Commentarie Upon the Catechisme of Christian Religion Which Is Taught in the Scholes and Churches Both of the Lowe Countries and of the Dominions of the Countie Palatinate.* Cambridge: John Legatt, 1593.

Batka, L'Ubomir. 'Luther's Teaching on Sin and Evil.' In *The Oxford Handbook of Martin Luther's Theology*, edited by Robert Kolb, Irene Dingel, and L'Ubomir Batka, 233-53. Oxford: Oxford University Press, 2014.

Baxter, Richard. *The Life of Faith. In Three Parts.* Vol. 3. *The Practical Works of the Late Reverend and Pious Mr. Richard Baxter*, 513-664. 1660; London: Thomas Parkhurst, Jonathan Robinson, and John Lawrence, 1707.

Beale, G. K. 'The Descent of the Eschatological Temple in the Form of the Spirit at Pentecost: Part I.' *Tyndale Bulletin* 56/1 (2005): 73-102.

_____. 'The Descent of the Eschatological Temple in the Form of the Spirit at Pentecost: Part II.' *Tyndale Bulletin* 56/2 (2005): 63-90.

_____. *The Erosion of Inerrancy in Evangelicalism: Responding to New Challenges to Biblical Authority.* Wheaton: Crossway, 2008.

_____. *Handbook on the New Testament Use of the Old Testament: Exegesis and Interpretation.* Grand Rapids: Baker, 2012.

_____. *A New Testament Biblical Theology: The Unfolding of the Old Testament in the New.* Grand Rapids: Baker, 2011.

_____. 'The Old Testament Background of Reconciliation in 2 Corinthians 5-7 and Its Bearing on the Literary Problem of 2 Corinthians 6:14-7:1.' In *The Right Doctrine from the Wrong Texts: Essays on the Use of the Old Testament in the New,* edited by G. K. Beale, 217-47. Grand Rapids: Baker, 1994.

_____. *The Temple and the Church's Mission: A Biblical Theology of the Dwelling Place of God.* Downers Grove: InterVarsity Press, 2004.

Beale, G. K. and D. A. Carson, editors. *Commentary on the New Testament Use of the Old Testament.* Grand Rapids: Baker, 2007.

Beatrice, Pier Franco. *The Transmission of Sin: Augustine and the Pre-Augustinian Sources.* Translated by Adam Kamesar. Oxford: Oxford University Press, 2013.

Berkouwer, G. C. *Sin.* Translated by Philip C. Holtrop. Studies in Dogmatics. Grand Rapids: Eerdmans, 1977.

Beza, Theodore. *The New Testament of our Lord Jesus Christ.* Translated by I. Tomson. London: Christopher Barker, 1586.

_____. *Theses Theologicae.* Geneva: Eustathium Vignon, 1586.

Bierma, Lyle D., Charles D. Gunnoe Jr., Karin Y. Maag, and Paul W. Fields, editors. *An Introduction to the Heidelberg Catechism: Sources, History and Theology.* Grand Rapids: Baker, 2005.

Bird, Michael F. 'Justification as Forensic Declaration and Covenant Membership: A *Via Media* Between Reformed and Revisionist Readings of Paul.' *Tyndale Bulletin* 57/1 (2006): 109-30.

_____.'Incorporated Righteousness: A Response to Recent Evangelical Discussion Concerning the Imputation of Christ's Righteousness in Justification.' *Journal of the Evangelical Theological Society* 47/2: (2004): 253-75.

_____. 'Progressive Reformed View.' In *Justification: Five Views*, edited by James K. Beilby and Paul Rhodes Eddy, 145-52. Downers Grove: InterVarsity Press, 2011.

_____. *The Saving Righteousness of God: Studies on Paul, Justification, and the New Perspective*. Milton Keynes: Paternoster, 2007.

Bonaiuti, Ernesto. 'The Genesis of St. Augustine's Idea of Original Sin.' *Harvard Theological Review* 10/2 (1917): 159-75.

Bonner, Gerald. 'Les Origenes Africaines de la doctrine Augustinienne sur la chute et le péché originel.' In *God's Decree and Destiny: Studies on the Thought of Augustine of Hippo*, 97-116. Variorum Collected Studies Series, 255. London: Variorum Reprints, 1987.

Bovell, Carlos R. 'Genesis 3:21: The History of Israel in a Nutshell?' *Expository Times* 115/11 (2004): 361-66.

Braulik, Georg. 'The Development of the Doctrine of Justification in the Redactional Strata of the Book of Deuteronomy.' In *The Theology of Deuteronomy: The Collected Essays of Georg Braulik, O. S. B.*, translated by Ulrika Linblad, 151-64. Bibal Collected Essays 2. North Richland Hills, TX: Bibal Press, 1994.

Breckinridge, Robert J. *The Knowledge of God Objectively Considered Being the First Part of Theology Considered as a Science of Positive Truth, Both Inductive and Deductive*. New York: Robert Carter & Brothers, 1858.

Brown, John. *The Life of Justification Opened*. Utrecht: 1695.

Bucer, Martin. *Metaphrases et Enarrationes perpetuae Epistolarum…*, vol. 1, *Continens Metaphrasim et Enrrationem in Epistolam ad Romanos*. Rihel: 1536.

Bucer, Martin. *Common Places of Martin Bucer*. Edited and translated by David F. Wright. Appleford: Sutton Courtenay Press, 1972.

Bultmann, Rudolph. *Theology of the New Testament: Complete in One Volume*. New York: Charles Scribner's Sons, 1951, 1955.

_____. 'New Testament and Mythology: The Mythological Element in the Message of the New Testament and the Problem of Its Re-interpretation.' In *Kerygma and Myth*. Edited by Hans Werner Bartsch, 1-44. New York: Harper & Row, 1961.

Burgess, Anthony. *The Doctrine of Original Sin*. London: Thomas Underhill, 1659.

Calvin, John. 'Canons and Decrees of the Council of Trent, with the Antidote, 1547.' In *John Calvin: Tracts and Letters*, vol. 3, 17-188. Edited and translated by Henry Beveridge. 1851; Edinburgh: Banner of Truth, 2009.

_____. *The Epistles of Paul the Apostle to the Romans and to the Thessalonians*. Translated by R. MacKenzie. Calvin's New Testament Commentaries. Edited by David W. Torrance and Thomas F. Torrance. 1961; Grand Rapids: Eerdmans, 1996.

_____. *The Gospel According to St. John 1-10*. Translated by T. H. L. Parker. Calvin's New Testament Commentaries. Edited by David W. Torrance and Thomas F. Torrance. 1960; Grand Rapids: Eerdmans, 1996.

_____. *Institutes of the Christian Religion*. Translated by John Allen. Grand Rapids: Eerdmans, 1949.

_____. *Institutio Christianae Religionis*. Geneva: Roberti Stephani, 1559.

Campbell, Constantine R. *Paul and Union with Christ: An Exegetical and Theological Study.* Grand Rapids: Zondervan, 2012.

Carson, D. A. 'Adam in the Epistles of Paul.' In *In the Beginning.* Edited by Nigel M. de Cameron, 28-44. Glasgow: Biblical Creation Society, 1980.

_____. 'The Vindication of Imputation: On Fields of Discourse and Semantic Fields.' In *Justification: What's At Stake in the Current Debates.* Edited by Mark Husbands and Daniel J. Treier, 46-78. Downers Grove: InterVarsity, 2004.

Catharinus, Ambrogio. *De Lapsu Hominis et Peccato Originali Liber Unus.* In *Opuscula.* Lugduni: apud Mathiam Bonhomme, 1542.

Cathcart, Kevin J. and Robert P. Gordon. *The Targum of the Minor Prophets: Translated, with a Critical Introduction, Apparatus, and Notes.* Wilmington, DE: Michael Glazier, Inc., 1989.

Charlesworth, James H., editor. *The Old Testament Pseudepigrapha.* 2 vols. New York: Doubleday, 1983.

Chemnitz, Martin. *Examination of the Council of Trent.* Translated by Fred Kramer. 4 vols. 1971; St. Louis: Concordia Publishing House, 2007.

Cheynell, Francis. *The Rise, Growth, and Danger of Socinianisme, Together with a Plaine Discovery of a Desperate Designe of Corrupting the Protestant Religion.* London: Samuel Gellibrand, 1643.

Chrysostom. 'Homily X.' Translated by J. Walker, J. Sheppard and H. Browne, and revised by George B. Stevens. In *A Select Library of Nicene and Post-Nicene Fathers.* Edited by Philip Schaff, Series 1, vol. 11, 401-08. 1899; Peabody, MA: Hendrickson Publishers, 1994.

Chrysostom. *Baptismal Instructions.* Edited Johannes Quasten and Walter J. Burghardt. Ancient Christian Writers, vol. 31. Mahwah: Paulist Press, 1963.

Clement of Alexandria. 'The Stromata, or Miscellanies.' Translated by William Wilson. In *The Ante-Nicene Fathers*, edited by Alexander Roberts and James Donaldson, vol. 2, 299-569. 1885; Peabody, MA: Hendrickson Publishers, 1994.

Clines, David J. A. *Job 1-20.* Word Biblical Commentary. Vol. 17. Dallas: Word, 1989.

_____. *Job 21-37.* Word Biblical Commentary. Vol. 18a. Nashville: Thomas Nelson, 2006.

_____. 'The Tree of Knowledge and the Law of Yahweh (Psalm XIX).' *Vetus Testamentum* 24 (1974): 8-14.

Collins, C. John. 'Adam and Eve in the Old Testament.' In *Adam, the Fall, and Original Sin: Theological, Biblical, and Scientific Perspectives.* Edited by Hans Madueme and Michael Reeves, 3-32. Grand Rapids: Baker, 2014.

_____. *Did Adam and Eve Really Exist? Who They Were and Why You Should Care.* Wheaton: Crossway, 2011.

A Confession of Faith, Put forth by the Elders and Brethren of Many Congregations of Christians (Baptized upon Profession of their Faith) in London and the Country. London: John Harris, 1688.

Coxe, Nehemiah. *A Discourse of the Covenants That God made with Men Before the Law.* J. D., 1681.

Cranmer, Thomas. *An Answer To A Crafty and Sophistical Cavillation Devised by Stephen Gardiner.* 1555; Cambridge: Cambridge University Press, 1844.

Crisp, Oliver D. *Jonathan Edwards on God and Creation.* Oxford: Oxford University Press, 2012.

_____ . 'Original Sin.' In *Christian Dogmatics: Reformed Theology for the Church Catholic*. Edited by Michael Allen and Scott R. Swain, 194-215. Grand Rapids: Baker, 2016.

_____. *Retrieving Doctrine: Essays in Reformed Theology*. Downers Grove: InterVarsity Press, 2010.

Cunningham, William. *The Reformers and the Theology of the Reformation*. Vol. 1. *The Collected Works of the Rev. William Cunningham*. Edinburgh: T & T Clark, 1862.

Curtis, Byron G. 'Hosea 6:7 and Covenant-Breaking like/at Adam.' In *The Law Is Not of Faith: Essays on Works and Grace in the Mosaic Covenant*, edited by Bryan D. Estelle, J. V. Fesko, and David VanDrunen, 170-209. Phillipsburg: P & R, 2009.

Dabney, Robert L. 'The Doctrine of Original Sin.' In *Discussions: Theological and Evangelical*, vol. 1,143-68. 1890; Edinburgh: Banner of Truth, n. d.

_____. *Syllabus and Notes of the Course of Systematic and Polemic Theology*. 2nd edition. St. Louis: Presbyterian Publishing Co., 1878.

Davenant, John. *An Exposition of The Epistle of St. Paul to the Colossians*. 1627; London: Hamilton, Adams, and Co., 1831.

Davidson, Roichard M. *Typology in Scripture: A Study of Hermeneutical τύπος Structures*. Berrien Springs, MI: Andrews University Press, 1981.

De Campos Jr., Heber Carlos. 'Johannes Piscator (1546-1625) and the Consequent Development of the Doctrine of the Imputation of Christ's Active Obedience.' PhD diss., Calvin Theological Seminary, 2009.

De Valdés, Juan. *Commentary Upon St. Paul's Epistle to the Romans*. Translated by John T. Betts London: Trübner & Co., 1883.

_____. *Seventeen Opuscules.* Edited and translated by John T. Betts. London: Trübner & Co., 1882.

De Witte, Petrus. *Catechizing upon the Heidelbergh Catechisme, of the Reformed Christian Religion.* Amsterdam: Printed by Gillis Joosten Saeghman, 1664.

A Declaration of the Faith and Order Owned and Practiced in the Congregational Churches in England. London: John Field, 1659.

Dempster, Stephen G. *Dominion and Dynasty: A Theology of the Hebrew Bible.* Downers Grove: InterVarsity Press, 2003.

Denlinger, Aaron. 'Calvin's Understanding of Adam's Relationship to His Posterity: Recent Assertions of the Reformer's "Federalism" Evaluated.' *Calvin Theological Journal* 44 (2009): 226-250.

_____. *Omnes in Adam Ex Pacto Dei: Ambrogio Catarino's Doctrine of Covenantal Solidarity and Its Influence on Post-Reformation Reformed Theologians.* Göttingen: Vandenhoeck & Ruprecht, 2010.

Denzinger, Heinrich, editor. *Compendium of Creeds, Definitions, and Declarations on Matters of Faith and Morals*, 43rd ed., revised and edited by Peter Hünermann. San Francisco: Ignatius Press, 2012.

Dickson, David. *Truths Victory Over Error.* Edinburgh: John Reed, 1634.

Dillard, Raymond. 'David's Census: Perspectives on 2 Samuel 24, 1 Chronicles 21.' In *Through Christ's Word: A Festschrift for Dr. Philip E. Hughes.* Edited by W. Robert Godfrey and Jesse L. Boyd III, 94-107. Phillipsburg: P & R, 1985.

Diodati, Giovanni. *Pious and Learned Annotations Upon the Holy Bible: Plainly Expounding the Most Difficult Places Thereof.* London: Nicholas Fussell, 1651.

Dodd, C. H. *According to the Scriptures: The Sub-Structure of New Testament Theology*. London: Nisbet & Co, Ltd., 1952.

Domning, Daryl P. and Monika K. Hellwig. *Original Selfishness: Original Sin and Evil in the Light of Evolution*. Aldershot: Ashgate, 2006.

Douglas, Mary. *Purity and Danger: An Analysis of the Concepts of Pollution and Taboo*. London: Routledge & Kegan Paul, 1966.

Downame, John. *The Christian Warfare against the devil world and flesh*. London: William Stansby, 1634.

Dunn, James D.G. *The Theology of Paul the Apostle*. Grand Rapids: Eerdmans, 1998.

Dunson, Ben C. *Individual and Community in Paul's Letter to the Romans*. Tübingen: Mohr Siebeck, 2012.

_____. 'Do Bible Words Have Bible Meaning? Distinguishing Imputation as a Word and Doctrine.' *Westminster Theological Journal* 75 (2013): 239-60.

Edwards, Jonathan. *Original Sin*. Vol. 3, *Works of Jonathan Edwards*. New Haven: Yale University Press, 1970.

Enns, Peter. *The Evolution of Adam: What the Bible Does and Doesn't Say about Human Origins*. Grand Rapids: Brazos, 2012.

_____. *Inspiration and Incarnation: Evangelicals and the Problem of the Old Testament*. Grand Rapids: Baker, 2005.

Estelle, Bryan D. 'The Covenant of Works in Moses and Paul.' In *Covenant, Justification, and Pastoral Ministry: Essays by the Faculty of Westminster Seminary California*, edited by R. Scott Clark, 89-132. Phillipsburg: P & R, 2007.

_____. 'Leviticus 18:5 and Deuteronomy 30:1-14 in Biblical Theological Development: Entitlement to Heaven Foreclosed and Proffered.' In *The Law Is Not of Faith: Essays on Works and Grace in the Mosaic Covenant*, edited by Bryan Estelle, J. V. Fesko, and David VanDrunen, 109-46. Phillipsburg: P & R, 2009.

Featley, Daniel. *Dippers Dipt, or The Anabaptists Duck'd and Plung'd Over Head and Ears.* London: 1647.

Fenner, Dudley. *Sacra Theologia sive Veritas quae Est Secundum Pietatem.* Geneva: Eustathium Vignon, 1589.

Fesko, J.V. *The Covenant of Redemption: Origins, Development, and Reception.* Göttingen: Vandenhoeck & Ruprecht, 2015.

_____. *Last Things First: Unlocking Genesis 1-3 with the Christ of Eschatology.* Fearn: Mentor, 2007.

_____. *The Theology of the Westminster Standards: Historical Context and Theological Insights.* Wheaton: Crossway, 2014.

_____. *The Trinity and the Covenant of Redemption.* Fearn: Mentor, 2016.

Fichter, Joseph H. *James Layñez: Jesuit.* St. Louis: Herder Book Co., 1944.

Fifth Ecumenical (Constantinople) Council (553). 'The Anathemas Against Origen.' Translated by Henry Percival. In *A Select Library of Nicene and Post-Nicene Fathers.* Edited by Philip Schaff and Henry Wace, Series 2, vol. 14, 318-320. 1900; Peabody, MA: Hendrickson Publishers, 1994.

Fishbane, Michael. *Biblical Interpretation in Ancient Israel.* Oxford: Clarendon, 1988.

Fisher, Edward. *The Marrow of Modern Divinity: Touching both the Covenant of Works, and the Covenant of Grace.* London: G. Calvert, 1645.

Fisher, George Park. *History of Christian Doctrine*. New York: Charles Scribner's Sons, 1911.

Fitzmyer, Joseph A. *Romans*. Anchor Bible. Vol. 33. New York: Doubleday, 1992.

France, R. T. *Jesus and the Old Testament: His Application of Old Testament Passages to Himself and His Mission*. Vancouver: Regent College Publishing, 1998.

Furnish, Victor Paul. *II Corinthians*. Anchor Bible. Vol. 32a. New York: Doubleday, 1984.

Garrett, James Leo. *Systematic Theology*. 2 vols. Grand Rapids: Eerdmans, 1990.

Garrissoles, Antoine. *Decreti Synodici Carentoniensis De Imputatione Primi Peccati Adae Explicatio et Defensio*. Montalbani: Petrum & Phlippum Braconerios, 1648.

Gignilliat, Mark. *Paul and Isaiah's Servants: Paul's Theological Reading of Isaiah 40-66 in 2 Corinthians 5:14-6:10*. London: T & T Clark, 2007.

Gillespie, Patrick. *The Ark of the Testament Opened*. London: R. C., 1681.

Goldingay, John. *Message of Isaiah 40-55: A Literary-Theological Commentary*. London: T & T Clark, 2005.

Gomes, Alan W. 'Faustus Socinus' *De Jesu Christo Servatore*, Part III: Historical Introductions, Translation and Critical Notes.' PhD diss., Fuller Theological Seminary, 1990.

Gootjes, Nicolaas H. *The Belgic Confession: Its History and Sources*. Grand Rapids: Baker, 2007.

Goppelt, Leonhard. *Typos: The Typological Interpretation of the Old Testament*. Grand Rapids: Eerdmans, 1982.

Greenwood, Kyle R. 'Labor Pains: The Relationship between David's Census and Corvée Labor.' *Bulletin of Biblical Research* 20/4 (2010): 467-78.

Grundke, Christopher L. K. 'A Tempest in a Teapot? Genesis III 8 Again.' *Vetus Testamentum* 51/4 (2001): 548-51.

Gunkel, Hermann. *Genesis.* Macon, GA: Mercer University Press, 1997.

Hafemann, Scott J. *2 Corinthians.* NIV Application Commentary. Grand Rapids: Zondervan, 2000.

Halpern, Baruch. 'The Ritual Background of Zechariah's Temple Song.' *Catholic Biblical Quarterly* 40 (1978): 167-90.

Harlow, Daniel C. 'After Adam: Reading Genesis in an Ages of Evolutionary Science.' *Perspectives on Science and Christian Faith* 62/3 (2010): 170-95.

Harris, Murray J. *The Second Epistle to the Corinthians.* New International Greek Testament Commentary. Grand Rapids: Eerdmans, 2005.

Hart, D. G. & John R. Muether. *Seeking a Better Country: 300 Years of American Presbyterianism.* Phillipsburg: P & R, 2007.

Haynes, Daniel. 'The Transgression of Adam and Christ the New Adam: St. Augustine and St. Maximus the Confessor on the Doctrine of Original Sin.' *St. Vladimir's Theological Quarterly* 55/3 (2011): 293-317.

Heidegger, Johannes. *Medulla Theologiae Christianae: Corporis Theologiae Praevia Epitome.* 2nd edition. Tiguri: Henrici Bodmeri, 1713.

Helm, Paul. *Faith and Understanding.* Grand Rapids: Eerdmans, 1997.

Henley, William Ernest. *Echoes of Life and Death: Forty-Seven Lyrics by William Ernest Henley*. Portland, ME: Thomas B. Mosher, 1908.

Hess, Richard S. *Joshua: An Introduction and Commentary*. Tyndale Old Testament Commentaries. Downers Grove: InterVarsity Press, 1996.

Hiestand, Gerald. 'Augustine and the Justification Debates: Appropriating Augustine's Doctrine Of Culpability.' *Trinity Journal* 28/1 (2007): 115-139.

Hoad, John. 'Some New Testament References to Isaiah 53.' *Expository Times* 68 (1956-57): 254-55.

Hodge, A. A. *Outlines of Theology*. 1860; Edinburgh: Banner of Truth, 1991.

Hodge, Charles. *A Commentary on the Epistle to the Romans*. New York: Robert Carter & Brothers, 1880.

_____.'The Christian Spectator on The Doctrine of Imputation.' *The Biblical Repertory and Princeton Review* 3 (1831): 407-43.

_____. 'The Doctrine of Imputation.' In *Theological Essays: Reprinted from the Princeton Review*, 195-217. New York: Wiley and Putnam, 1846.

_____. 'Inquiries Respecting the Doctrine of Imputation.' *The Biblical Repertory and Princeton Review* 2 (1830): 425-72.

_____. *Systematic Theology*. 3 vols. Reprint; Grand Rapids: Eerdmans, 1993.

Hoekema, Anthony A. *Created In God's Image*. Grand Rapids: Eerdmans, 1986.

Hoeksema, Herman. *Reformed Dogmatics*. Grand Rapids: Reformed Free Publishing Association, 1966.

Hofius, Otfried. 'The Fourth Servant Song in the New Testament Letters.' In *The Suffering Servant: Isaiah 53 in Jewish and Christian Sources*, edited by Bernd Janowski and Peter Stuhlmacher, 163-88. Grand Rapids: Eerdmans, 2004.

Hooker, Morna. 'Did the Use of Isaiah 53 to Interpret His Mission Begin with Jesus?' In *Jesus and the Suffering Servant: Isaiah 53 and Christian Origins*. Edited by William H. Bellinger, Jr. and William R. Farmer, 88-103. Eugene: Wipf & Stock, 1998.

Hooker, Thomas. *The Unbeleevers Preparing for Christ*. London: Andrew Crooke, 1638.

Hopkins, Samuel. *The System of Doctrines Contained in Divine Revelation*. 2 vols. Boston: Isaiah Thomas, 1793.

Horton, Michael. *God of Promise: Introducing Covenant Theology*. Grand Rapids: Baker, 2006.

Howard, Thomas Albert. *Protestant Theology and the Making of the Modern German University*. Oxford: Oxford University Press, 2006.

Humphrey, Z. M. 'Review of Henry Boynton Smith: His Life and Work (1881).' *The Presbyterian Review* 2 (1881): 474-499.

Hutchinson, George P. *The Problem of Original Sin in American Presbyterian Theology*. Phillipsburg: P & R, 1972.

Irenaeus. 'Against Heresies.' Translated by Alexander Roberts and William Rambaut. In *The Ante-Nicene Fathers*, edited by Alexander Roberts and James Donaldson, vol. 1, 309-567. 1885, 1899; Peabody, MA: Hendrickson Publishers, 1994.

Irons, C. Lee. '*Dikaiosyne Theou*: A Lexical Examination of the Covenant-Faithfulness Interpretation.' PhD diss., Fuller Theological Seminary, 2011.

Johnson, Jr., S. Lewis. 'Romans 5:12—An Exercise in Exegesis and Theology.' In *New Dimensions in New Testament Study*. Edited by Richard N. Longenecker and Merrill C. Tenney, 298-316. Grand Rapids: Zondervan, 1974.

Jue, Jeffrey K. 'The Active Obedience of Christ and the Theology of the Westminster Standards: A Historical Investigation.' In *Justified in Christ: God's Plan for us in Justification*. Edited by K. Scott Oliphint, 99-130. Fearn: Christian Focus, 2007.

Junkin, George. *The Vindication, Containing A History of the Trial of the Rev. Albert Barnes by the Second Presbytery and the by the Synod of Philadelphia*. Philadelphia: Wm. S. Martien, 1836.

Kant, Immanuel. *Religion Within the Limits of Reason Alone*. Translated by Theodore M. Greene & Hoyt H. Hudson. New York: Harper & Row, 1960.

Keckerman, Bartholomäus. *Systema S. S. Theologiae Tribus Libris*. Hanovia: Guilielmum Antonium, 1610.

Keele, Zach and Michael G. Brown. *Sacred Bond: Covenant Theology Explored*. Grandville, MI: Reformed Fellowship, 2012.

Kelly, J. N. D. *Early Christian Doctrines*. Revised edition. San Francisco: Harper San Francisco, 1978.

Kim, Seyoon. *The Son of Man as the Son of God*. Grand Rapids: Eerdmans, 1983.

Kirk, J. R. Daniel. 'The Sufficiency of the Cross (1): The Crucifixion as Jesus' Act of Obedience.' *Scottish Bulletin of Evangelical Theology* 24/1 (2006): 36-64.

Kitchen, Kenneth A. *On the Reliability of the Old Testament*. Grand Rapids: Eerdmans, 2003.

Kitz, Anne Marie. *Cursed Are You! The Phenomenology of Cursing in Cuneiform and Hebrew Texts.* Winona Lake: Eisenbrauns, 2014.

Klauber, Martin I. 'The Helvetic Formula Consensus (1675): An Introduction and Translation.' *Trinity Journal* 11 (1990): 103-23.

Kline, Meredith G. *Glory in Our Midst: A Biblical-Theological Reading of Zechariah's Night Visions.* Overland Park, KS: Two Age Press, 2001.

_____. *Images of the Spirit.* 1980; Eugene: Wipf & Stock, 1998.

Kolb, Robert. 'Luther on the Two Kinds of Righteousness: Reflections on His Two-Dimensional Definition of Humanity at the Heart of His Theology.' *Lutheran Quarterly* 13 (1999): 449-66.

_____. 'Luther on Two Kinds of Righteousness.' In *Harvesting Martin Luther's Reflections on Theology, Ethics, and the Church.* Edited by Timothy J. Wengert, 38-55. Grand Rapids: Eerdmans, 2004.

Kolb, Robert and Timothy J. Wengert, editors. *The Book of Concord: The Confessions of the Evangelical Lutheran Church.* Translated by Charles P. Arand. Minneapolis: Fortress, 2000.

Kraus, Hans-Joachim. *Psalms 1-59.* Continental Commentary Series. Minneapolis: Fortress, 1993.

Landis, Robert W. *The Doctrine of Original Sin as Received and Taught by the Churches of the Reformation.* Richmond: Whittet & Shepperson, 1884.

Layñez, Diego. 'Disputatio de justitia imputata.' In *Jacobi Laínez Disputationes Tridentiae*, vol. 2, 153-192. Edited by Hartmannus Grisar. Ratisbonae: Feliciani Rauch, 1886.

Legaspi, Michael C. *The Death of Scripture and the Rise of Biblical Studies*. Oxford: Oxford University Press, 2010.

Leigh, Edward. *Body of Divinity*. London: William Lee, 1662.

Letham, Robert. 'The *Foedus Operum*: Some Factors Accounting For Its Development.' *Sixteenth Century Journal* 14/4 (1983): 457-67.

Levenson, Jon D. *Sinai and Zion: An Entry Into the Jewish Bible*. San Francisco: Harper San Francisco, 1985.

Lillback, Peter Alan. 'Ursinus' Development of the Covenant of Creation: A Debt to Melanchthon or Calvin?' *Westminster Theological Journal* 43 (1981): 247-88.

Lohfink, Norbert. *The Christian Meaning of the Old Testament*. Milwaukee: Bruce Publishing Co., 1968.

Lombard, Peter. *The Sentences*. 4 vols. Translated by Giulio Silano. Toronto: Pontifical Institutes of Medieval Studies, 2007-10.

Longman, III, Tremper. *Job*. Baker Commentary on the Old Testament Wisdom and Psalms. Grand Rapids: Baker, 2012.

_____. *The Book of Ecclesiastes*. New International Commentary on the Old Testament. Grand Rapids: Eerdmans, 1998.

Lugioyo, Brian. *Martin Bucer's Doctrine of Justification: Reformation Theology and Early Modern Irenicism*. Oxford: Oxford University Press, 2010.

Luther, Martin. *Luther's Works*. 55 vols. St. Louis: Concordia Publishing House, 1957-86.

Luzaraga, J. *Las Tradiciones de La Nube en la Biblia y en el Judaismo Primitivo*. Rome: Biblical Institute Press, 1973.

Machen, J. Gresham. *The Christian View of Man*. 1937; Edinburgh: Banner of Truth, 1999.

Madueme, Hans and Michael Reeves, editors. *Adam, the Fall, and Original Sin: Theological, Biblical, and Scientific Perspectives.* Grand Rapids: Baker, 2014.

Marshall, I. Howard. *The Pastoral Epistles.* International Critical Commentary. Edinburgh: T & T Clark, 1999.

Mattes, Mark. 'Luther on Justification as Forensic and Effective.' In *The Oxford Handbook of Martin Luther's Theology.* Edited by Robert Kolb, Irene Dingel, and L'Ubomir Batka, 264-73. Oxford: Oxford University Press, 2014.

Maxcey, Carl E. 'Double Justice, Diego Layñez, and the Council of Trent.' *Church History* 48/3 (1979): 269-78.

Maximus the Confessor. *On the Cosmic Mystery of Jesus Christ.* Translated by Paul M. Blowers and Robert Louis Wilken. New York: St. Vladimir's Seminary Press, 2003.

McComisky, Thomas. *Zechariah.* In *The Minor Prophets: An Exegetical & Expository Commentary,* edited by Thomas McComsky. Vol. 3, 1003-1244. Grand Rapids: Baker, 1998.

McCormack, Bruce L. 'Jus*titia aliena*: Karl Barth in Conversation with the Evangelical Doctrine of Imputed Righteousness.' In *Justification in Perspective: Historical Developments and Contemporary Challenges.* Edited by Bruce L. McCormack, 167-93. Grand Rapids: Baker, 2006.

McGrath, Alister E. *Iustitia Dei: A History of the Christian Doctrine of Justification.* 3rd edition. Cambridge: Cambridge University Press, 2005.

McLeod, Donald. 'Original Sin in Reformed Theology.' In *Adam, the Fall, and Original Sin: Theological, Biblical, and Scientific Perspectives.* Edited by Hans Madueme and Michael Reeves, 129-46. Grand Rapids: Baker, 2014.

Melanchthon, Philip. *Loci Communes 1543.* Translated by J. A. O. Preus. St. Louis: Concordia Publishing House, 1992.

_____. 'Confutation of Osiander.' In *Documents from the History of Lutheranism 1517-1750.* Edited by Eric Lund, 208-09. Minneapolis: Fortress, 2002.

Merrill, Eugene H. *Haggai, Zechariah, Malachi: An Exegetical Commentary.* Chicago: Moody Press, 1994.

Mettinger, N. D. *The Eden Narrative: A Literary and Religio-Historical Study of Genesis 2-3.* Winona Lake: Eisenbrauns, 2007.

Middleton, J. Richard. *The Liberating Image: The Imago Dei in Genesis 1.* Grand Rapids: Brazos, 2005.

Milgrom, Jacob. *Leviticus.* Anchor Bible, vol. 3. New Haven: Yale University Press, 1991.

Mitchell, Alex F. and John Struthers, eds. *Minutes of the Sessions of the Westminster Assembly of Divines.* Edinburgh: Blackwood and Sons, 1874.

Moberly, R. W. L. 'Did the Serpent Get It Right?' *Journal of Theological Studies* 39, no. 1 (1988): 1-27.

Moo, Douglas J. *The Epistle to the Romans.* New International Commentary on the New Testament. Grand Rapids: Eerdmans, 1996.

Morales, L. Michael. *The Tabernacle Pre-Figured: Cosmic Mountain Ideology in Genesis and Exodus.* Leuven: Peeters, 2012.

Motyer, J. Alec. *The Prophecy of Isaiah: An Introduction & Commentary.* Downers Grove: InterVarsity Press, 1993.

Muller, Richard A. 'The Covenant of Works and the Stability of Divine Law in Seventeenth-Century Reformed Orthodoxy: A Study in the Theology of Herman Witsius and Wilhelmus à Brakel.' *Calvin Theological Journal* 29 (1994): 75-101.

_____. *Dictionary of Latin and Greek Theological Terms: Drawn Principally from Protestant Scholastic Theology*. Grand Rapids: Baker, 1986.

_____. 'Divine Covenants, Absolute and Conditional: John Cameron and the Early Orthodox Development of Reformed Covenant Theology.' *Mid-American Journal of Theology* 17 (2006): 11-56.

Murray, John. 'The Adamic Administration.' In *Collected Writings of John Murray*, vol. 2, *Systematic Theology*, 47-59. Edinburgh: Banner of Truth, 1977.

_____. *The Imputation of Adam's Sin*. Philipsburg: P & R, 1977.

_____. *Romans*. New International Commentary on the New Testament. 2 vols. Grand Rapids: Eerdmans, 1959, 1965.

Musculus, Wolfgang. *Common Places of Christian Religion*. London: 1563.

Nassif, Bradley L. 'Toward a "Catholic" Understanding of St. Augustine's View of Original Sin.' *Union Seminary Quarterly Review* 39/4 (1984): 287-99.

Neder, Adam. *Participation in Christ: An Entry into Karl Barth's Church Dogmatics*. Louisville: Westminster John Knox, 2009.

Neusner, Jacob, trans. *Genesis Rabbah: The Judaic Commentary to the Book of Genesis*. 3 vols. Atlanta: Scholars Press, 1985.

Niehaus, Jeffrey. 'In the Wind of the Storm: Another Look at Genesis 3:8.' *Vetus Testamentum* 44/2 (1994): 263-67.

Nieto, José. *Juan de Valdés and the Origins of the Spanish and Italian Reformation*. Geneva: Droz, 1970.

Oberman, Heiko A. *The Harvest of Medieval Theology*. 1963; Grand Rapids: Baker, 1983.

Oden, Thomas C., editor. *The Justification Reader*. Grand Rapids: Eerdmans, 2002.

O'Malley, John W. *Trent: What Happened at the Council*. Cambridge: Belknap Press, 2013.

Orr, James, John Nuelsen, Edgar Mullins, Morris Evans, and Melvin Grove Kyle, editors. *International Standard Bible Encyclopedia*. 5 vols. 1915; Grand Rapids: Eerdmans, 1974.

Osiander, Andreas. *Disputatio de Iustificatione (1550)*. In *Gesamtausgabe*. Vol. 9. Gütersloh: Gütersloher Verlagshaus, 1994.

Oswalt, John. *The Book of Isaiah: Chapters 40–66*. New International Commentary on the Old Testament. Grand Rapids: Eerdmans, 1998.

Owen, John. *The doctrine of Justification by Faith Through the Imputation of the Righteousness of Christ, Explained, Confirmed, & Vindicated*. London: R. Boulter, 1677.

_____. *The Doctrine of Justification by Faith*. In *The Works of John Owen*. Vol. 5. Edited by William H. Goold. 1850-53; Edinburgh: Banner of Truth, 1998.

Papageorgiou, Fr. Panayiotis. 'Chrysostom and Augustine on the Sin of Adam and Its Consequences.' *St. Vladimir's Theological Quarterly* 39/4 (1995): 361-78.

Pareus, David. 'The Epistle of D. *David Parie* to the Illustrious and Noble Count, Lord *Ludovick Witgensteinius* Concerning *Christs Active and Passive Justice*.' In Zacharias Ursinus, *Certain Learned and Excellent Discourses*. Edited by David Parreus, 792-93. London: H. L., 1613.

Parker, T. H. L. *Commentaries on Romans: 1532–42*. Edinburgh: T & T Clark, 1986.

Pedersen, J. *Israel, Its Life and Culture*. Vol. 1-2. Oxford: Oxford University Press, 1926.

Pelagius, *Pelagius's Commentary on St Paul's Epistle to the Romans.* trans. Theodore de Bruyn. Oxford: Clarendon Press, 1998.

Pemble, William. *Vindiciae fidei, or A Treatise of Justification by Faith.* 1625; Oxford: John Adams, Edw. and John Forrest, 1659.

Perkins, William. *A Clowd of Faithfull Witnesses, Leading to the Heavenly Canaan: Or, a Commentarie Upon the 11. Chapter to the Hebrewes.* In *The Works of That Famous and Worthy Minister of Christ, in the Universitie of Cambridge, Mr. William Perkins.* London: Cantrell Legge, 1618.

_____. *A Golden Chaine: or the Description of Theology,* In *The Workes of that Famous and Worthie Minister of Christ W. Perkins.* Vol. 1. London: 1612.

Péter, René. 'L'Imposition des Mains dans L'Ancien Testament.' *Vetus Testamentum* 27/1 (1977): 48-55.

Pictet, Benedict. *Christian Theology.* Translated by Frederick Reyroux. London: R. B. Seeley and W. Burnside, 1834.

Piper, John. *Counted Righteous in Christ: Should We Abandon the Imputation of Christ's Righteousness?* Wheaton: Crossway, 2002.

Piscator, Johannes. *Aphorismes of Christian Religion: or, A Verie Compendious Abridgement of M. I. Calvins Institutions.* London: Richard Field, 1596.

_____. *A Learned and Profitable Treatise on Man's Justification.* London: 1599.

Placaeus, Josua. *De Imputatione Primi Peccati Adami Josue Placaei in Academia Salmuriensi S. s. Theologiae Professoris Disputatio.* Saumur: Ioannem Lesnerium, 1661.

Polanus, Amandus. *The Substance of Christian Religion.* London: 1595.

Polyander, Johannes, Antonius Walaeus, Antonius Thysius, and Andreas Rivetus. *Synopsis Purioris Theologiae*, vol. 1. Edited by Dolft te Velde and translated Riemer A. Faber. Leiden: Brill, 2014.

Postell, Seth D. *Adam as Israel: Genesis 1-3 as the Introduction to the Torah and Tanakh*. Cambridge: James Clarke and Co., 2012.

Poythress, Vern. 'Adam versus Claims from Genetics.' *Westminster Theological Journal* 75/1 (2013): 65-82.

_____. *The Shadow of Christ in the Law of Moses*. Phillipsburg: P & R, 1991.

Preston, John. *The Breastplate of Faith and Love*. London: Nicolas Bourne, 1630.

_____. *The New Covenant or the Saints Portion*. London: Nicolas Bourne, 1639.

The Proceedings of the Assembly of Divines Upon the Thirty-Nine Articles of the Church of England, appended to The Humble Advice of the Assembly of Divines, Now by Authority of Parliament Sitting at Westminster. London: Company of Stationers, 1647.

Quick, John. ed., *Synodicon in Gallia Reformata, or The Acts and Decisions and Decrees of the XVII National Synod of the Reformed Churches of France, Held in the Town of Gap, and Providence of Dolphiny*. 2 vols. London: Thomas Parkhurst, 1692.

Rijssen, Leonhard. *Summa Theologiae Elencticae Completa*. Bern: Danielem Tschisselii, 1703.

Rist, John M. 'Augustine on Free Will and Predestination.' *Journal of Theological Studies* 20/2 (1969): 420-47.

Rivet, Andre. 'On Imputation.' Translated by Charles Hodge. In *Theological Essays: Reprinted from the Princeton Review*, 196-217. New York: Wiley & Putnam, 1846.

Roberts, Francis. *Mysterium & Medulla Bibliorum. The Mysterie and Marrow of the Bible. viz. God's Covenants with Man.* London: George Calvert, 1657.

Robertson, O. Palmer. 'Genesis 15:6: New Covenant Exposition of an Old Covenant Text,' *Westminster Theological Journal* 42/2 (1980): 259-89.

Rollock, Robert. *A Treatise of God's Effectual Calling.* In *The Select Works of Robert Rollock.* Vol. 1. Edited by William Gunn. Edinburgh: The Woodrow Society, 1849.

Rondet, Henri. *Original Sin: The Patristic and Theological Background.* Shannon, Ireland: Ecclesia Press, 1969.

Rutherford, Samuel. *The Covenant of Life Opened: Or, a Treatise of the Covenant of Grace.* Edinburgh: Robert Brown, 1654.

Schleiermacher, Friedrich. *The Christian Faith.* London: T & T Clark, 1999.

Schoonenberg, Piet. *Man & Sin: A Theological View.* Notre Dame: University of Notre Dame Press, 1965.

Schwartz, Baruch. 'The Bearing of Sin in the Priestly Literature.' In *Pomegranates & Golden Bells: Studies in Biblical, Jewish, and Near Eastern Ritual, Law, and Literature in Honor of Jacob Milgrom,* edited by David P. Wright, David Noel Freedman, and Avi Hurvitz, 3-21. Winona: Eisenbrauns, 1995.

Shaw, Robert. *An Exposition of the Westminster Confession of Faith.* 1845; Fearn: Christian Focus, 1998.

Shedd, W. G. T. *A Critical and Doctrinal Commentary upon the Epistle of St. Paul to the Romans.* New York: Charles Scribner's Sons, 1879.

_____. *Dogmatic Theology.* 3 vols. 1888; Grand Rapids: Zondervan, 1969.

_____. 'Original Sin.' In *Discourses and Essays*, 218-71. Andover: W. F. Draper, 1856.

Sheldon, Henry Clay. *History of Christian Doctrine*. 2 vols. New York: Harper & Brothers, 1886.

Smith, Henry Boynton. *System of Christian Theology*. 2nd edition. New York: A. C. Armstrong and Son, 1884.

Smith, Morton. *Studies In Southern Presbyterian Theology*. Phillipsburg: P & R, 1987.

Snoddy, Richard. *The Soteriology of James Ussher: The Acts and Object of Saving Faith*. Oxford: Oxford University Press, 2014.

Son, Sang-Won (Aaron). *Corporate Elements in Pauline Anthropology: A Study of Selected Terms, Idioms, and Concepts in the Light of Paul's Usage and Background*. Rome: Pontifico Instituto Biblico, 2001.

Sprinkle, Preston M. *Law and Life: The Interpretation of Leviticus 18:5 in Early Judaism and in Paul*. Tübingen: Mohr Siebeck, 2008.

Stansbury, A.J. *Trial of the Rev. Albert Barnes, Before the Synod of Philadelphia, in Session at York, October 1835, On a Charge of Heresy, Preferred Against Him by the Rev. George Junkin*. New York: 1836.

Stapfer, Johannes Friederich. *Institutiones Theologiae Polemicae Universae*. Vol. 1. Zurich: Heideggerum et Socios, 1757.

Steters, John Van. *Prologue to History: The Yahwehist as Historian in Genesis*. Louisville: Westminster John Knox, 1992.

Stordalen, T. *Echoes of Eden: Genesis 2–3 and Symbolism of the Eden Garden in Biblical Hebrew Literature*. Leuven: Peeters, 2000.

Strange, Alan D. 'Imputation of the Active Obedience of
Christ at the Westminster Assembly.' In *Drawn into
Controversie: Reformed Theological Diversity and Debates
within Seventeenth-Century British Puritanism*. Edited by
Michael A. G. Haykin and Mark Jones, 31-51. Göttingen:
Vandenhoeck & Ruprecht, 2011.

Strehle, Stephen. *Calvinism, Federalism, and Scholasticism: A Study
of the Reformed Doctrine of Covenant*. New York: Peter Lang,
1988.

Sweeney, Douglas A. *Nathaniel Taylor, New Haven Theology, and
the Legacy of Jonathan Edwards*. Oxford: Oxford University
Press, 2003.

Tertullian. 'A Treatise on the Soul.' Translated by Peter Holmes.
In *The Ante-Nicene Fathers*. Edited by Alexander Roberts
and James Donaldson. Vol. 3, 669-79. 1885, 1905; Peabody,
MA: Hendrickson Publishers, 1994.

_____. 'On Baptism.' Translated by S. Thelwell. In *The Ante-
Nicene Fathers*. Edited by Alexander Roberts and James
Donaldson, vol. 3, 181-235. 1885, 1905; Peabody, MA:
Hendrickson Publishers, 1994.

Thiselton, A. C. 'The Supposed Power of Words in the Biblical
Writings.' *Journal of Theological Studies* 25/2 (1974): 283-99.

Thornwell, John Henly 'Nature of Our Interest in the Sin of
Adam, Being a Review of Baird's Elohim Revealed.' In
Collected Writings, vol. 1, 515-68. Edited by John B. Adger.
Richmond: Presbyterian Committee of Publication, 1871.

_____. 'Theology, Its Proper Method and Its Central
Principle Being a Review of Breckinridge's Knowledge
of God Objectively Considered.' In *Collected Writings*,
vol. 1, 445-488. Edited by John B. Adger. Richmond:
Presbyterian Committee of Publication, 1871.

Tolkien, J. R. R. *The Fellowship of the Ring: The Lord of the Rings, Part I.* 1954; Boston: Mariner Books, 1994.

Trelcatius, Lucas. *Briefe Institution of Common Places of Sacred Divinitie.* London: Francis Burton, 1610.

Trueman, Carl R. 'The Harvest of Reformation Mythology? Patrick Gillespie and the Covenant of Redemption.' In *Scholasticism Reformed: Essays in Honour of Willem J. van Asselt.* Edited by Maarten Wisse, Marcel Sarot, and Willemien Otten, 196-214. Leiden: Brill, 2010.

_____. *John Owen: Reformed Catholic, Renaissance Man.* Aldershot: Ashgate, 2007.

_____. 'Original Sin in Modern Theology.' In *Adam, the Fall, and Original Sin: Theological, Biblical, and Scientific Perspectives.* Edited by Hans Madueme and Michael Reeves, 167-86. Grand Rapids: Baker, 2014.

Turner, Kenneth J. *The Death of Deaths in the Death of Israel: Deuteronomy's Theology of Exile.* Eugene: Wipf & Stock, 2010.

Turretin, Francis. *Institutes of Elenctic Theology.* 3 vols. Translated by George Musgrave Giger and edited by James T. Dennison, Jr. Phillipsburg: P & R, 1992-97.

Ursinus, Zacharias. *The Commentary of Dr. Zacharias Ursinus on the Heidelberg Catechism.* Translated by G. W. Williard. 1852; Phillipsburg: P & R, n. d.

Ussher, James. *A Body of Divinitie, or The Summe and Substance of Christian Religion.* London: Tho. Downes and Geo: Badger, 1645.

Van Doodewaard, William. *The Quest for the Historical Adam: Genesis, Hermeneutics, and Human Origins.* Grand Rapids: Reformation Heritage Books, 2015.

Van Limborch, Philip. *A Compleat System, or Body of Divinity*, vol. 1 (1702).

Van Mastricht, Petrus. *Theoretico-Practica Theologia*, 9th edition. Trajecti ad Rhenum: apud W. van der Water, 1724.

Van Stam, F. P. *The Controversy Over the Theology of Saumur, 1635-1650: Disrupting Debates Among the Huguenots in Complicated Circumstances.* Amsterdam: APA-Holland University Press, 1988.

Van Til, Cornelius. *An Introduction to Systematic Theology.* Phillipsburg: P & R, 1974.

VanDixhoorn, Chad. 'Reforming the Reformation: Theological Debate at the Westminster Assembly 1643-52.' 7 vols. PhD diss., University of Cambridge, 2004.

VanDrunen, David. *Divine Covenants and Moral Order: A Biblical Theology of Natural Law.* Grand Rapids: Eerdmans, 2014.

Vanhoozer, Kevin. *First Theology: God, Scripture, and Hermeneutics.* Downers Grove: InterVarsity Press, 2002.

Venema, Cornelis. 'Calvin's Doctrine of the Imputation of Christ's Righteousness: Another Example of "Calvin vs. the Calvinists"?' *Mid-America Journal of Theology* 20 (2009): 15-47.

_____. *The Gospel of Free Acceptance in Christ: An Assessment of the Reformation and New Perspective on Paul.* Edinburgh: Banner of Truth, 2006.

_____. 'Recent Criticisms of the Covenant of Works in the Westminster Confession of Faith.' *Mid-America Journal of Theology* 9/3 (1993): 165-98.

Venema, Herman. *Institutes of Theology.* Translated by Alex W. Brown. Edinburgh: T &T Clark, 1854.

Versteeg, J. P. *Adam in the New Testament: Mere Teaching Model or First Historical Man?* 2nd edition. 1977; Phillipsburg: P & R, 2012.

Vickers, Brian. *Jesus' Blood and Righteousness: Paul's Theology of Imputation.* Wheaton: Crossway, 2006.

Visscher, Gerhard H. *Romans 4 and the New Perspective on Paul: Faith Embraces the Promise.* New York: Peter Lang, 2009.

Visser, Derk. 'The Covenant in Zacharias Ursinus.' *Sixteenth Century Journal* 18/4 (1987): 531-44.

Vitringa, Campegius. *Doctrina Christianae Religionis per Aphorismos Summatim Descripta , 4th edition.* Francker: Fransiscum Halmam, 1702.

Von Harnack, Adolf. *The History of Dogma.* 7 vols. Edited by T. K. Cheyne and A. B. Bruce and translated by James Millar. London: Williams & Norgate, 1895-1900.

Vos, Geerhardus. *The Pauline Eschatology.* 1930; Phillipsburg: P & R, 1996.

_____. 'Paul's Eschatological Concept of the Spirit.' In *Redemptive History and Biblical Interpretation: The Shorter Writings of Geerhardus Vos.* Edited by Richard B. Gaffin, Jr., 91-125. Phillipsburg: P & R, 1980.

_____. *Reformed Dogmatics.* 5 vols. Edited by Richard B. Gaffin, Jr. Bellingham, WA: Lexham Press, 2012 - .

Walker, George. *Socinianisme in the Fundamentall Point of Justification Discovered, and Confuted.* London: John Bartlet, 1641.

Wallis, John. *A Brief and Easie Explanation of the Shorter Catechism.* London: Peter Parker, 1662.

Waltke, Bruce. *An Old Testament Theology: An Exegetical, Canonical, and Thematic Approach*. Grand Rapids: Zondervan, 2007.

Walton, John H. *The Lost World of Adam and Eve: Genesis 2-3 and the Human Origins Debate*. Downers Grove: InterVarsity Press, 2015.

Warfield, B.B. 'Edwards and the New England Theology.' In *The Works of Benjamin B. Warfield*. 10 vols., vol. 9, 515-38. 1932; Grand Rapids: Baker, 1989.

_____. *Evolution, Science, and Scripture: Selected Writings*. Edited by Mark A. Noll and David Livingstone. Grand Rapids: Baker, 2000.

_____. 'Imputation.' In *Studies in Theology*, 301-09. 1932; Edinburgh: Banner of Truth, 1988.

_____. 'Review of God's Image in Man by James Orr,' in *The Works of B. B. Warfield*, 10 vols., vol. 10, 136-41; 1932; Grand Rapids: Baker, 1981.

Watson, Thomas. *A Body of Practical Divinity*. London: Thomas Parkhurst, 1692.

Wellhausen, Julius. *Prolegomena to the History of Israel*. Edinburgh: Adam & Charles Black, 1875.

Wengert, Timothy J. 'Philip Melanchthon and John Calvin against Andreas Osiander: Coming to Terms with Forensic Justification.' In *Calvin and Luther: The Continuing Relationship*. Edited by R. Ward Holder, 63-87. Göttingen: Vandenhoeck & Ruprecht, 2013.

Wenham, Gordon J. *Leviticus*. New International Commentary on the Old Testament. Grand Rapids: Eerdmans, 1979.

_____. *Numbers*. Tyndale Old Testament Commentary. Downers Grove: InterVarsity Press, 1981.

Weir, David. *The Origins of the Federal Theology in Sixteenth-Century Reformation Thought*. Oxford: Oxford University Press, 1990.

Westminster Confession of Faith. 1646. Reprint, Glasgow: Free Presbyterian Publications, 1995.

Whitaker, William. *An Answer to the Ten Reasons of Edmund Campian*. London: Felix Kyngston, 1606.

_____. *A Disputation on Holy Scripture*. 1588; Cambridge: Cambridge University Press, 1849.

Witsius, Herman. *Conciliatory, or Irenical Animadversions*. Translated by Thomas Bell Glasgow: W. Lang, 1807.

Woolsey, Andrew A. *Unity and Continuity in Covenantal Thought: A Study in the Reformed Tradition to the Westminster Assembly*. Grand Rapids: Reformation Heritage Books, 2012.

Woudstra, Marten H. *The Book of Joshua*. New International Commentary on the Old Testament. Grand Rapids: Eerdmans, 1981.

Wright, David P. 'The Gesture of Hand Placement in the Hebrew Bible and Hittite Literature.' *Journal of the American Oriental Society* 106/3 (1986): 433-46.

Wright, N.T. *The Climax of the Covenant: Christ and the Law in Pauline Theology*. Minneapolis: Fortress Press, 1993.

_____. *Justification: God's Plan and Paul's Vision*. Downers Grove: InterVarsity Press, 2009.

_____. *The New Testament and the People of God*. Philadelphia: Fortress, 1992.

_____. *Paul and the Faithfulness of God*. Minneapolis: Fortress, 2013.

_____. *The Resurrection of the Son of God*. Minneapolis: Fortress, 2003.

_____. 'The Letter to the Romans: Introduction, Commentary, and Reflections.' In *The New Interpreter's Bible*. Edited by Leander E. Keck. Vol. 10, 393-770. Nashville: Abingdon, 2002.

_____. 'Romans and the Theology of Paul.' In *Pauline Theology*. Edited by David M. Hay & E. Elizabeth Johnson, 30-67. Minneapolis: Fortress, 1995.

_____. *Surprised by Scripture: Engaging Contemporary Issues*. San Francisco: Harper One, 2014.

_____. *What St. Paul Really Said: Was Paul of Tarsus the Real Founder of Christianity?* Grand Rapids: Eerdmans, 1997.

Wyttenbach, Daniel. *Tentamen Theologiae Dogmaticae Methodo Scientifica Pertractata*. Vol. 1 Frankfurt: Andreae et Hort, 1747.

Yeo, John J. *Plundering the Egyptians: The Old Testament and Historical Criticism at Westminster Theological Seminary (1929-98)*. Lanham: University Press of America, 2010.

Young, E. J. *The Book of Isaiah*. 3 vols. New International Commentary on the Old Testament. 1965; Grand Rapids: Eerdmans, 1974.

Zanchi, Girolamo. *Omnium Operum Theologicorum*. Vol. 4. Geneva: Ioannis Tornaesij, 1649.

Scripture Index

Subject Index

Also available from this author...

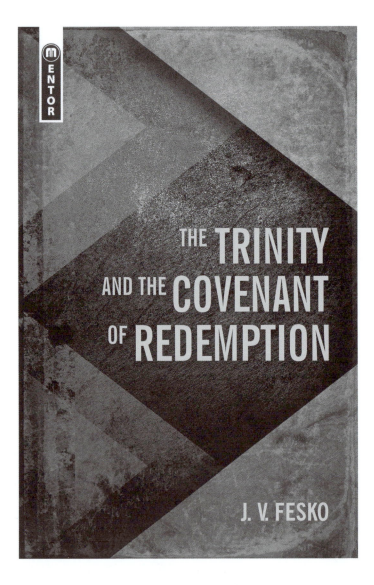

ISBN 978-1-78191-765-7

The Trinity and the Covenant of Redemption

J.V. Fesko

When Christians reflect on the gospel, their attention is rightly drawn to the cross and empty tomb. But is this it? Or is there much more to the story? In a ground-breaking work, J.V. Fesko reminds us that the great news of this gospel message is rooted in eternity, whereby a covenant was made between the persons of the Trinity in order to redeem sinners like you and me. J. V. Fesko, in the first of a three-part series on covenant theology featuring Redemption, Grace and Works, aims to retrieve and recover classic Reformed covenant theology for the church.

Some books today exegete the shining truths of the Holy Scriptures, others mine the treasures of Reformed orthodoxy, and yet others interact with influential theologians of the modern era. This book is one of the few that does all three, and does them well.

JOEL R. BEEKE
President, Puritan Reformed Theological Seminary
Grand Rapids, Michigan

... shows historical care, exegetical soundness, and doctrinal wisdom. I commend it heartily as a wonderful entryway to considering this most profound facet of the Christian confession.

MICHAEL ALLEN
Associate Professor of Systematic and Historical Theology,
Reformed Theological Seminary, Orlando, Florida

Christian Focus Publications

Our mission statement –

STAYING FAITHFUL

In dependence upon God we seek to impact the world through literature faithful to His infallible Word, the Bible. Our aim is to ensure that the Lord Jesus Christ is presented as the only hope to obtain forgiveness of sin, live a useful life and look forward to heaven with Him.

Our Books are published in four imprints:

CHRISTIAN FOCUS

popular works including biographies, commentaries, basic doctrine and Christian living.

CHRISTIAN HERITAGE

books representing some of the best material from the rich heritage of the church.

MENTOR

books written at a level suitable for Bible College and seminary students, pastors, and other serious readers. The imprint includes commentaries, doctrinal studies, examination of current issues and church history.

CF4•K

children's books for quality Bible teaching and for all age groups: Sunday school curriculum, puzzle and activity books; personal and family devotional titles, biographies and inspirational stories – because you are never too young to know Jesus!

Christian Focus Publications Ltd,
Geanies House, Fearn, Ross-shire,
IV20 1TW, Scotland, United Kingdom.
www.christianfocus.com